Central Works of Philosophy

Central Works of Philosophy is a multi-volume set of essays on the core texts of the Western philosophical tradition. From Plato's *Republic* to the present day, the volumes range over 2,500 years of philosophical writing covering the best, most representative, and most influential work of some of our greatest philosophers. Each essay has been specially commissioned and provides an overview of the work and clear and authoritative exposition of its central ideas. Together these essays introduce the masterpieces of the Western philosophical canon and provide an unrivalled companion for reading and studying philosophy.

Central Works of Philosophy
Edited by John Shand

Central Works of Philosophy Volume 3
The Nineteenth Century

Edited by John Shand

McGill-Queen's University Press
Montreal & Kingston • Ithaca

In memory of my parents, Alexander Hesketh Shand and Muriel Olive Shand

© Editorial matter and selection, 2005 John Shand. Individual contributions, the contributors.

ISBN 0-7735-3052-5 (hardcover)
ISBN 0-7735-3053-3 (paperback)

Legal deposit fourth quarter 2005
Bibliothèque nationale du Québec

Published simultaneously outside North America
by Acumen Publishing Limited

McGill-Queen's University Press acknowledges the financial support of the Government of Canada through the Book Publishing Development Program (BPIDP) for its activities.

Library and Archives Canada Cataloguing in Publication

Central works of philosophy / edited by John Shand.

Includes bibliographical references and indexes.
Contents: v. 1. Ancient and medieval — v. 2. The seventeenth
    and eighteenth centuries — v. 3. The nineteenth century.
ISBN 0-7735-3015-0 (v. 1 : bound).—ISBN 0-7735-3016-9 (v. 1 : pbk.).—
ISBN 0-7735-3017-7 (v. 2 : bound).—ISBN 0-7735-3018-5 (v. 2 : pbk.).—
ISBN 0-7735-3052-5 (v. 3 : bound).—ISBN 0-7735-3053-3 (v. 3 : pbk.)

1. Philosophy—Introductions. I. Shand, John, 1956-

B21.C45 2005   100   C2005-902037-7

Designed and typeset by Kate Williams, Swansea.
Printed and bound by Biddles Ltd., King's Lynn.

Contents

Contributors

Curtis Bowman has published articles on Kant, Fichte, Husserl, Heidegger, and Derrida, and is one of the translators of *Notes and Fragments*, volume 13 of the Cambridge Edition of the Works of Immanuel Kant. He has taught at the University of Pennsylvania, Bryn Mawr College, and Haverford College.

C. Stephen Evans is University Professor of Philosophy and Humanities at Baylor University, Texas and has also taught at Calvin College, Michigan and St. Olaf College, Minnesota. He is the author of many articles and fifteen books, including, most recently, *Kierkegaard's Ethic of Love*.

Michelle Grier is Professor of Philosophy at the University of San Diego. In addition to numerous articles on Kant's philosophy, she is the author of *Kant's Doctrine of Transcendental Illusion*.

Michael Inwood has taught philosophy at Trinity College, Oxford since 1967. Besides his publications on Hegel, he is also the author of *Heidegger* and *A Heidegger Dictionary*. He has also written on Plato and Aristotle, and is particularly interested in the relationship between Greek and German philosophy.

Dale Jacquette is Professor of Philosophy at The Pennsylvania State University. He is the author of *The Philosophy of Schopenhauer* (Acumen) and editor of *Schopenhauer, Philosophy, and the Arts*.

Jonathan Riley is Professor of Philosophy at Tulane University, New Orleans, and editor of *Politics, Philosophy and Economics*. His most recent book is *Mill's Radical Liberalism*.

Tom Rockmore is Professor of Philosophy at Duquesne University, Pittsburgh. He is the author of many books concerned with different thinkers and themes from modern European philosophy.

John Shand is an Associate Lecturer in Philosophy at the Open University and is the author of *Philosophy and Philosophers: An Introduction to Western Philosophy* (second edition Acumen) and *Arguing Well* and editor of *Fundamentals of Philosophy*.

Rex Welshon is Associate Professor of Philosophy, Chair of the Department of Philosophy, and Associate Dean of the College of Letters, Arts, and Sciences at the University of Colorado at Colorado Springs. His primary research interests are in the philosophy of mind and the philosophy of Nietzsche. He is the author of *The Philosophy of Nietzsche* (Acumen).

Preface

The works in the *Central Works of Philosophy* volumes have been chosen because of their fundamental importance in the history of philosophy and for the development of human thought. Other works might have been chosen; however, the underlying idea is that if any works should be chosen, then these certainly should be. In the cases where the work is a philosopher's *magnum opus* the essay on it gives an excellent overview of the philosopher's thought.

Chapter 1 by Michelle Grier introduces Kant's *Critique of Pure Reason*. Few works have been more influential in philosophy. Kant's transcendental idealism attempted to set the limits of what could be known within the bounds of possible experiences (phenomena). In this way he could give grounds, *contra* empiricism, as to why the basic assumptions of science such as causality applied to the world, and why, *contra* rationalism, we should refrain from metaphysical speculation concerning things-in-themselves (noumena) – things as they are independently of how they can appear to us – where no experience could possibly settle the problems raised. We know that the world will conform to our basic conceptual categories for understanding it because those categories are the structure of any possible experience imposed by the mind as a condition for having those experiences, and the world just is the sum of possible experiences, if it is anything at all to us. He aimed also to leave a realm beyond science, beyond phenomenal experience, that would provide room for moral responsibility and faith in God.

Chapter 2 by Curtis Bowman looks at Fichte's *Foundations of the Entire Science of Knowledge*. Fichte saw himself as the true heir to Kant. He seeks to

rectify two main defects in Kant's philosophy. The first is the problematic notion of things-in-themselves, necessarily unknowable, but in some sense existing beyond how things appear to us. The second is the link of theoretical and
practical reason, left unconnected in Kant. In Fichte theoretical reason cannot
be understood in separation from its practical engagement with the world; the
world is a soundingboard for our moral endeavours. Fichte's solution to the first
defect starts by examining the pure I or ego. The I is not a thing, but exists in
virtue of the self-creating normative activity of positing itself – a "self-positing
I", where the self-positing activity is the very essence of the I – and in so doing
it must limit itself by positing a non-I, something not itself. When it is viewed
through the categories – principally, space, time and causality – the thing-in-
itself is what we call the external world. He goes further than Kant and holds
that the thing-in-itself cannot even be thought about, let alone known. The I
encounters a block at the limits of thought, and that gets posited as the thing-
in-itself.

Chapter 3 by Michael Inwood elucidates Hegel's *Phenomenology of Spirit*.
Hegel aims to show how we can overcome the restriction that we can know the
world only as an appearance, and thus not come to know things-in-themselves.
He tries to accomplish this by showing that the mind and the world must in the
end form an identity in an absolute conception that renders the whole intelligible.
The dualism of mind, which does the conceptualizing, and the world, which is
conceptualized, is collapsed and overcome, as is the dualism of knowledge and
the object of knowledge. This is not to argue for subjective idealism, where the
individual mind and the world are one; rather, the world as an intelligible whole
is a manifestation of infinite mind or spirit, which the individual mind may
to some degree reflect through ever-increasing understanding. Hegel presents
various lesser ways of understanding reality as steps leading to a final absolute
conception that give a complete view of reality in which mind and world are
one. The understanding of the world is thus mind understanding the development of itself.

Chapter 4 by Dale Jacquette discusses Schopenhauer's *The World as Will and
Representation*. Schopenhauer thought of himself as being true to Kant's project
of transcendental idealism, but thought he had found a way of making sense of
things-in-themselves so that they do not contravene the strictures defining the
project. He posits that the reality behind appearances or representations is a
blind striving Will. We have an inkling of this through our awareness of the one
case of something that is not presented to us as a representation, which unlike a
representation may not be subsumed under Kantian categories. We are aware from
"within", directly and non-representationally, of our will as bodily action, and in a
different way from how we view from "without" the movement of other physical

objects. This leads Schopenhauer to some grim conclusions about the human condition. We are in reality driven, as products of the Will, by a restless striving, interspersed with periods of boredom following the accomplishment of some aim, all of which is in the end pointless. Our conscious awareness provides only a spurious surface rationale of aims and projects for our lives, and we mistakenly take this appearance for reality.

Chapter 5 by Jonathan Riley introduces Mill's *On Liberty*. This is the classic statement of the principles of a liberal society. Because he is a utilitarian Mill cannot base his account of liberal society on a presumption of inalienable natural rights, but has to justify liberal values, in particular personal liberty, by showing that they increase overall happiness both for the individual and for society as a whole. Mill insists that happiness should be considered in its broadest sense, and not be identified with mere animal pleasure. Indeed Mill's notion of happiness is best taken to mean full human flourishing. Mill's outline of society is then quite simple: people should be allowed to do as they choose so long as it does no harm to others. The utilitarian justification of this, which would give rise to various "experiments in living", is that it propagates the happiness of both the individual and society. Liberty within the constraint of not harming others propagates individual happiness because it is essential to the fulfilment of human nature that we do not just have a certain sort of life, but that we choose the certain sort of life that we have. It propagates the happiness of society because it releases and promotes talent, facilitates the discovery of the truth and reveals better ways of living.

Chapter 6 by Stephen Evans discusses Kierkegaard's *Philosophical Fragments*. Kierkegaard is an anti-systematic iconoclast. He extols the irreplaceability of religious faith over bloodless fragile rational philosophical systems, which are in any case rationally incompleteable. In particular, he is concerned with Christian religious faith, which could not, he argued, be replaced, dressed up as a rational philosophical system, as Hegel attempted to do. Kierkegaard emphasizes that in the end one's life must be a personal choice without ultimate rational justification, and not something one can live out by simply clothing it in a philosophical system. Priority is given to the self, to subjective personal experience, taking responsibility and choosing for oneself; making what one lives by a part of one's nature, and not following, by merely reading them off, a system of abstract rules. It is a delusion to think that one may hand over the decision as to how to live to something external to oneself. In this, he battled against depersonalized mass opinion, and for an independent authentic self that has truly chosen its life.

Chapter 7 by Tom Rockmore discusses Marx's *Capital*. Marx in his youth studied and was inspired by Hegel's ideas. It is debatable to what extent Marx's thought constitutes a continuity or discontinuity with Hegel's philosophy. What is clear is that Marx's ideas have a deep philosophical underpinning. The most prominent factor here is a developmental and directional view of human history built on a material base, whereby each epoch – including bourgeois capitalism – gives rise to an ideology, a way of thinking and values, that reinforces the economic and social system as being inevitable and natural. The conditions of man are chiefly determined by the material economic structures of the society, where men are to a considerable degree blind pawns of economic forces that arise as a function of the economic structures. The structures contain within them forces that precipitate change between epochs. This motion of history is not endless, however. It will culminate inevitably in communism, which will mark the end of history. In that communal state people will be truly free – as opposed to the illusion given by political liberty – through regaining a relation to labour in which they are no longer alienated through their work being either unworthy or something to which they are driven by economic forces over which they have no control.

Chapter 8 by Rex Welshon gives an account of Nietzsche's *On the Genealogy of Morals*. Nietzsche is highly suspicious of philosophical systems. His approach is iconoclastic, and seeks to free us from our sense that there must be a single system that may give a final true picture of reality. Rather he emphasizes the diversity of perspectives on the world, and the senselessness of the attempt to talk about the world independently of a perspective. It is not as if there is "a world" that the perspectives are all perspectives on. The striving for absolutes is an attempt to replace God following His death, by which "death" Nietzsche means the demise of the work that the idea of God once did in our beliefs. In the book discussed here, he seeks out the philosophical and psychological grounds of the dominant morality, the unquestioned "herd morality" around us that we take for granted. He seeks to rewrite the story, according to which our current morality developed out of, and is a culminating improvement on, previous moralities. "Herd morality" has not grown, as Nietzsche's story goes, from our final recognition of there being a universally valid moral order, but in fact from a hidden process whereby a morality has arisen through which the weak may overcome the strong and noble by making a virtue of the characteristics of the weak and an evil of the characteristics of the strong individual. Thus, Nietzsche's account opposes, and is even an inversion, of the traditional account of morality.

John Shand

The Nineteenth Century
Introduction

John Shand

The nineteenth century is perhaps most notable for an intellectual pluralism and a conflict of ideas to a degree never before witnessed. The philosophy of the Enlightenment, which emerged during the seventeenth century and reached its apogee in the eighteenth century, advocated the vigorous unrestricted application of argument and the studious appeal to evidence. It did not, in the nineteenth century, throw up one clear set of rationally based conclusions as to the nature of reality, knowledge, values and the best social order, as one might suppose it would given the ideals of argument and evidence. It did not deliver a singular definitive worldview or *Weltanschauung* (a term that came to have its modern philosophical meaning during the nineteenth century). Negatively it did, nevertheless, forever cast suspicion on protected authority, divorced from truly penetrating questioning and argument. Positively, it delivered up an abundance of scientific and technical success, which in the nineteenth century accelerated and increased to a level never before seen. It was at the intellectual foundation, in philosophy, that it failed to ground the whole edifice of human understanding once and for all. This was because of a problem that persists in philosophy to this day: the intellectual tools that would be used to attempt to ground the whole of human understanding themselves necessarily come into question in such an attempt. This is clearly a case of trying to lift oneself up by one's own bootstraps. Various answers have since been developed to try to avoid, dismiss or at least ameliorate this problem; or else, finally, accept it as inevitable.

The new thinking of the seventeenth and eighteenth centuries was increasingly successful in explaining the natural order, where once religion and appeal to God had pretensions to do so, and so God and religion were pushed aside in this respect. The terminal blow to the value of religion in this area in the nineteenth century was Darwin's theory of evolution. This also emphatically made man a part of the natural world, so that the explanation of his existence and nature may be given entirely naturalistically without needing to appeal to the divine. But this was not the end of the decline of religious authority and the rise of secularism. The nineteenth century saw God and religion similarly losing their grip over the area where they sought refuge from their loss of authority in determining the natural order, that of values. The distinct moral status of a person, affirmed by religion, was also threatened by the inclusion of man within biological naturalism. The nineteenth century, which followed the Enlightenment, is informed by a curious combination of overweening confidence that at last all knowledge and values may be grounded in a grand philosophical system and a corrosive nihilism, according to which all knowledge and values are baseless and have a substantiality that upon examination evaporates. It was a century of the confident and the lost. It is this clash of certainty and doubt, and consequent bewilderment about what we should believe, that gives rise to the crisis of Western thought in the nineteenth century, marked as it was by intellectual and social turmoil. However, this crisis, some argued, should not be understood as an accidental failure somehow to get an indestructible philosophical worldview up and running once and for all. It dawned on thinkers such as Kierkegaard and Nietzsche that the lack of a final unified consummation of human ideas in a single complete worldview was in fact an ineradicable feature of the human condition that we have to learn to live with. One alternative is wilful adherence to an all-encompassing monist closed belief system, such as religion offers; but it is a system that only stands up and hangs together as an edifice of ideas through which we may guide our beliefs and our lives, because some areas are arbitrarily blocked off from examination; in particular those areas that would, if brought into doubt, make it vulnerable to collapse. Philosophy has not developed anything to replace such putative global certainty, although Hegel comes closest to thinking that he had developed such a philosophical system.

With the inevitability of intellectual diversity comes choice, with choice comes uncertainty, and with uncertainty comes insecurity and the anxiety or fear that what we hold dear is falling apart around us, leading at the limit to nihilism. *Angst* – a term introduced by Kierkegaard – is particularly appropriate for this sense of deep, vertiginous, unfocused dread. Living with a new kind of fundamental uncertainty in our beliefs and values was the price of intellectual and personal freedom that the collapse of the medieval worldview, precipitated by the Enlightenment, brought about. The medieval worldview was not about to be replaced with something similar, and some concluded it was irreplaceable. Some found that this delivered a disturbing intellectual vertigo, while others revelled in a new freedom to explore different and novel ways of thinking, albeit ways that could never be brought to a definitive resolution.

Sometimes from observations such as these, there is exaggerated talk of the fundamental failure of the Enlightenment, and of this failure resulting from flaws in reason itself. One should, however, only suppose that reason has been revealed as flawed through its not providing definitive intellectual consummation if one assumes it must, in order to succeed, throw up indisputable and settled answers across the whole range of human concerns. That it did not was certainly seen as a problem, and this has had repercussions to the present day, so that sometimes people are induced to seek consolation in irrational eternal certainties rather than live with the anxiety of perpetual decisions made on an uncertain or fallible basis. The nineteenth century evinces the fear of living with this kind of uncertainty. This contrasted with having once been promised so much in the way of final answers by those who extolled the value of the exercising of a new intellectual freedom. At the same time, there was no return to the comforting shelter of traditional authoritarian belief-monism. The uncertainty came as a delightful and romantic liberation to some, and this begot the view that man was the maker of his world, free of preordained prescriptions as to how the world is (rather, this has to be discovered) and how life should be lived (rather, this should be freely debated). Even so, such liberation could be tinged with more than a little fear born of the realization that this freedom granted man seemingly unlimited and disturbingly arbitrary choices.

Among the rapidly changing counterpoint of events, set against a new freedom and uncertainty of ideas, the people of the nineteenth century could see all around them the impressive technological and practical products of the application of determined reason and patient experimental enquiry, which were remarkable in themselves as well as increasing wealth unimaginably. Of course, many people remained poor; but there was a vast increase in population, and such people would not have existed at all were there not a remarkable general increase in wealth. This wealth was brought about by the industrial revolution.

The failure of the Enlightenment, in so far as it is correct to make such a claim at all, was not a consequence of intrinsic flaws in reason, but rather the over-optimistic estimation of the *power* of reason to determine people's beliefs; on the one hand positively through reasoning itself and, on the other hand, negatively by clearing away the clouds of fear caused by irrational superstition. Despite everything the rational-minded philosopher could do, people's

3

predilection to be swayed in their beliefs by the irrational, and by non-rational passions and desires, remained strong and probably ineradicable. If the failure of the Enlightenment means anything, then, it is the simplistic overestimation of the power of reason to control emotions, desires, wishes and other causes of belief, even when it is appropriate for reason to do so. By reason is meant open argument based on evidence, perhaps even systematic experimentation, which, when appropriate, should form the basis of our judgements and beliefs. Reason alone had been notably unable to settle matters such as the nature of the good life, or turn up a definitive system of ethics, while obviously being hugely successful in providing answers in other areas such as the physical sciences and mathematics. Again, this is only a problem for reason if one thinks a unified notion of the good life, perhaps as a basis for the ideal society, is possible, required and something we may expect reason to reveal, rather than our being content to live together with a plurality of views, allowing, as Mill called them, a variety of "experiments in living".[1] The reaction to this lack of a definitive conception of the good life led, in the nineteenth century, to an increasing call for liberalism. As doubt undermined the idea of a knowable unique view of how one should live, a view that in paternal high-handedness might and should be imposed on others, so the call grew stronger for how one should live to be determined as far as possible by the individual.

Indeed, this gives a clue as to where some sought refuge in nineteenth-century thought. It was in the philosophical elevation of the self or, more accurately, in selfhood: that in virtue of which we are aware of everything that we are aware of, beyond which there is nothing, or at least the utterly unknowable or ineffable. The self on this view is the locus, not only of values, as one might relatively uncontentiously suppose, but a determiner of the nature of reality. This "self" may refer in some philosophers to the individual self or mind; in others it refers to the universal generative nature of mind in general. In any event, the mind was seen as constitutive of the nature of reality, a reality that could no longer be "read off" independently of considering the mediating contribution of mind. Reality and values were no longer "out there" in the world in any straightforward objective sense, to be found naked after the contribution of mind is stripped away, but could rather only be understood with reference to, and exist through a dependence on, that sentience only through which awareness of reality and values is possible. The self was the new focus of philosophical concern both because of its being seen as an immovable shaping lens through which we view any world of which we could be aware, and because it is the residence of the will, the ultimate place where choices must be made as to what one should believe, value and do. Whatever we take "reality" or "the world" to be, we have to start by looking at the contribution of the self, from which they are inseparable, both perhaps epistemically and ontologically. Much of nineteenth-century philosophy is an exploration of what is seen as the new crucial role of the self.[2]

With the rise of radical pluralism in all sorts of fields, other than perhaps technology and science, came also what Nietzsche called the "death of God". It was not that in the nineteenth century there were not many people who still held strong religious belief. However, the determination of what place, if any, God, and the religious beliefs and trappings that were built on and adorned the supposition of His existence, should have in our lives was far more uncertain and this uncertainty more openly expressed. Among the educated, at least, belief in God became an increasingly private matter, bracketed off from other views about the world, where before it had been pervasive and all-inclusive. Some of the educated did indeed decisively reject belief in God, yet others were plagued by doubt; both on a scale, and to a degree, unthinkable in previous centuries, and certainly in any case little expressed publicly in earlier times. With this came the further decline, at least in the West, of the attractiveness of anything remotely resembling a systematic theocracy, even if religion still *de facto* pervaded the everyday life and thought of many people, as well as public and private institutions. Bit by bit secularism was chipping away at the last attempts of religion, in the name of God's known dictates, to lay down rules, solidified and enforced in law, as to how people should live. Some free spirits were able, through privilege and courage, to throw off the ruling of their lives by religion, which acted through the laws of the State and social convention. The nineteenth century was also a period of rapidity of change never before encountered. All these things showed themselves in political revolution, fecundity and experimentation in the arts, and individual soul-searching; all pointing to personal quests for credible ideas, firm ground on which to plant one's feet, which might then guide decisions in life. For the deepest thinkers it was the culmination of the agony of centuries.

The philosophers in this volume – Kant, Fichte, Hegel, Schopenhauer, Mill, Kierkegaard, Marx, Nietzsche – together fully reflect all these matters. They provide, through different lenses, views of the human condition that taken collectively encompass the range of conceptions explored in the nineteenth century. In them one finds grand plans, modest proposals and heroic desperation. Kant, although his work was published somewhat before the nineteenth century, is the intellectual powerhouse driving what is arguably most significant in nineteenth-century philosophy. Following the destructive undermining of the Enlightenment by Hume, Kant is seemingly its saviour, showing a way forwards. The salvation comes in the form of idealism: the solution to the problem of justifying our claims to grasp objective reality is that such reality, in so far as we can know it, is in fact in some way a product of, or dependent on, ourselves. Nothing can be known of reality apart from how it appears to ourselves considered as minds, and the fundamental structures we take to be features of the world – space, time, identity and causality – are not something we need to justify by deriving them from the world, but are rather what our minds bring to the world to form the experience we have in ways that cannot be otherwise, and without which experience would be impossible for us. The formative qualities of mind presented in Kant's philosophy of transcendental idealism are pervasive, but restricted to appearances; these formative qualities are extended to become all-pervasive in the philosophy of absolute idealism in Fichte and Hegel, and come to encompass the whole of reality. This goes beyond what Kant would have thought permissible and is just the sort of extension he sought to rule out by limiting knowledge to appearances, thereby, in an act of cognitive modesty, eliminating as futile metaphysical speculations that would seek to go beyond appearances. Nevertheless the argumentative momentum to absolute idealism – in which mind and world ultimately must become one – from Kant's transcendental idealism is powerful, and for Hegel and Fichte irresistible, since without it Kant's philosophy was seen as leaving a mysterious residual world "out there", an ontological dangler, of which we were always forbidden knowledge. Concepts are required for thought, they are the form of thought; direct access to an unconceptualized reality would be something literally unthinkable; thus reality must conform to the forms of thought. Such philosophy is driven to eliminate all ontological danglers and fill in all epistemic lacunas.

Hegel sees the progression to the eventual absolute conception of reality as something discernible in the increasing levels of understanding manifest in successive historical periods, and in the development of mind or spirit (*Geist*) itself. Indeed, it is the drive of the logical dialectic to remove inconsistency and incompleteness that moves history forwards, as it does human and individual understanding. Thus, *Geist* – mind or spirit – is manifest in an intertwined objective and subjective sense. What Marx takes from Hegel is his talk of long historical epochs that give a direction to history revealed in the movement from one epoch to another, and driven by underlying forces that stand behind the surface appearance of things. Where Marx differs from Hegel is in what he identifies as the engine of such change: not, as in Hegel, the state of the development of ideas manifest in the world-spirit (*Weltgeist*) of an epoch, but the tensions pent up in the material, economic and social, structures and processes.

In Mill we see someone less troubled by deep epistemic and metaphysical problems, relying on a sturdy empiricism that rejects the possibility of anything but houses of cards being built on speculative *a priori* reasoning alone. The purpose of science is to map the regularities of phenomenal experience, and questions that might arise from considering the metaphysical underpinnings of phenomena, which are inaccessible to science, are left neglected or their consideration rejected as futile. Mill's passionate advocating of experimental method, applied painstakingly and piecemeal, extends to his vision of society and ethics. Rather than present a blueprint for the good society, or lay down absolute *a priori* ethical rules, we should be guided by experience in considering what is best for people, and what we should value; his liberalism indeed advocates an open society in which these very matters – what is best for people, what we should value – can be debated and explored freely without the imposition of any paternalistic monist belief system, no matter how well intended. The structure of society should be such as to act as a laboratory for the exploration of values and the best ways for society to order itself. In order to explore effectively the proper bounds of liberty, as well as for the sake of liberty itself, a society must allow free speech and a plurality of values. Questions arise as to the limits of free speech and how we may accommodate such a plurality of values in a way that neither stymies them nor causes society to fragment under the pressure of people heading off in different directions. Mill attempts to give a utilitarian justification of liberal pluralism according to which liberal pluralism is itself valuable through being conducive to overall happiness. We need freedom in order to be happy because of human nature. We're not sheep. It is important for our happiness not just that we live a certain sort of life, but that whatever life we have is chosen by us.

Schopenhauer, like Fichte and Hegel, sees himself as the true heir to Kant. Yet, he too, although not an absolute idealist, may be seen as extending Kant beyond what he would have accepted. Schopenhauer argues that we can have awareness of things-in-themselves, but not in the representational manner by which we grasp appearances. Nor is there much of the optimism in Schopenhauer that one finds in Kant, for his view holds that the driving force of our lives is quite other than it seems, and when properly understood it renders life truly pointless. Our conscious understanding of the world is mostly as an appearance. Such an understanding gives merely a carapace of rationale that covers over a blind, striving, purposeless, inhuman reality, things-in-themselves – characterized as world-Will – whose essence is simply the striving for existence. As individual wills we are strapped to this mass of pointless striving; restlessly driven, individual pimple-wills on the face of the world-Will. Life is the futile attempt to satisfy our desires, interspersed with lagoons of boredom that only act to precipitate yet more striving. One may escape this unto-death alternation of boredom and striving, brought about by the tyranny of the will, only by a loss of self, as when one is fully absorbed in a work of art, or one engages in the ascetic denial of a saint; but either is possible for only the few.

A reaction rejecting idealism was not slow in coming in both Kierkegaard and Nietzsche. With Nietzsche we find a philosopher who tries fully to take on board the implications of bottomless uncertainty, and yet then to hold up triumphantly a heroic affirmation of life and values that overcomes the uncertainty in absolute awareness of it. Kierkegaard is a thinker equally troubled by the lack of a philosophical system that is not in truth a mere castle in the air, but who then concludes that without an individual decision to believe in God there can only be despair, and nothing can be built worth our emotional or intellectual affirmation; he therefore acknowledges that there is nothing else for it but to decide upon a leap of faith, without which we are lost. Otherwise, we shall be forever chasing our philosophical tails, or doomed to thoughtless conformity to the masses around us, or to a rudderless and despairing life. Kierkegaard is particularly mocking of Hegelian philosophical systems and their hubris. Nietzsche's rejection of philosophical systems and of God leads to a heroic attempt to live positively without either, this being the only honest way. For Kierkegaard, while also rejecting philosophical systems, Nietzsche's attempt must always be the impossible one of trying to hoist oneself up by a pulley that is floating unsupported in mid-air.

Once one passes through the full gamut of the nineteenth century's darkest speculations, the world never quite seems the same again, and afterwards there is no way back; we are thrown out forever from an innocent intellectual Garden of Eden of preordained order and adamantine certainty. The trajectory of nineteenth-century thought included modest hope in Kant, grand hope in Fichte and Hegel, grand despair in Schopenhauer, relatively untroubled escape into worldly matters in Marx and Mill, and explosions of both despair and affirmation in Kierkegaard and Nietzsche. All that forms the modern mind is present in the philosophers of this period. Standing back one may see that all are ruled by one regulative thought: to find the place of humanity in the world, a world in which old certainties were dead or dying. It is a search for a way to live with the stark truth about the human condition.

Kant is our beginning. Kant aims to solve the sceptical problems, as he saw it, left by the empiricism of Hume, by showing that the fundamental concepts Hume sought to derive from experience are in fact necessary conditions for experience. Kant also seeks to show that because both these necessary conditions for experience and experience itself are required for knowledge, metaphysical speculations, such as those found in the rationalism of Leibniz, that claim knowledge of reality beyond experience, must always be undecidable and futile. Rather than rushing headlong into trying to solve philosophical problems, Kant first critically examines the main tool of philosophical enquiry, that of reason, with the aim of drawing a boundary to proper philosophical speculation that uses reason. By having this boundary mark the limits of the knowable, he could contend that all the philosophical problems within could in principle be solved, while all the philosophical problems without should be seen as beyond solution and attempted solutions futile. In this way Kant sought to bring to an end once and for all the endless convolutions of centuries of grand philosophizing, leaving the remaining philosophical problems to be solved piecemeal from a modest firmly delineated platform, one where we would no longer be tempted to get carried away to endless speculations beyond the possibility of settlement in knowledge. The limits were the bounds of sense, or experience. Anything beyond the bounds of possible experience was beyond our knowledge. Within the bounds of sense are phenomena, or appearances; beyond the bounds are noumena, or things-in-themselves. Matters beyond such bounds could be thought about, but any problems arising there – such as free will, the existence of God, whether the universe had a beginning – could not be settled. The bounds of experience could be set because for experience to be possible it had to conform to certain necessary conditions imposed by the mind. This is the mind considered as transcendental self, not as an empirical self; the former is identified by, and determines, supposedly universal and necessary modes of human thought and experience. The imposed necessary conditions of possible experience are that it consists of objects existing in space and time and subject to the rules of causality. The senses alone are thoughtless and the understanding alone is empty. Knowledge of the world requires thought and experience in combination, and experience is given its form, but not its content, by mind.

The picture of the nineteenth century is somewhat complicated by two incompatible intellectual streams that deserve mention. The streams are neo-Kantianism, which perpetuated Kant's transcendental project in spirit, if not in letter, and naturalism, which opposed transcendentalism. The individual figures from these movements are largely forgotten, and have not, unlike the philosophers considered in this volume, stood the test of time; nevertheless, a good deal can be learnt from what they stood for. Naturalism opposed Hegelian idealism too, which developed out of Kant's philosophy. From around the middle of the century there was a relative decline in Hegelianism until its revival at the end of the century by the likes of Thomas Green and F. H. Bradley. The chief tenet of naturalism is to subsume all explanations, and indeed philosophy itself, under empirically known physical and causal scientific theories. Naturalism stands in contrast, most generally, to transcendentalism, of which Kant is the initiating and chief protagonist. A consideration of naturalism sheds considerable light on an underlying motivation of transcendentalism. If naturalism were true, then, according to the transcendentalist, there would be no room for normativity. By this is meant a realm of reasons and values, which makes no sense, it is argued, if the world can have a complete description in causal laws discovered through *a posteriori* empirical knowledge alone. The transcendentalist presents in some form a separate realm, accessible to *a priori* reasoning, which stands outside the causal nexus, without which talk of being correct or incorrect, according to non-natural rules, would make no sense. Under causal laws things either happen or they do not; there is no sense in saying that they are in error or making a mistake in happening or not happening, as one would be in drawing or failing to draw a conclusion in the course of an argument. There is a sense in which one should draw a logical inference that persists regardless of, and independently of, any facts concerning what happens or may happen. Most pressingly, the *should* of moral judgements (and aesthetic ones) seems to have no place in a purely causal world; indeed it is difficult to see how prescriptive morality can be reconstructed at all in a world with no place for anything but purely descriptive causal laws that leave room only for what *does* or *does not* happen, as opposed to what *should* or *should not* happen in a non-predictive normative sense. This naturalist strand is found prior to the nineteenth century in Hume, and Kant thought that if naturalism were true, then knowledge, moral and aesthetic judgements, and mathematics, would be impossible as their normativity could not be accounted for; therefore naturalism must be false. In Kant, the transcendental realm is provided by a notion of a transcendental self. The I as a mere natural object could not act normatively, in reasoning or values; it could not be a moral subject or moral object. Such a transcendental normative *a priori* realm also gives an autonomous subject matter for philosophy.

Kant's philosophy is the key to understanding the broad sweep of that which is most important and long lasting in nineteenth-century philosophy, and his ideas give it whatever unity it possesses. It connects together the diversity of the major nineteenth-century philosophers considered here by their being seen as various reactions to Kant. Much of nineteenth-century philosophy may be viewed as an affirmation or rejection of Kant. Not since Aristotle in the medieval period had one philosopher exerted such a pervasive influence, a defining framework within which philosophical problems are initially set up. Of those philosophers considered in this volume, Mill is an exception to this, for he derives his views directly from an earlier British empiricist tradition and largely circumvents Kant's influence.[3] As for the rest of the nineteenth-century philosophers in this volume, whichever way these philosophers take their ideas,

Kant is their starting-point, and the starting-point in Kant is the conception of a transcendental self. The transcendental self – as opposed to the contingent variation of individual selves – captures the notion of there being a set of necessary universal features, conceptual structures, in our minds that determine the way in which the world can be experienced as phenomena that is valid for all human beings, perhaps for all rational beings. The fundamental modes of human experience are in some sense necessary and universal for all mankind. As there is no way to remove these formative structures, there is no possibility of knowing what the world is like without them as noumena, and, as has been said, to speculate on such a world leads only to undecidable and thus futile metaphysical speculation. But this still leaves a hanging token "world", somehow existing in total independence of our subjectivity, but about which nothing can be known. Few philosophers were satisfied with this. Nor were they fully satisfied with the attempt to replace the sense of objectivity as something "out there", independent of the human mind, with objectivity as universal intersubjectivity based on common universal structures within human cognition. How could we be sure such structures are universally valid for all human beings? And even if they are, do they really deliver the full connotations of "objective"? Are such structures valid for all rational creatures or only for human beings? If only the latter, can it be truly claimed that they lay down the conditions of all possible experience and give the limits of knowledge? Dissatisfaction takes our philosophers in two opposing directions, albeit that what appears in each philosopher is significantly different in detail. There are those that affirm and extend the grasp of the transcendental self and its necessary conceptual structures, and those that reject the possibility of there being a transcendental self embodying such necessary conceptual structures.

Those that seek to extend the transcendental self or extend the supposed limits placed on our knowledge by it are Fichte, Hegel and Schopenhauer, and those that deny the existence of any transcendental self that might define universally valid modes of cognition are Kierkegaard and Nietzsche. In Fichte and Hegel, the transcendental self is extended to ultimately encompass the whole of reality. There is no longer a dummy "world" standing in the place of "the world as it is independent of any way we might have knowledge of it". This is accomplished by overcoming the subject and object distinction. The self and the world properly understood are one. So there is nothing left over that the mind cannot and may not know. Even in Marx, although the metaphysics is very different, there is a similar overcoming of the subject and object; but in Marx the collapse goes rather the other way, so that the objective material side becomes all-encompassing and the form and nature of the subject become largely determined by it. Schopenhauer abides, he thinks, by Kant's stricture

11

that knowledge proper may not extend beyond the bounds of possible experience, for knowledge requires conceptualization, and conceptualization only legitimately applies to the world as it is experienced. However, he argues that we nevertheless do have a non-experiential awareness from our own case of something that indicates what reality is like beyond our conceptualizations, namely our will as manifest in bodily action that we are directly aware of, and that Will as such is the ultimate nature of reality; reality as it is in itself beyond how we experience it.

There is, then, the other direction. There are those who reject the pretence of the transcendental self – Kierkegaard and Nietzsche – and hold that there is no necessary universally valid set of conceptual structures by which we have to grasp any world it is possible to know. In Nietzsche this rejection takes the form of saying that there can be a variety of perspectives, ways of conceptualizing the world, and none of them can meaningfully be said to give us *the* true structure of reality, for talk of such a reality makes no sense independently of some way of conceptualizing it, and there is no unique way of doing so. Some ways of conceptualizing reality may be better than others for certain purposes, but none can claim absolute ascendancy over the others. Kierkegaard too rejects the hubristic folly of the transcendental self and, even more, the preposterous extension of it to remove that modesty in its range that Kant thought vital in such a manner as to leave nothing that lies outside rational comprehension, so that the real and the rational become one. But nor does Kierkegaard think satisfactory, or liveable, the wide-open range of perspectives ushered in and welcomed by Nietzsche. It has to be said, however, that Nietzsche is clear that there is no possibility of simply switching with ease between cognitive perspectives and sensibilities that ground our sense of reality and values; rather, we are usually unaware of just how deeply they penetrate our very natures and form who we are and who we think we are. Nevertheless, for Nietzsche, an indefinite range of perspectives remain open as possibilities from which we may choose, through which we may attempt and achieve "self-overcoming", and in the course of which we should, most importantly, do our own work in thinking things out.[4] Kierkegaard rejects the extension, in the Hegelian manner, of the Kantian structures, because it produces spurious rational systems that crumble under the pressure of life. He also rejects Nietzsche's perspectival pluralism, because, if taken seriously, it can lead only to an abyss of nihilism that gives us no way of choosing how to live. In fact, we would probably end up simply buffeted into thinking the same as the thoughtless masses around us. Nietzsche is similarly suspicious of the thinking and morality of the masses, holding rather that we must make our own way and overcome our own limitations. Kierkegaard's answer is a return to faith, and to

Christian religion in particular, but we have to make a *personal* choice for which we alone are responsible as to what we believe and how we live; otherwise our lives are either inauthentic (because we thoughtlessly take on the views of those around us) or empty (because no rational ground exists on which to base our beliefs and lives). Nietzsche's answer is an overcoming of nihilism, a nihilism that seemingly follows as a consequence of the lack of a certain foundation to the whole of human thought; he asserts a defiant affirmation of life in the full glare of the truth about the human condition.

In a way, all these reactions can be seen as basically in thrall to the Kantian framework, although they try to go beyond it or throw it off. They all see the same problem: that of knowing that our basic conceptual structures apply to the world given that all we have is a subjective stance from which to view things. It is just that some solve this by leaving none of the world outside those conceptual structures, while others deny that there are universal conceptual structures at all. The first, however, threatens implausible conceptual absolutism, while the second threatens equally implausible conceptual relativism.

Kant's legacy extends into the twentieth century. As the twentieth century began, the division between those who took Kant as their philosophical starting-point and those who rejected such a starting-point as fundamentally misconceived opened up a divide between, respectively, continental European philosophy and Anglo-American philosophy. By the end of the twentieth century much had been done to bridge the rift through a greater common understanding and knowledge of the two traditions, and a new awareness of underlying similarities; but for many philosophers in both traditions a gap of comprehension as to each other's philosophy, and a disagreement about what philosophy should be doing, still remains.[5]

Notes

1. J. S. Mill, *On Liberty*, G. Himmelfarb (ed.) (Harmondsworth: Penguin, 1985 [1859]), Ch. 3, 120.
2. Consonant with the approach presented here is that to be found, in more extended form, in R. C. Solomon, *Continental Philosophy since 1750: The Rise and Fall of the Self* (Oxford: Oxford University Press, 1988). Central to his story overall is the rise and fall of an extraordinary conception of the self: that of the transcendental self, which in Kant, in an elaborately worked-out form, crucially for the account, gives rise to what Solomon calls the "transcendental pretence", and it is from this that many other philosophers, in various ways, have taken their cue.
3. Even so Mill's utilitarianism is usually thought to be illuminated by its standing in contrast to Kant's deontological ethical theory.
4. This latter point is brought out in a magnificent passage in Nietzsche's *Thus Spoke*

Zarathustra, where Zarathustra makes it clear that he does not want to be seen or treated as a traditional adored prophet who has subservient followers:

> "I now go away alone, my disciples! You too now go away and be alone! … Truly, I advise you: go away from me and guard yourselves against Zarathustra! And better still: be ashamed of him! Perhaps he has deceived you … One repays a teacher badly if one remains only a pupil … You say you believe in Zarathustra? But of what importance is Zarathustra? You are my believers: but of what importance are all believers? You had not yet sought yourselves when you found me. Thus do all believers; therefore all belief is of so little account. Now I bid you lose me and find yourselves; and only when you have all denied me will I return to you" (*Thus Spoke Zarathustra*, R. G. Hollingdale (trans.). (Harmondsworth: Penguin, 1980 [1883–85]), Part 1, "Of the Bestowing Virtue", §3, 103).

This passage, which expresses a vision of life without gods, or at least the thought of the possibility of such a life, could stand well as encapsulating a growing fundamental concern of its time; a prospect liberating and terrifying, hopeful and dangerous.

5. I am grateful to David E. Cooper for his insightful suggestions and comments on the Introduction. I should also like to thank Michael Inwood for his improving remarks on the Preface.

1

Immanuel Kant

Critique of Pure Reason

Michelle Grier

Immanuel Kant's *Critique of Pure Reason*, first published in 1781, is generally considered to be one of the most important and one of the most difficult texts in the history of philosophy.[1] In it, Kant develops his theory of *transcendental idealism*, which aims to provide a corrective to the problems generated by the theories offered by both his rationalist and his empiricist predecessors. The *Critique of Pure Reason* is thus where Kant lays out his own theory of knowledge (his "transcendental epistemology") and where he "critiques" metaphysics.

That reason needs a "critique" is demonstrated, according to Kant, by the fact that neither the empiricist nor the rationalist approaches had succeeded in resolving fundamental issues in epistemology and metaphysics. The methodological approach of the empiricists had, in the hands of Hume, only led to a form of pernicious scepticism, a scepticism that threatened to undermine empirical knowledge and science. That of the rationalists had opened up the floodgates for an unrestrained dogmatism, a dogmatism that flourished in the transcendent metaphysical theories about the soul, the world and God.

The problem of synthetic *a priori* knowledge

Kant's theoretical philosophy is often viewed as a response to a fundamental question: how are synthetic *a priori* propositions possible? Justifying such

principles is important to Kant because he believes that many of our judgements about the world are of this type; knowledge of nature is based on principles that state more than what can be known through logic alone, and yet such
principles cannot be justified by any particular experience. Previously, it was
generally held that there were two sorts of judgements or propositions: *a priori*, analytic, judgements and *a posteriori*, synthetic, judgements. Analytic
judgements are judgements in which the concept of the predicate is already
thought or contained in the concept of the subject. An obvious example of an
analytic judgement is "All triangles are three sided". Since the definition of a
triangle (a "three-sided figure") already, as it were, "contains" the predicate
("three-sided"), the judgement is true analytically. Because a mere analysis of
the concept (triangle) allows us to make this claim, it was held that such judgements were "*a priori*", or knowable independently of and not derivable from
any particular experience. This also links up with Kant's claim that analytic
judgements do not really extend our knowledge outside the concept of the
subject; they merely clarify it. Alternatively, a synthetic judgement ("Bodies are
heavy") is one in which the concept of the predicate is not already thought in
the concept of the subject, but is added to it in a way that extends our
knowledge.

Before Kant, it was generally held that only analytic judgements could be *a
priori* and necessary. Problems with this view arose, however, especially as a
result of the deconstructive analyses of David Hume. Hume began with a fundamental metaphysical principle: *every event has a cause*. Briefly, Hume noted
that this judgement, if coherent, would have to be either analytic/*a priori* or
synthetic/*a posteriori*. Hume basically showed that the principle did not fit
neatly into either category. It could not be justified by any appeal to experience
(*a posteriori*) because it presented itself as both universal (*all* events have causes)
and necessary, and no inductive procedure could ever accommodate these
features of the proposition. In short, the problem is that we are unable to examine *all* events, past, present and future. It could not be justified *a priori* (by
reason alone), however, because the connection between an event and its cause
is not analytic, and could never be discovered independently of experience. This
problem, the so-called "problem of induction", led Hume to suggest that the
principle was not philosophically justifiable at all. Left unresolved, Hume's
sceptical solution would be disastrous for natural science.

Kant is well aware of Hume's account of causality. Moreover, he agrees that
the principle of causality could never be justified by any appeal to experience.
Because the principle is necessary and universal, it asserts something well
beyond what any experience could prove, and presents as an *a priori* principle.
But Kant also agrees with Hume that the principle is synthetic. However, rather

than say that the principle is incoherent because it is both *a priori* and synthetic, Kant argues that what Hume had really illuminated was the possibility of an entirely different and previously unrecognized principle: a synthetic *a priori* principle. Kant holds that knowledge in mathematics and science is based upon synthetic *a priori* judgements. His transcendental idealism is thus supposed to account for the synthetic *a priori* principles in these disciplines. He argues, however, that the synthetic *a priori* propositions in the field of metaphysics are unjustified.

Transcendental idealism and the Copernican turn in philosophy

As above, Kant is well known for offering a unique form of idealism in philosophy. Kant's idealism, known as "transcendental idealism", examines the necessary (Kant calls them "transcendental") conditions in the human mind that make knowledge and experience possible. Kant's technical terminology poses one of the greatest obstacles to understanding his idealism, and the term "transcendental" occupies an important place in his lexicon. Unfortunately, Kant uses the term "transcendental" in a number of different, albeit closely associated, ways. Often, in claiming that something is "transcendental", Kant means to emphasize that it is non-empirical, or "pure", and does not have its source in experience. But Kant also uses this important term to refer to something's status as a "necessary condition". Kant is interested in disclosing subjective (mental) conditions that are transcendental in both of these senses (subjective conditions for knowledge and experience that are both *a priori* and necessary). Kant's original and revolutionary claim is that there are certain conditions that have to be met in order for us to have any experience at all. These conditions lie "in us", as part of the constitution of the human mind.

To understand this claim, it is important to see what Kant means by the "conditions" of human knowledge. Although Kant has been interpreted in a variety of ways, it seems clear that he at the least intends to say that whatever is able to count for us as an object must conform to certain cognitive conditions of the mind. In other words, Kant says that the way that we are constituted influences the way objects appear to us. One purpose of the *Critique of Pure Reason* is to identify the ways in which the human mind contributes to knowledge of objects. Kant does *not* argue that there can be any innate knowledge. He does, however, deny that the human mind is merely a passive recipient of the matter or data to be known and experienced. Instead, he suggests that we bring to experience certain kinds of necessary features, and that these features, imposed by the mind, play a role in constituting objectivity.

Kant begins by identifying two kinds of transcendental conditions. First, he claims that there are certain *sensible* conditions of knowledge, conditions that ground the possibility of sensibly intuiting (perceiving) any object. Secondly, he argues that there are certain *conceptual* conditions of knowledge, conditions that make possible the "thought" of the content given in sensibility. Kant thus first begins by identifying two distinct faculties or capacities of the mind: sensibility and understanding. *Sensibility* is defined as the receptivity of the mind by means of which objects can be given, and it gives rise to a unique kind of representation: an *"intuition"*. *Understanding* is the capacity for judgement, and the representations that ground its activities are called *concepts*.

This division of cognitive conditions reflects the Kantian view that human knowledge is *discursive*. To say that our knowledge is discursive is to say that it requires first that something be given to the human mind to intuit (perceive) as an object of the senses, and secondly that these intuitions (our sensory data) must be taken up and subsumed under (thought through) concepts. In other words, for us to know anything, we must both sense it and understand what we are sensing. Thus, for Kant, knowledge always requires both intuitions and concepts. Without intuitions, there could be no content to think about and know; without concepts, there would be no cognition or knowledge of what is given. In Kantian terms, "Thoughts without intuitions are empty, intuitions without concepts are blind" (A51/B76).

In making these claims, Kant introduces what he calls a "Copernican revolution" in philosophy. Early theorists had thought that the sun revolves around the earth. Copernicus, however, suggested that the apparent movement of a heavenly body is in fact owing to the earth's own motion relative to it. In an analogous way, Kant tells us that he intends to shift our perspective on the relation between the knowing subject (the mind) and objects of knowledge. Previously, Kant contends, philosophers had assumed that objects exist in a mind-independent manner: that they have an absolute existence independent of any possible human experience of them. On this assumption, knowledge consisted in having our beliefs and perceptions correspond and conform to the way that objects "really are", in themselves. Kant suggests that such an assumption, that knowledge has to conform to the absolutely independent constitution of objects, leads to problems. For there opens up an unbridgeable epistemological gap between the subject (the knower) and the object, and we can never be sure that our concepts or perceptions really do accurately map onto the object. Roughly, the problem is that things might appear to us (either perceptually or conceptually) in ways that are different from the ways they really are. In response to this, Kant presents his own hypothesis. Suppose that rather than knowledge having to conform to objects, objects have to conform to certain *a priori* epistemological conditions of the mind. This suggestion entails that what it means to be an object is in some sense antecedently dependent on the subject for whom it is an object. Analogously with the Copernican revolution, then, what thinkers had previously attributed to features of the world are in fact features of us.

Kant's Copernican revolution reflects an explicit shift away from a "theocentric" model of knowledge. Rather than trying to acquire knowledge of objects as they might exist in some absolute sense, from a non-human standpoint, or from God's point of view, we must consider such objects in their necessary connection with the epistemological conditions of the mind. In this case, our knowledge is always relative to the specifically human standpoint. Once again, Kant thinks that there are both sensible and intellectual (or conceptual) conditions of knowledge. In the *Critique of Pure Reason*, Kant discusses these in turn.

The sensible conditions of knowledge: Kant's transcendental aesthetic

The transcendental aesthetic is the section in Kant's *Critique of Pure Reason* devoted to examining the *a priori* conditions of sensibility. It is here that Kant famously (some might say notoriously) argues that space and time are the subjective conditions of the human mind under which objects can be given to us in sense. This position is striking in so far as it rejects what had been the more dominant conceptions of space and time. Kant explicitly poses the problem by distinguishing his view from both the Newtonian and the Leibnizian theories of space and time. According to Newton, absolute space and time were real existences, and operated as the ontological conditions for all things. In this, Newton held that space and time were logically prior to objects. Leibniz, however, had contended that space and time were not "real" in this sense. Rather, he argued that space and time were the ideal relations that hold between pre-existing monads. Although their views are opposed, note that both Newton and Leibniz agree that the properties of space and time hold of objects independently of any connection with our mind. More specifically, both Newton and Leibniz think that space and time are based on something systematic about a mind-independent reality. In Kantian terms, as we shall see below, both Newton and Leibniz take space and time to be *transcendentally real*: to hold of things independently of any human mind.

Kant rejects the transcendental reality of space and time. Instead, he argues that space and time are merely the subjective conditions under which the *human mind* intuits objects. All objects, according to Kant, are given in time, the form of inner sense. All outer objects (extended objects) are also given in space. To say this is to say that space and time operate as the *a priori* and necessary (that is, the transcendental) conditions under which beings with a certain kind of sensibility are constrained to be given objects. That is to say, space and time are "transcendentally ideal" and, independently of the human mind, they are not real existences. How can Kant show this?

Kant's arguments for the transcendental ideality of space and time are rather controversial. He begins with our representations of space and time. He first wants to show that these representations are *a priori*, that is, that we could never have acquired these representations from our experiences of objects. Secondly, he wants to show that these representations are *intuitions* (they are not "concepts"). Kant thinks that by showing that space and time function as *a priori* intuitions, he will prove that space and time are "in us", and that they only hold for objects of our (human) sensibility.

In stating that space and time are *a priori*, Kant insists that we could never have come up with any representation of space by deriving it (as the empiricists had said) from our experiences of objects. One might think, for example, that we could have come up with the idea of space simply by experiencing objects as next to or above one another, or as spatially distinct from us. The representation of space, in such a case, would be something we acquire through experience. But Kant argues that this is impossible, for in order to represent objects as distinct from us, or as next to or beside one another, space would already have to be presupposed. Kant also notes that even though it is possible for us to think of space and time as empty (without objects), we cannot represent objects except as in space and time. This shows, according to Kant, that space and time cannot be derived from our experience of objects. Indeed, he claims that it shows that space and time already necessarily condition and make possible our experience of objects.

Moreover, Kant contends that our representations of space and time are very different from any abstract concept. For concepts are general, and refer to a number of possible objects. My concept of a "human being", for example, refers to any one of a number of objects (any number of possible individual human beings). Intuitions, however, are not general in this way. An intuition is the immediate contact with a particular object. When I see John, for example, I am representing, in "empirical intuition", a singular person, not human beings in general. Space and time, according to Kant operate as the form or context within which we can *intuit* objects. Kant emphasizes this view by referring to space and time as "pure forms of sensibility", or "pure intuitions". Once again, what he means by this is that space and time are the conditions under which particular objects are intuited (sensed) *by us*. Because of this, Kant argues that independently of the human mind, space and time are "nothing": "Time is therefore merely a subjective condition of our human intuition (which is always sensible …) and in itself, outside the subject, is nothing" (A35/B52). Because space and time only hold for sensible beings, Kant thinks that objects given *in* space and time always have a necessary relation to the mind.

There are passages in the *Critique of Pure Reason* where Kant admits that there may be beings who share forms of sensible intuition like ours (perceive things under the conditions of space and time), but he quickly adds that if there are such beings, then all that this means is that such beings would be limited in the way that human beings are:

> It is not necessary to limit the kind of intuition in space and time to the sensibility of human beings; it may well be that all finite think-ing beings must necessarily agree with human beings in this regard (though we cannot determine this), yet even given such universal validity this kind of intuition would not cease to be sensible …
>
> (B72)

Kant's aim is to delineate our epistemological predicament, as finite discursive knowers, and to preclude any adoption of an absolutistic or theocentric stand-ard for knowledge. Space and time, therefore, are understood by Kant (for all intents and purposes) as forms of human sensibility. What this means is that human knowledge is always limited to the forms or conditions under which we (as discursive finite knowers) can be given objects.

This claim has a startling consequence: it entails that we need to draw a distinction between the way we talk about objects in their necessary connection to human sensibility, on the one hand (as spatial and temporal objects), and the way that we talk about them as they might be independently of this connection. Kant thinks that some of the most profoundly harmful errors in philosophy have occurred precisely because philosophers confused or conflated the consid-eration of objects from these different points of view.

The distinction between appearances and things-in-themselves

One of the most controversial and important distinctions in Kant's philoso-phy is the so-called "transcendental distinction" between "appearances" (or phenomena) and "things-in-themselves" (noumena). Although controversial, a solid grasp of this distinction is crucial for understanding Kant's idealism. The transcendental distinction between appearances and things-in-themselves follows from the analyses of space and time. Kant refers to the objects given to the mind under the conditions of human sensibility (in space and time) as "appearances". The word "appearance" has a unique connotation for Kant, and we must be careful in trying to interpret Kant's claim, for he uses the term in a rather technical, "transcendental", sense. He does not mean that there are no real objects independently of the human mind (e.g. objects outside our bodies), as though everything we experience is an illusion, a fiction, or "unreal". By an *appearance* Kant essentially means a spatiotemporal object. The reason Kant calls these objects *appearances* is that space and time are "in us". Because space and time are subjective conditions (forms) of our (human) sensibility, the objects experienced *in* space and time always have a necessary connection to the human mind too, and must always be viewed in their possible connection to human sensibility. This entails that we cannot meaningfully apply spatiotemporal properties to non-sensible objects. This claim, of course, goes hand in hand with Kant's Copernican revolution, that is, his view that as human beings we can only experience and know objects from our own human standpoint. We cannot experience any object from some mystical God's-eye point of view. Knowledge is relative to our own constitution as finite discursive knowers.

Kant's idealism is thus distinct from other traditional forms of idealism. Once again, Kant does not, for example, deny that there are real empirical, mind-independent, objects, nor does he claim that our knowledge is limited to our own subjective representative states (ideas in our minds) in such a way as to lack any objective validity. On the contrary, Kant claims that we can have genuine knowledge of empirical objects that really exist. Kant uses specific terminology to make his point. According to him, appearances are, like space and time, "*empirically real*". They are the real, empirical objects of human experience, about which we can acquire scientific knowledge. Nevertheless, appearances, again like space and time, are held to be at the same time "*transcendentally ideal*". These objects can only be experienced and known under the subjective (transcendentally ideal) conditions under which they can be given to and taken up by the mind. Once again, in Kantian terms, they can only be known "as appearances", in the transcendental sense. This claim, in turn, will ground Kant's efforts to undermine attempts to acquire knowledge of objects that are not given in sensible intuition. Indeed, it is Kant's claim that what such objects would be like independently of these sensible conditions is unknown to us.

We are now in a position to examine what Kant means by "things-in-themselves". A "thing-in-itself" is an object considered independently of human sensibility. The concept of the thing-in-itself is thus essentially a way of *thinking* objects in such a way that abstracts from our own sensible capacities. The problem, for Kant, is that when we abstract from all those conditions under which any real object could be given to us in sensation, we thereby abstract from all the empirical content. What we are left with is the bare *thought* of something that, to be known and experienced, would have to be given in space and time. One might ask, at this point, why Kant even speaks about the thought of objects as things-in-themselves. If all real objects are appearances in his unique (transcendental) sense, and if these are the only objects we can experience, then why bother talking at all about mysterious and unknowable "things-in-themselves"?

There are a number of possible responses to this question. One might say that Kant is committed to the real existence of some "thing" that "appears" to us under the forms of space and time, and that he requires the concept of the thing-in-itself in order to account for the cause of appearances in us. Such suggestions imply that there is some "unknown true reality" lurking out there that we can only access under certain human forms of perception. But if Kant is saying this, then he does seem to be adopting a non-human standpoint, for how can we even think about objects "independent of the human mind" if we are limited to our own decidedly human standpoint? Puzzles such as this have given rise to a variety of interpretations (and criticisms) of Kant's distinction.

Without minimizing the complexity of Kant's transcendental distinction, however, we might note that an obvious answer to this question lies in Kant's view that human beings have two capacities that ground knowledge. First, as we have seen, sensibility is the capacity to be given objects in intuition; but understanding is a capacity to conceptualize and make judgements about objects so given. Kant insists that these two capacities are different in kind, and cannot reduce to one another. Moreover, Kant maintains that our capacity to "think" goes *beyond* the bounds of sense, beyond the limits of sensibility. In short, Kant's view is that we can "think" in a way that abstracts from all empirical content. Although this capacity allows us to form a problematic *concept* of a thing as it might be in itself, we have also seen that such a "problematic concept" lacks content. In order to understand this claim, we must turn to Kant's discussion of the conceptual conditions of knowledge.

The conceptual conditions of knowledge: Kant's transcendental analytic

The transcendental analytic is the section of the *Critique of Pure Reason* wherein Kant examines the "conceptual conditions" of knowledge. As we have seen, Kant argues that human knowledge is discursive, and requires both intuitions and concepts. And we have seen as well that Kant maintains that any object of human experience has to conform to the conditions of space and time. If, in general, we now try to round out Kant's theory of knowledge, we must first consider the conceptual conditions he thinks the mind contributes to knowledge and to the experience of objects. Without some conceptual appropriation, without judgement, no experience of an object is possible.

Concepts are required in order to make judgements about that which is given in sensation. Kant's view is that even the most simple of perceptual experiences involves an act of conceptualization whereby the given is synthesized (combined) and ordered. The experience of perceiving a table in front of me involves applying concepts of existence and "table" and so on. Kant thus aligns himself against the empiricist tradition according to which the mind is a "blank slate" and simply receives sensory impressions from "objects" presented to us. According to Kant, these sensory impressions are themselves "perceived" only because they are "taken up" and "ordered" in the pure manifold of space and time. That is, the mind determines these data by subsuming them under the conceptual rules of the understanding. The specified procedures for subsuming objects under these rules are actually quite complex. Kant offers a robust and detailed account of the functions of the mind that ground judgements about phenomena. Nevertheless, the central point is that the mind plays an essentially active role in synthesizing the data of sense. Thus, even immediate perceptual experience is made possible only because the data are taken up by the mind and conceptualized in some way.

Kant goes further. He thinks that these ordinary acts of conceptualization (judgement) are rooted in various rules that have their source *a priori* in the mind. Kant calls these rules "the pure concepts of the understanding" or, alternatively, the "categories". What he argues is that *any* act of conceptualizing, and thus all our ordinary empirical concepts, are ultimately grounded in these *a priori* rules for thinking possible objects.

Kant is well known for claiming to have identified exhaustively the *a priori* rules for thinking objects, the most fundamental concepts in the mind that ground the thought of any object whatsoever. How did he find them? As a clue to discovering the most fundamental concepts, those that allow us to think any possible object that could be given, Kant turns to the forms of judgement. More specifically, Kant turned to the articulation of the fundamental "forms" of judgement that had already, he alleged, been exhaustively identified by general logic. Such "forms of judgement" include, for example, the form of a categorical judgement ("*A* is *B*") or the form of a hypothetical judgement ("If *A* then *B*"). Kant's essential point is that the mind is constrained to order appearances according to certain judgemental forms, and that to do so is to conceptualize the data of sense in specific ways. Because Kant believed that the forms of judgement had all been exhaustively identified, he took these fundamental forms of all thinking, and derived from them a corresponding set of pure concepts of the understanding. Such pure concepts (categories), examples of which are substance, causality, possibility, necessity, reality and so on, are the most general conceptual rules that ground our thought of objects as such. In Kantian terms, they are rules for thinking possible objects in general. Kant presents the table of categories as follows (cf. A80/B106):

Table of Categories

1. Of Quantity
Unity
Plurality
Totality

2. Of Quality
Reality
Negation
Limitation

3. Of Relation
Of Inherence and Subsistence
(*substantia et accidens*)
Of Causality and Dependence
(cause and effect)
Of Community (reciprocity
between agent and patient)

4. Of Modality
Possibility–Necessity
Existence–Non-existence
Necessity–Contingency

Having identified the necessary concepts, Kant subsequently attempts to justify their use as *a priori* modes of knowledge and experience. Such is the aim of the transcendental deduction. Kant's transcendental deduction is a notoriously difficult example of philosophical argumentation. It should be noted that, in addition to being notoriously difficult, the transcendental deduction is the subject of a variety of interpretations among scholars. Nevertheless, it is possible to identify the outlines of the argument. A "deduction" is a justification *for the use* of a concept. Notice that the principal aim of the transcendental deduction is to show that whatever is to count as an object or an objective order must conform to the categories. Here again, this claim goes hand in hand with Kant's Copernican revolution. What he is essentially trying to show is that anything that is going to count as an object must comply with the mind's fundamental structures. This radical claim entails that "objectivity" itself is in some necessary relation to subjectivity.

One central move in Kant's demonstration concerns his theory of self-consciousness, and it is important enough to consider in some detail here. According to Kant, if something is to count as an object for me, it has to be possible for me to become self-consciously aware of it as such. If I cannot become so aware, then it is not an object "for me". In attempting to isolate the pure (*a priori*) form of this self-consciousness, Kant abstracts from the empirical content of consciousness. He calls this form of self-consciousness "transcendental apperception". According to Kant:

> It must be possible for the "I think" to accompany all my representations; for otherwise something would be represented in me that could not be thought at all, which is as much as to say that the representation would either be impossible or else at least would be nothing to me.
> (B131–2)

Here Kant refers to the necessity of the possibility of connecting the manifold of intuition up to the same, singular, "I". This is formulated in terms of the analytic claim that in order for representations to be mine, they must one and all be capable of being connected up to me, the "I think". But Kant's further, and more important, claim is that knowledge requires that all representations be able to be connected up with the same (identical, unitary) "I". In Kantian terms, there must be a "unity" of consciousness. The claim that experience is grounded in self-consciousness proved to be the revolutionary inspiration and starting-point of the German idealists, such as Fichte, Schelling, Hegel and Schopenhauer.

As we shall see, when Kant argues for the necessity of an analytic unity of consciousness, he is not arguing (as Descartes had) that the "I" that thinks is a simple and unified being or substance, such as a soul. Kant's claim is very *formal*. What he maintains is that objects have to be connected up to the "I think", as a formal representation: that they have to be referred representationally back to the same *act* of self-consciousness. Why? Take a general case. Suppose I am aware of a set of discrete judgements, for example, "It is cold", "I want to go home" and "Bach makes beautiful music". Kant's claim is that in order for each of these to be represented as *my* thoughts, they must be connected up to the *same* "I think". Otherwise, the possibility remains that each thought is connected up with a distinct self, and there could be no "unity of consciousness": in Kant's words, there would be just as "many-colored and diverse a self as I have representations of which I am conscious to myself" (B134). The "I" who recognizes the talent of Bach might be entirely different from the "I" who wants to go home. In such a case, it is utterly impossible to account for coherent experience and knowledge.

The plot now thickens. In order for this to succeed, Kant notes that there must be a "synthesis of the manifold" in intuition. I could not represent myself as a singular "I" unless I (at the same time) synthesized the manifold into one representational unity. There would be no representation of the identity of the "I" throughout all these modifications of thought unless I could become aware, in one act, of myself as the "thinker" of each of these disparate thoughts. In the more general case above, I think that "it is cold" and "I want to go home" and that "Bach makes beautiful music", and it is the capacity to recognize the conjunction of these thoughts as all belonging to me that renders me capable of thinking myself as one singular self-consciousness, one self-consciousness that remains the same throughout changing judgements. Thus the very representation of myself as singular and identical presupposes a synthesis of the manifold into one whole. Because the combination or synthesis of the manifold of intuition is always accomplished through the application of the conceptual rules for combining the data of sense (the categories), it follows that all my experience conforms to these rules.

Kant goes even further. He does not simply say that these abstract categories are the rules for ordering our experience in order to make it coherent. He also wants to show how each concept yields a specific *principle of empirical knowledge* when it is applied to the manifold (roughly, the data given under the condition) of time. The category of "cause", for example, when it applies to objects given in time, tells us that any object (or event), any alteration in time, must be subject to the category of causality. And this means, specifically, that human experience and knowledge are guided by the necessary principle that "every event has some cause". Kant defends an entire system of such principles, each generated by applying a category to the manifold of time. This system of principles is outlined in detail by Kant in the sections of the analytic entitled "Axioms of Intuition", "Anticipations of Perception", "Analogies of Experience" and "Postulates of Empirical Thought". The upshot is that by means of a set of very complex arguments, Kant claims to be able to justify and ground the legitimate use of the synthetic *a priori* principles (such as the causal principle) that are presupposed in the natural sciences.

It should be noted that even though the concepts of the understanding are said to be necessary in determining any object that could be given to us, Kant also argues that the categories can only be legitimately employed in connection with the manifold of *sensible intuition*. Only in application to sensible intuition do the categories succeed in yielding the principles of knowledge. (In Kantian terminology, the categories have to be "*schematized*".) Apart from this, the categories are said to be purely empty "forms" for thinking objects in general. This claim follows from Kant's view that *knowledge*, as opposed to mere *thought*, requires both intuitions (content) and concepts (forms). In this connection, Kant emphasizes that the categories may seem to allow a more general application precisely because it is possible to *think* beyond the limits of sensible intuition. We can do this because these concepts are the most general rules in terms of which any rational being thinks about possible objects. We can think, for example, of a something in general that is not necessarily a spatiotemporal object. Kant's view, however, is that in so doing we are merely (and indeterminately) thinking some possible "object", without there being anything actual or determinate given to think about. Until, that is, the category is "applied" to some empirically given data (intuition), it lacks any real content, and so provides no knowledge.

Kant's theory of knowledge thus has two sides. On the positive side, he claims to have demonstrated the *a priori* possibility of real knowledge of objects of possible experience. Because whatever is to count as such an object must conform to the sensible and conceptual conditions of the mind, the possibility of real knowledge is secured. We can thus know, for example, that (*contra* Hume) objects of our experience really are themselves subject to the causal principle. Indeed, Kant thought that by demonstrating the necessary role played by the principles of the understanding, he had secured the foundation for empirical knowledge and science, and had, thereby, undermined scepticism. On the negative side, however, Kant argues that the principles and concepts of the mind have to be limited to objects of experience (phenomena). Indeed, the *positive* results of Kant's efforts to justify the application of the concepts and principles of the understanding to appearances or phenomena (objects of experience) entail the *negative* result that these do not yield knowledge of any non-phenomenal object. Our concepts and principles only yield knowledge of objects given to us in sensibility.

The restrictive aspect of Kant's epistemology, his claim that we can only have knowledge of objects given to us in experience, is one of the most influential aspects of his work. Indeed, a major goal of Kant's idealism is to "curb the pretensions of the understanding": to limit our knowledge claims to objects considered in their necessary relation to the human standpoint (appearances, or phenomena). This entails that human knowledge can only extend to objects given in experience, and thus that the hope of acquiring metaphysical knowledge of objects that transcend the bounds of sense is doomed to fail.

A problem of course remains, and it is one that we have encountered in connection with the discussion of things-in-themselves. The problem is that the human mind is characterized by an intellectual capacity to think in abstraction from the domain of sensibility and experience. This capacity has proved to be so powerful that it has seduced us into making claims that go well beyond anything that could be confirmed by or given in experience. The effort to acquire knowledge beyond the bounds of sense manifested itself traditionally in the staggering array of metaphysical doctrines in the rationalist tradition. After securing empirical knowledge and the possibility of science, therefore, Kant considers the synthetic *a priori* propositions advanced in metaphysics. Kant's claim will be that the metaphysical doctrines involve the error of confusing appearances (phenomena) with things-in-themselves (noumena).

To anticipate, we can already see that if the principle of causality only applies to objects of human sensibility (appearances), it makes no sense to try to ask ourselves what, if anything, preceded the world (understood as the sum total of all appearances) in time. Similarly, if the category of substance only applies to sensible (spatiotemporal) objects, it makes no sense to ask ourselves whether the soul is a "substance", since the soul is never encountered as a sensible object. Exposing these errors in the field of metaphysics is the task of Kant's transcendental dialectic.

The critique of metaphysics: Kant's transcendental dialectic

The transcendental dialectic contains Kant's criticisms of traditional metaphysics. More specifically, Kant directs his attack at the three branches of special metaphysics in the rationalist tradition: rational psychology, rational cosmology and rational theology. Rational psychology is the branch of metaphysics concerned to identify the nature and the constitution of the "soul". (Is the soul a simple substance? Is it identical, and distinct from the body?) In rational cosmology, we want to acquire knowledge about the nature of the "world". (Is the universe finite or infinite?) Finally, rational theology is devoted to proving the existence of God. Kant uses his own transcendental epistemology (his theory of knowledge) in order to show that such knowledge is *impossible*. It is essentially here, then, in the transcendental dialectic, that Kant offers his "critique" of "pure reason", for it is precisely the field of metaphysics that seems to hold the last remaining promise of acquiring knowledge that goes beyond any experience. The promise under Kant's gaze is, unfortunately, one that cannot be met.

We might ask why Kant needs to discuss these metaphysical disciplines at all. In so far as he has already shown, in the transcendental analytic, that all of our concepts and principles can only apply to sensible objects, it seems that the task of undermining metaphysics has already been accomplished. Nevertheless, Kant avers that human reason is so constituted that it inevitably defies the boundaries outlined in the transcendental analytic. A major part of Kant's effort, then, will be in showing that despite all critical warnings, reason is subject to an *illusion* that leads it to transcend experience in a quest for ultimate knowledge.

Reason and transcendental illusion

Kant defines "dialectic" as "the logic of illusion" (A61–2/B86–7). In his transcendental dialectic, he will be concerned to "expose the illusion" involved in our attempts to acquire knowledge of transcendent objects (A298/B355). Kant's general view is that the traditional efforts to acquire knowledge in metaphysics involve going well beyond the bounds of experience in order to make assertions about objects (e.g. the soul) that we could never be given in our sensible experience. Thus, even though he takes himself to have shown in the transcendental analytic that the concepts of the understanding can only yield knowledge of objects considered as appearances, he thinks that human reason has an unavoidable interest in going beyond these objects in its vain quest to acquire metaphysical knowledge of "things-in-themselves". It is thus important to note that even though Kant will reject the metaphysical arguments, he nevertheless thinks that it is the *very nature of human reason* to try to acquire knowledge of things that transcend all experience. Our interests in this regard are essentially twofold: first, Kant suggests that we have a theoretical or scientific interest in achieving completeness of knowledge; secondly, he contends that we have practical (moral) interests in establishing the immortality of the soul, freedom and the existence of God. None of these interests, however pressing, can be satisfied by explanations derived from sensible experience.

In the introduction to the dialectic, Kant identifies reason as a unique capacity, one characterized by an ability and a tendency to think beyond all objects of sense. Unlike the understanding, which Kant claims is concerned to "secure the unity of appearances by means of rules", reason is said to be a faculty of "principles" (B359). What Kant generally suggests, then, is that reason is to be construed as a higher-order capacity to take the knowledge given through the understanding, and unify it under ever fewer principles. Such a capacity is essential both to the unification of knowledge into scientific theory, and to our moral endeavours. These demands of reason link up, for Kant, with what he calls a demand for the "unconditioned". The demand for the "unconditioned" essentially amounts to a demand for ultimate explanations. Thus, Kant claims that reason is characterized by the following prescription: "*Find for the conditioned knowledge given through the understanding, the unconditioned whereby its unity is brought to completion*" (A308/B364, emphasis added).

Reason, that is, expresses our interest in providing an explanatory account that is complete. This fuels, for example, our efforts to go beyond explanations for various empirical phenomena in the world, and to find an ultimate explanation for the world itself.

In the process of performing its unavoidable function, Kant suggests, reason posits the "unconditioned" (roughly, the ultimate ground of explanation) as given, and there to be found. In Kantian terms, we slide from the above rational *prescription to seek* completeness of knowledge to a principle stating that "If the conditioned is given, the absolutely unconditioned … is also given" (A308/B366). Herein lies the problem: the "unconditioned", or the ultimate explanatory ground that we seek, is nowhere given to us in the field of appearances. If we ask, for example, "What caused the universe?", there is nowhere in our human sensible experience that we can find ultimate answers of this sort: original uncaused causes. Thus, reason is led inevitably to go beyond the bounds of experience in order to find a resting place for thought. This assumption, that the "unconditioned" is given, is linked up for Kant with what he refers to as "transcendental illusion [*tranzendentale Illusion*]".

Kant characterizes transcendental illusion as a tendency to "take a subjective necessity of a connection of our concepts … for an objective necessity in the determination of things in themselves" (A297/B354). Basically, Kant suggests that reason has an unavoidable tendency to take our subjective interests and principles (such as the interest in securing explanatory completeness) to hold "objectively" independently of us. How is this illusion manifested? Kant's claim is that in its efforts to bring knowledge to completion, reason posits certain ideas that serve to explain phenomena. Kant focuses on three such ideas of reason in the dialectic: the soul, the world and God. What he suggests is that we arrive at, for example, the idea of the soul because we want to give a complete or exhaustive account of psychological phenomena (we want to understand what it is that ultimately grounds all thinking). Similarly, we posit the world (that is, the totality of all things in time) in our efforts to provide complete explanations about the sum of all appearances. Each of the ideas of reason, in other words, is conceived in our efforts to account for various kinds of phenomena.

The problem, as we shall see, is that even though reason represents these ideas *as* objects, the ideas do not refer to anything that is or could ever be given to us in sensible experience. The soul, the world and God are not objects of any possible sensible experience. In Kantian terms, these ideas lack "*objective reality*"; they refer to no real object. It is common, therefore, to find Kant referring to the ideas of reason as "pseudo objects", "fictions of the brain" or "mere thought entities". What he is saying is that the so-called (transcendent) "objects" that are the subject of metaphysical enquiries are merely *ideas in us*, and do not refer to any object of possible knowledge.

Although Kant argues that reason's ideas are illusory, and fail to refer to any knowable object, it is not the case that he thinks they are arbitrary or avoidable. Indeed, Kant thinks that the reason why metaphysics is so seductive is precisely because reason has an unavoidable interest in providing ultimate explanations. Moreover, as we shall see, Kant will actually want to defend the use of these ideas in *some sense*. His claim will be that, even though the ideas of reason do not yield *knowledge* of any real object, they nevertheless play an important, indeed an indispensable, role in guiding our enquiries. Before considering this claim, it is important to see why he thinks the ideas of reason do not, and cannot, yield knowledge.

Rational psychology, the soul, and the paralogisms

Is the soul an immaterial being? Is it simple, and identical? One longstanding metaphysical interest has been in providing answers to such questions. Many philosophers before Kant had developed arguments about the nature and the constitution of the soul. René Descartes, for example, famously stated, "I think, therefore I am". Descartes thought that his existence could be proved simply from an analysis of the activity of his own thinking. When Descartes asked himself, "What is this I?", he responded by claiming that the "I" is a "thing that thinks", by which he meant a soul. Descartes is thus an example of a philosopher who suggested that the soul is an object whose existence and nature could be determined independently of any sensible experience. Indeed, since the soul is not an object of sensation and experience, the only knowledge we could have would seem to be through reason.

The branch of metaphysics concerned with arguments about the soul is referred to by Kant as "rational psychology". In the section entitled "Paralogisms of Pure Reason", Kant undertakes to show that none of the synthetic *a priori* conclusions drawn about the soul are justified. Indeed, Kant wants to show that any effort to acquire knowledge about the soul through concepts alone is doomed to fail. In this it is clear that Kant is not arguing against empirical accounts of the self (i.e. he is not criticizing empirical psychology). Rather, his target is all those theories, such as those of Descartes or Leibniz, that purport to derive conclusions about a metaphysical self purely *a priori*, simply from an analysis of the activity of thinking. Kant emphasizes this purely conceptual basis for the metaphysical doctrines of the soul by telling us that in rational psychology, the "I think" is the sole text (A343–4/B401–2). In short,

Kant is criticizing as insupportable those doctrines that move from pure (transcendental) self-consciousness to a theory of the soul as an object.

Kant identifies two errors in these attempts. First, he says that the "soul" is not an object that could be known, for it is nowhere given to us in space and time. Rather, the "soul" is merely an *idea* of reason, one to which we are led in our quest for the "unconditioned", so that we can find an ultimate ground or explanation for psychological phenomena. Thus a metaphysics of the soul is motivated by reason's demand for the "absolute (unconditioned) unity of the thinking subject itself" (A334/B391). In accordance with such a demand, the rational psychologists attempt to prove the substantiality, simplicity and personal identity of the soul. More specifically, he thinks that reason's tendency towards illusory representations leads us to take what is merely an idea in us to be a real metaphysical object about which we could acquire knowledge. Indeed, according to Kant, a "natural illusion" compels us to take the apperceived unity of consciousness for an intuition of an object" (B402).

Kant's complaint is that the rational psychologist mistakenly moves from certain subjective features of self-consciousness to a metaphysics of the self as an object. Beginning with the formal and *a priori* representation characteristic of transcendental apperception (the "I" or the "I think"), the metaphysician tries to argue that the "I" is an object that can be known. In each case, according to Kant, a feature of self-consciousness gets transmuted into a metaphysics of the self as an object. Thus, owing to the fact that in transcendental self-consciousness the "I" is a subject of thought, we conclude that the "I" is a substance in the metaphysical sense (a self-subsistent being). Similarly, because the "I" of self-consciousness is always represented as unitary and identical, we conclude that the "I" is an object that can be known to be simple, and to have identity. Kant goes to considerable lengths to remind us that transcendental self-consciousness is merely a *form of thinking*, and that by itself it gives us no *object to think about*. The judgement that "I am thinking", for example, expresses an activity of thought. But taken by itself alone, according to Kant, there is no *object* that is given that corresponds to this "I". Kant thus tells us that the "I" of apperception is not an object, but is merely the transcendental condition for thinking *about* objects that must be given in sensibility.

Because the rational psychologist takes the soul to be an object that we can access through reason alone (independent of sensation), Kant thinks he is seduced into erroneously applying concepts of the understanding outside the bounds of experience. Kant tries to demonstrate the fallacies or errors (the "paralogisms") involved in the rational psychologist's project in an exceptionally detailed way. The central point, however, is that in attempting to say something substantive about the "I", the metaphysician tries to apply categories of the understanding (such as "substance") to a pseudo-object in order to make a knowledge claim. These include the claim that the soul is a "substance" (a being or thing), that the soul is "simple" (non-extended), that the soul is numerically "identical" and so on. Here again, then, Kant contends that disastrous consequences follow from our failure to limit the application of our concepts to objects of sense.

Kant's critique of the rational psychologist's project is of considerable interest not only to philosophers concerned to examine the legitimacy of metaphysical doctrines of the soul. Indeed, his accounts have been enormously influential in contemporary discussions in the philosophy of mind. Many see in Kant an early and powerful statement about the forms of human cognition.

Rational cosmology, the world and the antinomies

One of the most dramatic sections of Kant's *Critique of Pure Reason* is found in the section entitled "Antinomies of Pure Reason". The antinomies are sets of arguments (there are fours sets) about the cosmos, or the world. The background for Kant's arguments is the metaphysical disputes relating to the nature of the world. Is the world infinite in space and time, or does it have a beginning and a limit in space (is it finite)? Are objects in the world composed of some ultimately simple and irreducible particles or substances, or is matter infinitely divisible? Is there room for freedom (uncaused causes) in the world, or is everything in the world caused? Is there some necessary being that grounds the existence of objects, or is everything contingent? Such questions attract us at the same time as they confound us. In the history of philosophy, these different options proved to be the basis for protracted metaphysical debate. Kant claims that in trying to answer these questions human reason finds itself at an impasse. Both sides to these disputes seem to have cogent arguments, and reason, in its efforts to decide upon the matter, falls into "contradiction" with itself. The spectacle of reason at odds with itself is what first awakened Kant from what he called his "dogmatic slumber".

There are, as already noted, four sets of arguments (four conflicts, or "antinomies") that are addressed by Kant. He thinks that in each of the disputes, one side (the so-called "thesis positions") tries to find some ultimate explanation, some first beginning. Thus, the proponent of the thesis arguments wants to say that the world is finite, and has a first beginning in time, and a limit in space, or that there is some ultimately simple substance of which objects are composed. This attempt to find some first beginning, or some elementary substance, reflects reason's desire to have a complete explanation for the world, and things in the world. We want here to find that our explanation stops somewhere, with a final answer. In keeping with this, the thesis arguments go on to defend the view that there is a first, or uncaused cause (e.g. freedom), and that there is some absolutely necessary being.

We have a strong need, according to Kant, to defend these views. Why? Suppose that we say that the world goes on infinitely in space and time. In such a case, we can never answer the question "How can the beginning of the world be accounted for?" Or suppose that everything is caused. Then, in such a case, the series of causes goes on infinitely, and we never can reach the ultimate cause of the world. Kant thinks human reason seeks, however, ultimate and complete explanations, and is deeply frustrated and bewildered in their absence. The problem with the thesis positions, however, is that we cannot anywhere in our experience encounter a "first beginning" or a limit in time; nowhere can we find for any event in time a beginning that is not itself preceded by an earlier event from which it follows. Thus, in making these claims, reason is forced to move outside human experience, and to posit some ultimate (intelligible) explanation.

This is exactly what the other side to the dispute (advanced by the so-called "antithesis" positions) criticizes. According to the antithesis positions, the world is infinite in time and space, bodies are infinitely divisible, there is no first or uncaused cause, and no necessary being. As a defence of these views, the proponent of the antithesis positions will often appeal to "nature's own resources". Here, the antithesis positions reflect a desire to stay within the realm of experience, and to consider things in their necessary relationship to space and time. Because, according to the antithesis positions, space and time are infinite, there can be nothing outside space and time, no non-temporal beginning. Similarly, because space is infinitely divisible, everything in space is infinitely divisible too, and so there can be no simple indivisible substance.

Kant tries to resolve these disputes by appealing to his own distinction between appearances and things-in-themselves. According to him, the conflicts are all fuelled by the fact that both parties to the dispute fail to distinguish between the standpoint of appearances and the consideration of things as they are "in themselves". Indeed, according to Kant both the thesis and the antithesis positions are unsatisfying. To accommodate reason's need for ultimate (intelligible) beginnings is to assert something "too big" for the understanding, something that can never be experienced in space and time (freedom, ultimately simple particles). Adopting the antithesis positions is, however, equally unsatisfying. For the antithesis positions can never give us any ultimate explanation that satisfies our necessary demand for completeness. In such a case, the conclusion is "too small" for reason. Worse, in appealing to spatiotemporal considerations to make transcendent metaphysical claims, the antithesis arguments erroneously assume that space and time are transcendentally real, that they hold of things "absolutely", independently of the human mind.

Kant contends that his own distinction between appearances and things-in-themselves resolves these issues once and for all. In the case of the first two conflicts (whether the world is finite or infinite, and whether there is an ultimately simple substance), Kant argues that the conclusions on both sides are *false*. Both parties claim to be talking about the world in space and time. The problem is that they both assume that "there is a world", understood as the sum total of all appearances, and that it is either finite or infinite. Herein lies the problem, according to Kant. The "world" is not an object, and it is therefore neither finite nor infinite.

With regard to the second set of conflicts (freedom versus causality, or whether there is some necessary being), Kant *again* argues that the conflict is resolvable. Here, however, he argues that there is room for both sides to be *true*. This is possible, he tells us, because in these cases the proponents of the positions are arguing at cross-purposes. The third antinomy is of particular importance in this regard. In this conflict, the thesis contends that in addition to mechanistic causality, we must posit some first, uncaused, causal power (freedom). The opponent rejects the possibility of freedom, and claims that everything is subject to the principle of causality. The resolution to this conflict consists in giving each side its due, but in carefully limiting the domain over which the claims hold. The thesis demand for an absolute causal beginning (freedom) *might* well be allowed to stand, but certainly *not* as an explication of appearances in nature. The antithesis claim that everything has a cause is true, but only as an explication of objects in nature, understood as *appearances*. In this way, Kant thought that he had accomplished two important tasks. First, he rescued the principle of universal causality, the claim that "every event has a cause". Since this principle is essential to scientific enquiries into nature, Kant forestalled scepticism, and secured the "order of nature". At the same time, however, the fact that Kant limits the application of this principle to spatiotemporal objects (appearances) leaves open *the possibility* of securing freedom outside the subjective conditions of space and time. Although Kant does not claim to *prove* that there is such freedom in this argument, he claims to succeed in establishing at the very least the "compatibility" of human freedom and mechanistic causality. Securing the possibility that freedom and mechanistic causality might be reconciled was a main interest for Kant in writing the *Critique of Pure Reason*.

A similar result is achieved with respect to the topic at hand in the fourth antinomy, which concerns the possibility of a necessary being. The thesis position that such a being is necessary might well be allowed, but not as relating to the field of appearances in nature. Thus, the antithesis denial that there is any necessary being (that everything is contingent) holds, but only in so far as it relates to *appearances*. If such conclusions limit *knowledge* to the epistemological conditions of the human mind, they at the same time leave open the right of reason to appeal to these same necessary ideas of freedom and a necessary being (God) from a different (a moral) standpoint. Kant's theoretical philosophy thereby paves the way for his later, highly influential, moral theory.

Rational theology, God, and the ideal of pure reason

The last branch of metaphysics that Kant tackles is theology and the attendant arguments for the existence of God. The rational demand for an unconditioned explanation for all things comes to a natural resting place with the idea of God, understood as an absolutely necessary and supremely real being that is the ultimate cause of all things. Kant takes the idea of God to be one that "contains a wherefore for every therefore" (A585/B613), and he refers to this specific idea as the "ideal of pure reason". Kant's view is that the idea of God is the idea in which our great need for completeness of knowledge culminates in the notion of a single, individual, thing.

The first thing to note, then, is that Kant does not think that the idea of God is an arbitrary or useless one. He is not arguing that the idea is without any legitimacy in philosophy. On the contrary, he refers to the idea as indispensable and "inescapable" (A584/B612). Moreover, he thinks we have strong philosophical reasons for forming the idea of God. The idea of a supremely real being is one to which we are inevitably led in our philosophical attempts to account for the pure possibility of things.

Because of its importance, Kant spends a great deal of time trying to account for the rational origin of the idea of God. His account is difficult in the extreme, but the essential point is this: suppose we want to explain the source of everything that is. In our efforts to do this, we form the idea of a being that contains all possible reality (the *ens realissimum*). This idea, the idea of a being that contains the source, material and explanation for everything in reality, is important for us in our philosophical attempts to account for things. The problem is that, as a result of the illusion characteristic of reason, we erroneously take this idea to be a self-standing object, and then try to prove that it "exists necessarily".

Although the *idea* of God plays an important role for reason in its quest for knowledge, then, Kant argues that it actually corresponds to no *real object* that could ever be given to us. Thus Kant claims that our subjectively necessary idea of God should not lead us to "presuppose the existence of a being that corresponds to this ideal, but only the idea of such a being, and this only for the purpose of deriving from an unconditioned totality of complete determination the conditioned totality, that is, the totality of the limited" (A578/B606). Here then, as with the idea of the soul and the idea of the world, Kant contends that there is no actual object of knowledge given about which we are entitled to draw speculative conclusions. The ideas of reason express subjective (rational) interests in seeking explanations, but they do not correspond (objectively) to anything that could ever be given to us in experience.

Kant's account of the rational origin of the idea of God provides the framework within which he seeks to undermine the traditional arguments for God's existence. There are three such arguments: the ontological, the cosmological and the physico-theological (the argument from design). Each of these arguments seeks to show that the idea of God (the *ens realissimum*, the supremely real being) is an idea of an actual being that exists necessarily.

An ontological argument seeks to deduce the necessary existence of God from concepts alone, and thus claims to establish God's existence completely *a priori*. Various versions of the argument have appeared in the history of philosophy, of course, but Kant distils these down to the following syllogism:

1. God (the *ens realissimum*) is the concept of a being that contains all reality, or predicates.
2. Existence is a reality/predicate.
3. Therefore God exists.

Kant offers a number of criticisms of this argument, but the most famous criticism is that "existence" is not a real predicate. In the above argument, we are trying to deduce the necessary existence of God simply from the concept of the *ens realissimum*. But this is only accomplished by assuming that "existence" is a real, determining predicate. A real predicate for Kant is one that enlarges the concept to which it is attached. But according to Kant, "existence" does not add anything at all to the definition of the concept. To say that something *exists* is not to expand its definition; it is rather to posit an object as corresponding to our concept. Since there is no real object given to us in experience corresponding to the concept, however, the argument only succeeds by begging the question.

Whereas the ontological argument begins with the concept of the *ens realissimum* (God) and attempts to show that such a being exists necessarily, both the cosmological and physico-theological arguments argue in the opposite direction. Each, that is, seeks to show that there is something that exists necessarily, and then argues that the only thing that could answer to this description is the *ens realissimum* (God). Kant has two general responses to these arguments. The first is that we cannot conclude from the contingent existence of appearances that there is a necessary being. More problematically, he claims that even if we could so conclude, the cosmological and physico-theological arguments could only succeed by showing that the necessary being in question is identical to the *ens realissimum*. Thus, both of these later arguments presuppose the success of the ontological argument. Since the latter fails, so (according to Kant) do the arguments.

The positive use of reason

Despite his destructive treatment of metaphysics, Kant does not want to rule out the use of reason altogether. Indeed, in his Appendix to the transcendental dialectic, Kant defends reason's principles and ideas. Although he denies that these yield any metaphysical *knowledge* of transcendent objects, he does think that reason plays an important role in science. According to Kant, the ideas of reason are "indispensably necessary" to us in our efforts to expand our empirical knowledge. Such ideas (the soul, world and God) serve to guide our empirical investigations by postulating goals for further explanation. He therefore emphasizes the importance of what he refers to as the "regulative" use of reason. Reason may not yield knowledge "beyond the bounds of sense", but it does serve to orient our investigations by positing the goal of ever more complete and systematically unified theories. Moreover, the principles and ideas of reason take us well beyond the theoretical sphere, and illuminate our non-sensible capacities to act in accordance with the dictates of morality and justice.

As an enlightenment philosopher, Kant remained deeply committed to the defence of human reason. It is the principles and ideas of reason, he contended, that ground human progress and dignity. Although reason's pretences to transcendent knowledge in the theoretical sphere need to be subjected to "critique", he nevertheless held that reason has a positive and necessary role to play in virtually all human endeavours. It is the disciplined use of our reason, our capacity to think freely and for ourselves, that gives us our human worth.

Note

1. References in the body of this chapter to Kant's *Critique of Pure Reason* are to the standard A and B pagination of the first and second editions. Quotations in English are from Norman Kemp Smith's translations, *Immanuel Kant's Critique of Pure Reason*, 2nd edn

(New York: St Martin's Press, 1929). Passages in German are from Raymund Schmidt's German edition (Hamburg: Felix Meiner Verlag, 1954).

Further reading

Kant, I. 1929. *Critique of Pure Reason*, N. Kemp Smith (trans.). New York: St Martin's Press.
Kant, Immanuel (1998) *The Cambridge Edition of the Works of Immanuel Kant: The Critique of Pure Reason,* Trans. and ed. by Paul Guyer and Allen Wood, Cambridge: Cambridge University Press.

Secondary sources

Al-Azm, S. 1972. *The Origins of Kant's Argument in the Antinomies*. Oxford: Oxford University Press.
Ameriks, K. 1992. "The Critique of Metaphysics: Kant and Traditional Ontology". In *Cambridge Companion to Kant*, P. Guyer (ed.). Cambridge: Cambridge University Press.
Ameriks, K. 1982. *Kant's Theory of Mind*. Oxford: Clarendon Press.
Allison, H. 2004. *Kant's Transcendental Idealism, and Interpretation and Defense* (revised and enlarged edition). New Haven, CT: Yale University Press.
Bennet, J. 1966. *Kant's Analytic*. Cambridge: Cambridge University Press.
Bennet, J. 1974. *Kant's Dialectic*. Cambridge: Cambridge University Press.
Bird, G. 1973. *Kant's Theory of Knowledge: An Outline of One Central Argument in the Critique of Pure Reason*. New York: Humanities Press.
Britton, G. G. 1978. *Kant's Theory of Science*. Princeton, NJ: Princeton University Press.
Brook, A. 1994. *Kant and the Mind*. Cambridge: Cambridge University Press.
Buchdahl, G. 1969. *Metaphysics and the Philosophy of Science*. Cambridge, MA: MIT Press.
England, F. E. 1968. *Kant's Conception of God*. New York: Humanities Press.
Ewing, A. C. 1938. *A Short Commentary on Kant's Critique of Pure Reason*. London: Methuen.
Gardner, S. 1999. *Routledge Philosophy Guidebook to Kant and the Critique of Pure Reason*. London: Routledge.
Grier, M. 2001. *Kant's Doctrine of Transcendental Illusion*. Cambridge: Cambridge University Press.
Guyer, P. 1987. *Kant and the Claims of Knowledge*. Cambridge: Cambridge University Press.
Guyer, P. (ed.) 1992. *The Cambridge Companion to Kant*. Cambridge: Cambridge University Press.
Kemp Smith, N. 1923. *A Commentary to Kant's Critique of Pure Reason*. London: Macmillan.
Kitcher, P. 1990. *Kant's Transcendental Psychology*. Oxford: Oxford University Press.
Kuehn, M. 2001. *Kant: A Biography.* Cambridge: Cambridge University Press.
Körner, S. 1977. *The Philosophy of Kant*. Harmondsworth: Penguin.
MacFarland, P. 1970. *Kant's Concept of Teleology*. Edinburgh: Edinburgh University Press.
Paton, H. J. 1936. *Kant's Metaphysics of Experience*, 2 vols. London: Allen & Unwin.
Powell, C. T. 1990. *Kant's Theory of Self-Consciousness*. Oxford: Clarendon Press.
Scruton, R. 1982. *Kant*. Oxford: Oxford University Press.

Strawson, P. F. 1966. *The Bounds of Sense: An Essay on Kant's Critique of Pure Reason*. London: Methuen.

Walsh, W. H. 1975. *Kant's Criticisms of Metaphysics*. Edinburgh: Edinburgh University Press.

Wilkerson, T. E. 1976. *Kant's Critique of Pure Reason: A Commentary for Students*. Oxford: Clarendon Press.

Wolff, R. P. 1963. *Kant's Theory of Mental Activity*. Cambridge, MA: Harvard University Press.

Wood, A. (ed.) 1984. *Self and Nature in Kant's Philosophy*. Ithaca, NY: Cornell University Press.

Wood, A. 1978. *Kant's Rational Theology*. Ithaca, NY: Cornell University Press.

Wood, A. 2005. *Kant*. Oxford: Blackwell.

2

Johann Gottlieb Fichte

Foundations of the Entire Science of Knowledge

Curtis Bowman

Introduction

Johann Gottlieb Fichte developed a system of philosophy known in German as the *Wissenschaftslehre*. The proper translation of this technical term has always been disputed, but Fichte scholars have usually settled on "Science of Knowledge", "Doctrine of Science", or "Theory of Scientific Knowledge". None of these translations has ever been very informative, and they are even less helpful now that modern English tends to associate that which is scientific with the natural sciences and, to a lesser degree, the social sciences. Given the burden that the German term must bear, contemporary scholars routinely leave it untranslated in their discussions of Fichte's thought. Therefore, throughout this chapter Fichte's system will simply be called the *Wissenschaftslehre*.

German philosophers in the late-eighteenth and early-nineteenth centuries had a more expansive concept of science than we have today. Consequently, although the *Wissenschaftslehre* is not a science in our sense of the term, Fichte felt no discomfort in regarding his system as a scientific one. In so far as he considers the *Wissenschaftslehre* a science, Fichte argues not only that (i) it possesses a systematic form, but also that (ii) it possesses a systematic form in virtue of its being derived from a single first principle that is known with certainty. Moreover, he argues that (iii) the *Wissenschaftslehre* is the foundational discipline that grounds all theoretical and practical knowledge and demonstrates their fundamental unity; therefore, he sometimes refers to the

Wissenschaftslehre as "the science of science". Fichte's *Foundations of the Entire Science of Knowledge* attempts to demonstrate these three aspects of the *Wissenschaftslehre*.

Because of the alleged scientific character of the *Wissenschaftslehre*, Fichte claims not only to be the sole legitimate heir to Kant's Critical Philosophy, but also to have corrected the great man's errors and oversights. Fichte even claims to have put philosophy on a proper foundation for the first time in its history. In fact, according to Fichte, there is no philosophy besides the *Wissenschaftslehre*. Whatever may be said in criticism of Fichte, no one may rightly say that he is not a robust thinker. The philosophical project embodied in the *Wissenschaftslehre* is an ambitious one.

Fichte's *Foundations of the Entire Science of Knowledge* (henceforth the 1794/95 *Foundations*) was published in three parts in 1794 and 1795. Because it was initially written as a handbook for his students, Fichte assumed that any defects in the manuscript could be clarified in the classroom; consequently, he was not bothered by the book's manifest sketchiness. Furthermore, Fichte also thought that the underdeveloped nature of the book would encourage independent thinking in his students and readers. He often said that he wanted his audience to think the *Wissenschaftslehre* for themselves. Therefore, the particular manner in which his system was expressed in writing was never all that important to him. Such indifference has always been one cause of the widely varying interpretations of Fichte's work.

Unfortunately for those of us who were not his students, the 1794/95 *Foundations* is a wildly imperfect piece of writing. It is obscure, repetitive and inconclusive. It begins with a brief preface that says very little about what is to follow. Part I, a discussion of the fundamental principles of the *Wissenschaftslehre*, is such a dense and difficult beginning of a great work of philosophy that many overwhelmed readers have refused to read any further. Parts II and III investigate the foundations of theoretical and practical knowledge, and are only slightly less obscure, although much longer, than Part I. The book simply ends with Part III. There is no conclusion or summary. Everything, from start to finish, is fearsomely abstract.

Nonetheless, there is no substitute for the 1794/95 *Foundations*, if only because it was the fullest articulation of the fundamental principles of the *Wissenschaftslehre* to appear in Fichte's lifetime. Fichte left behind unpublished manuscripts that attempted to reformulate the thinking embodied in the 1794/95 *Foundations*, but this first version of the foundations of his system was the only one to appear in book form during his lifetime. Consequently, Fichte scholars agree that it is essential reading for anyone wishing to understand Fichte's thought.

The 1794/95 *Foundations* is sometimes called the *Wissenschaftslehre*. As its full title explicitly indicates, however, Fichte's book provides the foundations for his system, and thus ought not to be identified with the entire system. Later works attempt to fill out the rest of the system, especially as it applies to issues in moral and political philosophy. This chapter will focus on the most important elements of the 1794/95 *Foundations* while seeking to avoid the scholarly controversies that inevitably gather around such a complicated work. Unfortunately, numerous complex interpretive issues will remain unresolved by the end of this brief survey. Perhaps, however, it will be possible to attain a more modest goal; namely, the clarification of enough of the work to allow readers to begin to think the *Wissenschaftslehre* for themselves. This is what Fichte would have wished.

The background to the *Wissenschaftslehre*

The best way to begin to unravel the 1794/95 *Foundations* is to look at some of the philosophical issues that confronted Fichte in the early 1790s. We know little about his views prior to 1790, but we can be certain that during the summer of that year he became a devoted Kantian after accepting a job tutoring a university student in Kant's writings. Apparently, Fichte had not yet studied Kant's works with any care, and his immersion in them turned out to be a life-transforming experience. For the rest of his life Fichte would be preoccupied with the Kantian turn in German philosophy.

Fichte met Kant in person for the first time on 4 July 1791. The meeting did not go well, and Kant seems not to have been much impressed by his visitor. Fichte resolved to write something that would prove his philosophical merit. He quickly composed a manuscript, sent it to Kant on 18 August, and was gratified to learn a few days later that Kant thought well enough of it to recommend that it be published by his own publisher. After some delay the revised manuscript appeared in the spring of 1792 as a book entitled *Attempt at a Critique of all Revelation*.

Fichte's book demonstrates a deep understanding of Kant's thought. The basic argument is inspired by Kant's moral theology as it is formulated in the *Critique of Practical Reason*. Just as Kant argues in that work that belief in the existence of God and the immortality of the soul must be constrained by various moral considerations if it is to be rational belief, Fichte argues in the *Attempt* that any alleged revelation of God's activity in the world must pass a moral test before it can be the object of rational belief. According to Fichte, nothing that violates the moral law can be attributed to God. Consequently, no legitimate revelation can ever represent God as giving an immoral command or performing an immoral action. But this criterion falls short of telling us when an alleged revelation is a genuine revelation. At best, Fichte gives us a necessary condition, not a sufficient one, for judging something a genuine revelation. The test, though, is a moral one, not a theoretical one.[1]

For reasons that are still mysterious, Fichte's name and preface were omitted from the first edition of *Attempt at a Critique of all Revelation*. To the rest of the German intellectual world it looked as if Kant had finally published a work devoted solely to religious questions, and that he had done so anonymously in order to avoid trouble with Prussian censors. Consequently, Fichte's *Attempt* was hailed as the latest great work to come from Kant's pen. Naturally, everyone was flabbergasted to learn that a complete unknown had published a book that was thought to have been written by Kant. Once Fichte was revealed as the author, everyone realized that a new philosophical star had risen over Germany.

Fichte's sudden celebrity changed his life completely. By the end of 1792 he had given up tutoring and devoted himself to working out his philosophical views. In 1793 he brought out an enlarged edition of his book on revelation, which was properly credited to him this time. He published works defending freedom of thought and the French revolution, thereby acquiring a reputation as a supporter of radical ideas and causes. In late 1793 and early 1794 Fichte published several reviews in the *Allgemeine Literatur-Zeitung*, a leading intellectual periodical of the day. One of these reviews is extremely important for understanding the inspiration behind the creation of the *Wissenschaftslehre*, and thus for understanding the 1794/95 *Foundations*.

Fichte took on the task of reviewing a book entitled *Aenesidemus, or on the Foundations of the Elementary Philosophy Propounded in Jena by Professor Reinhold, Including a Defense of Scepticism Against the Pretensions of the Critique of Reason*.[2] Despite its having been published anonymously in 1792, *Aenesidemus* was widely known to have been written by G. E. Schulze, a sceptical opponent of all things Kantian. Schulze criticized not only the views of K. L. Reinhold, who at the time was Kant's most famous interpreter and follower, but also those of Kant himself.

In the late 1780s Reinhold had helped to popularize the Critical Philosophy. He then developed his own system of philosophy, the so-called *Elementarphilosophie* ("Elementary Philosophy"), in order to remedy what he regarded as the deficiencies in the foundations of Kant's system.[3] Schulze's book deploys many arguments against Kant and Reinhold and attempts to demonstrate, among other things, that both philosophers fall prey to sceptical objections.

As a member of the younger generation of Kantians, Fichte quickly recognized the importance of Schulze's assault on the Kantian philosophy. Schulze was especially critical of three things: (i) Kant's doctrine of the thing-in-itself; (ii) Kant's doctrine of the primacy of practical reason; and (iii) Reinhold's so-called "principle of consciousness", that is, the foundational principle of the *Elementarphilosophie* that was supposed to turn the Critical Philosophy into a properly grounded system. The details of these criticisms, as we should expect, are very complicated. Therefore, a brief discussion of the manner in which Schulze's criticisms motivated Fichte to create the *Wissenschaftslehre* must suffice for the purposes of this chapter.[4]

Even casual students of Kant are familiar with the thing-in-itself. As is the case with Kant's most important doctrines, the proper interpretation of the thing-in-itself is a matter of controversy. At the very least, however, Kant argues in the *Critique of Pure Reason* not only that (i) we can have *a priori* knowledge of appearances but not of things as they are in themselves, but also that (ii) things as they are in themselves are beyond all possible experience. We can, he maintains, only *think* things as they are in themselves; therefore, for Kant, we can at least conceive of them. Kant's so-called transcendental idealism – that is, his general conception of the nature of his system – can be encapsulated in the motto that we can know things only as they appear to us, not as they are in themselves.

Kant's doctrine of the primacy of practical reason is less well known. In short, Kant argues in the *Critique of Practical Reason* that practical reason can justify propositions about theoretical matters when its judgements (i) do not conflict with the deliverances of theoretical reason and (ii) are grounded in *a priori* principles derived from practical rather than theoretical reason. It is in this manner that Kant's moral theology argues in favour of belief in the existence of God and the immortality of the soul.

Because Fichte shares Schulze's scepticism about the thing-in-itself, this aspect of Schulze's critique is congenial to him. Therefore, one important element of the *Wissenschaftslehre* is the rejection of the thing-in-itself. But Fichte goes further than Kant, for he denies that we can even think the thing-in-itself (Fichte 1988a [1794a]: 72–3). Kant, as we just saw, allows that it is possible to think of things existing apart from our representations of them. It seems, then, that Fichte's *Wissenschaftslehre* is a more thoroughgoing form of idealism than Kant's Critical Philosophy. The nature of Fichte's idealism is an important topic that will be addressed below in "Experimental Conclusions".

Fichte's views on revelation embody an application of the doctrine of the primacy of practical reason to a realm of our experience that Kant had not yet investigated when Fichte's *Attempt* was published in 1792. Consequently, it is hardly surprising that Fichte retains the doctrine in his own system. He claims that Schulze misunderstands Kant on this particular point, and then briefly, although somewhat obscurely, defends the doctrine (Fichte 1988a [1794a]: 74–7). The concept of striving, which plays an extremely important role in the *Wissenschaftslehre*, is introduced in the context of this defence. The important point is that Fichte wishes to defend the doctrine of the primacy of practical reason. Ultimately, he expands its significance until it becomes one of the basic constituents of the *Wissenschaftslehre*.

Unlike Kant's doctrines of the thing-in-itself and the primacy of practical reason, Reinhold's principle of consciousness is a part of the history of German philosophy between Kant and Hegel that is largely neglected today. Nonetheless, it is vital for understanding Fichte's *Wissenschaftslehre*.

Reinhold worries that Kant's system lacks an explicitly formulated foundation capable of unifying the various doctrines and distinctions scattered across Kant's three Critiques. He purports to fill this lacuna in Kant's system with the principle of consciousness, which is typically formulated as follows: "In consciousness representation is distinguished through the subject from both object and subject and is related to both".[5] Reinhold claims that this principle is a fact – in German, a *Tatsache* – known by means of reflection, and thus that it is not known by means of argument or inference. Reinhold applies this principle to the Critical Philosophy, attempting to use it, for example, to deduce the distinction between the faculties of sensibility and understanding and to prove the existence of the thing-in-itself. In this fashion Reinhold hopes to secure the foundations of Kant's project against sceptical doubt.

Schulze argues that Reinhold's *Elementarphilosophie* is just another form of philosophical dogmatism, given that it interprets the thing-in-itself as the cause of the sensations received in sensibility and organized by the categories of the understanding. The Critical Philosophy itself admits that we cannot know the thing-in-itself; consequently, Schulze concludes, we must be sceptical about the correspondence of our representations with things outside us. (Schulze's form of scepticism depends on construing truth as the correspondence of our representations with things-in-themselves, whereas Kant and his followers tend to interpret truth as the conformity of our representations to the *a priori* laws of thought.)

Furthermore, Schulze argues that (i) the principle of consciousness cannot be a fundamental principle, if only because it must be free of contradiction, and thus is subject to the laws of logic; and that (ii) it cannot be known with certainty, because it is derived from merely empirical reflection on the contents of consciousness. As Hume teaches, certainty cannot be derived from empirical evidence. An empirically known principle that is less than fundamental is not what Reinhold claims to be offering as the foundation of the Critical Philosophy.

Finally, with regard to the primacy of practical reason, Schulze claims that theoretical reason actually possesses primacy, since we can never argue about what we *ought* to do before we know what we *can* do. In the *Critique of Practical Reason* Kant derives our belief in God's existence and the immortality of the soul from our duty to pursue the highest good, arguing that these two beliefs are conditions for the possibility of rationally pursuing the highest good. Schulze wishes to deny this argumentative strategy to Kant, since he claims that it depends on Kant's simply assuming that we can bring about the highest good.

Although Fichte agrees that Reinhold's principle of consciousness is a merely empirical principle, he continues to subscribe to Reinhold's vision of systematic philosophy. Any fundamental principle is subject to the logical constraint of non-contradiction. But Fichte counters that this is only a formal constraint. What we need, he says, is a material principle – that is, one that possesses some sort of content – that is not founded on any other material principle. Fichte accepts the principle of consciousness, but claims that it is derivable from a higher material principle that is genuinely fundamental and known with certainty. Consequently, he requires a different first principle for the *Wissenschaftslehre*. Reinhold's error, Fichte claims, is to assume that the first principle must express a fact. Instead, Fichte suggests that the first principle can express something besides a fact (Fichte 1988a [1794a]: 64).

It is at this point in the *Aenesidemus* review that Fichte introduces another of his famous technical terms. The German word for "fact" is the perfectly ordinary term "*Tatsache*". When Fichte provides an alternative to a fundamental fact that the first principle of his system will express, he takes advantage of the ability of the German language to create new compound words. Instead of expressing a *Tatsache*, Fichte says that the first principle can also express a *Tathandlung*. The German term "*Handlung*" is often translated as "act" or "deed". Therefore, Fichte's *Tathandlung* has something to do with activity. At this point, though, he says nothing about what sort of activity should be associated with the *Tathandlung*.

Somewhat later in the review Fichte identifies the *Tathandlung* with what he calls "the self-positing I", which is said to be absolutely autonomous and independent (Fichte 1988a [1794a]: 75). In several places Fichte seems to indicate that the self-positing I is a form of intellectual intuition (*ibid.*: 65, 70, 75). There is some controversy on this point, however. Fichte could simply be saying that we become aware of the self-positing I by means of intellectual intuition; in other words, the I has an immediate intuition of its own activity. But it is more likely that Fichte is making a radical claim about the very nature of the self-positing I. That is, it seems as if Fichte is claiming that the I is self-creating in some as yet unexplained fashion. This more ambitious reading sheds light on

some of Fichte's more puzzling pronouncements, as we shall see below in §
"The vicissitudes of the self-positing I" (p. 53). Furthermore, he intimates – albeit somewhat obscurely – that the self-positing I is the source of the unity of
theoretical and practical reason (*ibid.*: 75).

Without too much difficulty we can begin to imagine how Fichte intends to
ground a new Kantian-style system on this unusual form of activity, even if we
cannot yet see exactly how he will develop it into the *Wissenschaftslehre*. Fichte's
doctrine of the self-positing I is his stand-in for Kant's concept of rational
agency. The Kantian context of Fichte's philosophizing suggests that the self-
positing I performs the same work in the *Wissenschaftslehre* as autonomous
reason in the Critical Philosophy.

Fichte is fond of saying that he philosophizes in accordance with the spirit,
although not the letter, of the Critical Philosophy. This is why he continues to
regard himself as a Kantian. Consequently, it is perfectly legitimate to draw on our
understanding of Kant in our efforts to interpret Fichte's *Wissenschaftslehre*, as long
as we recognize that Fichte is not simply renaming various elements of the Critical Philosophy and incorporating them into his system. Often, although admittedly not always, Fichte reinterprets Kant in important ways.

Fichte characterizes the I as activity – and thus not as an object or a thing – and
as self-creating activity, as if the I is pure agency in the absence of an agent. The
self-creating aspect of the I follows from the claim that it is a form of intellectual
intuition. That is, the I creates itself in so far as it intuits itself. This is a rather
baffling assertion, to say the least. That Fichte is adapting Kant's doctrine of
intellectual intuition for his own purposes should be obvious, but what he intends
to achieve by means of this transformation is as yet far from clear.

Much of the remainder of this chapter will be devoted to exploring the nature
of the peculiar activity of the self-positing I as it is presented in Fichte's 1794/
95 *Foundations*. In this section we have looked at the *Aenesidemus* review as a
means of orientating ourselves towards some of the basic concerns of the
Wissenschaftslehre. But before we investigate the train of thought that begins
with the self-positing I, we must look at Fichte's methodology; otherwise, we
shall certainly fail to untangle his arguments. Once again, we must turn to a
work that Fichte published before the 1794/95 *Foundations*.

The methodology of the *Wissenschaftslehre*

In January 1794 Fichte was asked to fill Reinhold's vacant chair in philosophy
at the University of Jena. Fichte could hardly turn down such a prestigious offer,
even though he had only just begun to work out his new views in a systematic

fashion. Before he arrived in Jena in May 1794, he hurriedly wrote an essay entitled "Concerning the Concept of the *Wissenschaftslehre* or, of So-called 'Philosophy'". This work marks the first published appearance of the term "*Wissenschaftslehre*". Fichte's essay was intended as an invitation to prospective students, and thus was designed to introduce his expectant audience to his philosophical point of view. The title alone reveals Fichte's conviction that the *Wissenschaftslehre* is to be identified with philosophy in its entirety. How could students have resisted the temptation to attend his classes?

"Concerning the Concept of the *Wissenschaftslehre*" deals primarily with the methodology of the *Wissenschaftslehre*. Strictly speaking, this essay is not a part of the *Wissenschaftslehre*. Instead, it reflects on the nature of the *Wissenschaftslehre* and concludes with several undeveloped ideas that are discussed more thoroughly in the 1794/95 *Foundations*. At the beginning of this chapter we encountered, in summary form, the most important elements of Fichte's concept of science. Those earlier statements can be reformulated as follows: Fichte construes science as a systematic body of propositions that are known with certainty, and the certainty they possess is derived from an absolute first principle that is itself known with certainty (Fichte 1988b [1794b]: 101–3). A pressing epistemological issue now comes to the fore: how can we know that we are in possession of an absolute first principle that is known with certainty (*ibid.*: 105)?

Fichte sometimes gives the impression that our knowledge of this absolute first principle is based on some sort of mental act that is akin to introspection. We sit down, as it were, reflect in some mysterious fashion, and thereby discover the self-positing I in all its glorious self-evidence. Then, in good logical fashion, we deduce the various propositions that make up the content of the *Wissenschaftslehre*, thereby transferring the certainty with which we know the self-positing I to the propositions that are derived from it. As a result, Fichte's system arises before our very eyes in an utterly impeccable manner.

Fortunately, Fichte possesses a more subtle alternative to such an improbable way of justifying the claim that he has certain knowledge of his philosophical starting-point. It should be stressed that "Concerning the Concept of the *Wissenschaftslehre*" contains much more useful information regarding this matter than the 1794/95 *Foundations*. Because many of Fichte's original readers had not read the earlier essay, his book was largely greeted with incomprehension. But since Fichte never works out his alternative view in a fully rigorous way, even extended acquaintance with the methodological essay leaves many issues unresolved.

The gist of the view, though, is as follows. To assert that some principle is an absolute first principle is to imply that it is not derivable from any other principle. Something that is absolutely first is, well, absolutely first. Therefore, whatever we adopt as our absolute first principle cannot be demonstrated on the basis of other principles to be an absolute first principle. If, however, we simply claim that our preferred principle is an absolute first principle, then we beg the question in favour of our own starting-point. No one need agree with us in such circumstances. The process of reflection caricatured two paragraphs ago can rightly be construed as begging the question in favour of Fichte's theory. What else, then, can we do in order to make Fichte's vision of systematic philosophy more plausible?

According to Fichte (1988b [1794b]: 113, 127), we must experiment. That is, we must make an attempt at constructing a system of philosophy grounded on an indemonstrable first principle. We must choose a principle with which to begin. Since our choice must be a legitimate candidate for an absolute first principle, it must not be derivable from another principle. This is a necessary limitation on what we are allowed to choose as our starting-point. Although Fichte chooses the self-positing I as his starting-point, his methodology allows for the possibility that a different first principle could be an equally good or even superior starting-point.

Fichte often refers to this act of choosing as the free act with which the *Wissenschaftslehre* begins. He also frequently claims that some people are not capable of it, and that we need not argue with those who cannot make this free choice. Their inability to begin constructing a system of philosophy is no reason for us not to try. We are not guaranteed success, but neither are we condemned to failure. As Fichte tersely declares, "Everything depends on the experiment" (1988b [1794b]: 113).

Once we have chosen a principle that is a legitimate candidate for an absolute first principle, we must then actually attempt to construct the entire system of human knowledge in theoretical and practical terms. The best test of our success or failure is whether or not the system so erected adequately accounts for the intricate nature of human knowledge. If we succeed, then we will have offered the best possible reason for believing that we initially chose the proper first principle. At the same time, though, our systematic efforts to unravel and trace out the consequences of our starting-point may perhaps allow us to articulate the underlying rational structure of human knowledge in ways that are new to us. The Kantian inspiration should be plain: Fichte hopes to set out the conditions for the possibility of theoretical and practical knowledge, and he proposes to do so by beginning with the self-positing I.

The preceding methodological remarks on experimentation indicate that the self-positing I is a philosophical postulate. That is, we freely adopt it as our starting-point and then see what work it can do for us. But the labour that we wish it to perform depends on the purposes behind its adoption. As we follow Fichte's experiment with the self-positing I in the rest of this chapter, we should recall the earlier discussion of his *Aenesidemus* review. There we looked at various useful hints about the motives and goals behind the creation of the *Wissenschaftslehre*. They should be kept in mind as we work through Fichte's arguments.

The self-positing I is adopted as our starting-point in order to address various *philosophical* issues. Consequently, Fichte does not attempt, within the *Wissenschaftslehre*, to refute or modify our convictions about the *non-philosophical* sciences. Instead, their contents are set aside at the very beginning of the *Wissenschaftslehre*. Therefore, if properly formulated, the *Wissenschaftslehre* should not interfere with physics, chemistry or any of the other sciences.[6]

Rather than delving any further into Fichte's methodological reflections, it will be more helpful if we now turn to some of the major arguments of the 1794/95 *Foundations*. Once we complete a survey of Fichte's chief results, we can return to the two unresolved questions of this section: (i) how can we know that we have constructed a system that adequately accounts for the entirety of human knowledge; and (ii) is the *Wissenschaftslehre* entirely neutral with respect to the non-philosophical sciences?

The vicissitudes of the self-positing I

We must begin with at least a partial clarification of Fichte's concept of the self-positing I. Otherwise, what follows in the rest of this section will be little more than an exercise in jargon-mongering of a very unenlightening sort.

The English language typically uses the word "I" as a first-person pronoun; consequently, the noun phrase "the self-positing I" sounds odd to our ears. Because the original German phrase is "*das selbstsetzende Ich*", translators have traditionally chosen from "the self-positing ego", "the self-positing self" and "the self-positing I". Nowadays most scholars prefer "the self-positing I" for being more literal (and thereby usefully avoiding the many psychological connotations that the terms "ego" and "self" carry in modern English).[7] Furthermore, the very oddity of the English phrase is a boon to Fichte's Anglophone audience, given that he wishes all of his readers to reflect on themselves in ways that are likely to be new to them. The ungainly English locution helps to create an atmosphere of philosophical discovery.

We saw above that the concept of the self-positing I is Fichte's stand-in for Kant's concept of rational agency. This implies, with respect to theoretical reason, that Fichte is concerned with the spontaneity of the human mind in the formation of judgements. For Kant, the process of judging is not a haphazard or solipsistic one. Instead, we weigh evidence, make inferences and provide reasons. That is, our judgements claim to be justified, and thus they implicitly demand that others agree with us. But to attribute justifications to our judgements is to enter the realm of normativity, and to acknowledge this fact about our judgements is to take one step forwards in understanding the nature of theoretical reason.

Fichte follows Kant in these matters. That the I is self-positing indicates that Fichte conceives of its normative activity as self-determining. That is, we authorize ourselves to make judgements; moreover, we determine and impose the appropriate standards of judgement on ourselves. This is not, however, to give ourselves licence to engage in pigheaded table-thumping. The pursuit of theoretical knowledge is a form of public debate, since none of us are infallible regarding such matters. Therefore, any claim to knowledge is open to revision and correction.

With respect to practical reason, Kant regards the determining of the will not merely as arbitrarily choosing some course of action from among the many others that are open to us, but also as the application of reasons to our choices. The categorical imperative is our guide in practical matters, but we determine its content for ourselves. The realm of normativity, once again, turns out to be essential, this time for understanding how it is that we justify our choices.

Fichte's view of practical reason is much the same. The self-positing I authorizes itself to be the moral authority that sits in judgement of its own actions. It decides for itself how it ought to act. But, as is the case in theoretical matters, the self-positing I is also fallible in practical matters. Others can assist us in thinking through the reasons for our actions, and we can do the same for them.

Fichte's free choice to begin his system with the self-positing I is a declaration of independence. The I posits itself absolutely, he says. Although the I posits itself as independent, and hence as free, it discovers various restrictions on its independence as it begins to work out the consequences of its initial act of self-positing. In other words, to declare our independence is not sufficient to make us independent. Consequently, according to Fichte, we must *strive* to make ourselves free.

As we saw earlier, Schulze argues that Reinhold's principle of consciousness is a mere empirical fact. Fichte agrees with Schulze's assessment, which leads him to suggest that we begin our philosophical system with a *Tathandlung*, not with a *Tatsache*. That is, Fichte proposes to begin with a deed instead of a fact. What does this mean?

Fichte seems to have the following in mind. The fact of representation, with which Reinhold begins his system, requires, according to Fichte, acts that are prior to representation. This priority should not be understood in temporal terms. Because Fichte is not a psychologist, he is not concerned with the temporal order of mental events studied by the empirical science of psychology. Instead, he is concerned with the necessary conditions of representation in so far as they are understood from a philosophical point of view. These conditions are slowly clarified in the unfolding discussion of the activity of the self-positing I. We already know, however, that they will somehow involve normativity. Consequently, we might say that the priority in question is epistemological, not psychological.

When Fichte describes the activity of the self-positing I in the 1794/95 *Foundations*, he does not explicitly make use of the concept of intellectual intuition. Given what was said above in § "The background to the *Wissenschaftslehre*" (p. 45), this omission should come as a surprise to us. It is reasonable, though, to assume that the 1794/95 *Foundations* continues to regard the self-positing I as a form of intellectual intuition. Such an interpretation makes sense of much that Fichte says. Furthermore, this Kantian notion reappears in the two introductions to *An Attempt at a New Presentation of the Wissenschaftslehre*, a book that Fichte began in 1797 but abandoned uncompleted in 1798. That he resumed his habit of referring to the I as a form of intellectual intuition indicates that he never ceased to regard it as such, even though the 1794/95 *Foundations* does not explicitly speak of it in his earlier manner.

Now that these preliminaries have been taken care of, we can begin to make sense of Fichte's various arguments involving the self-positing I. We must always keep in mind that Fichte is presenting us with the foundations of his system. Consequently, he argues at the highest level of generality that the *Wissenschaftslehre* can attain, thereby erecting imposing obstacles to understanding the precise nature of what he is saying.

What we have seen so far in this chapter leads us to expect that Fichte will restrict himself to a single principle in Part I of the 1794/95 *Foundations*. Yet, somewhat disconcertingly, he discusses three principles in this section. Only the first one, though, satisfies the conditions described earlier for serving as the absolute first principle of a philosophical system, and Fichte clearly states that this is so.

The argument in support of the first of Fichte's three principles begins as we should expect (Fichte 1982 [1794/95]: 93). That is, Fichte declares that (i) his task is to discover the absolute first principle of the entirety of human knowledge, and that (ii) this principle will express the *Tathandlung* that is the basis of all consciousness.[8] If the *Tathandlung* is the basis of all consciousness, then, according to Fichte, it cannot appear in consciousness. That is, the *Tathandlung* is not to be found among the empirical states that make up ordinary mental life.

Fichte attempts to establish the *Tathandlung* by appealing to the law of identity, or, as he puts it, $A = A$ (Fichte 1982 [1794/95]: 94). Yet he is careful enough to claim that he is *not* logically deducing the *Tathandlung* from $A = A$. To do that would ultimately involve deducing the first principle that expresses the activity of the self-positing I from something more fundamental than itself; and thus Fichte would not actually be grounding the *Wissenschaftslehre* on an absolute first principle. That is, the law of identity would be more fundamental than the proposition that the I posits itself absolutely. The opposite is true, he claims. According to Fichte, all logical laws are to be derived from the *Tathandlung*.

If Fichte's procedure seems circular, at least he honestly acknowledges it as such, but he claims that its circularity is unavoidable yet unproblematic, given the subject matter under discussion. We must begin, he says, with a proposition that everyone grants as absolutely certain. Then we must show that the *Tathandlung* is necessarily thought along with that proposition. Elsewhere in the *Wissenschaftslehre* we can show how the laws of logic are derived from the *Tathandlung*; however, at the beginning of the project, says Fichte, we may appeal to the universally acknowledged certitude of logic as our chosen means of showing that we implicitly think the *Tathandlung* when we explicitly think of the laws of logic as absolutely certain.

Everyone, says Fichte, accepts $A = A$ as absolutely certain, and does so in the absence of any ground that proves that this proposition is known with absolute certainty. Therefore, we can begin an argument with $A = A$ without fear of immediate disagreement, for even those who might not be Fichteans will agree that $A = A$. That we so agree, according to Fichte, is just a fact of empirical consciousness. That is, we all occupy some minimal common ground for the argument to follow.

But, according to Fichte, to assert that $A = A$ is not to assert that A exists. Instead, says Fichte, it is to assert that if A exists, then A exists (Fichte 1982 [1794/95]: 94–5). That is, the proposition $A = A$ implicitly contains an inference, and in so far as we assert that $A = A$ is absolutely certain, we give ourselves permission to make an inference that no one may deny us the right to make. But if everyone – by agreeing that $A = A$ is absolutely certain – implicitly acknowledges that no one may deny us the right to assert that $A = A$, then it follows that everyone agrees that we are absolutely justified in making the inference that is implicitly contained in $A = A$.

In so far as we implicitly make an inference when we assert that $A = A$, we are, quite literally, doing something. Yet we should not think of this action in psychological terms. That is, Fichte's point is not that we mentally pass, so to speak, from the antecedent to the consequent of the conditional that he claims is implicitly contained in $A = A$. Naturally, individual inferences, understood as mental events, have numerous psychological aspects, but Fichte is not interested in them. Once again, to repeat a point made earlier, we are dealing with epistemology, not psychology.

In the case of asserting that $A = A$, we not only authorize ourselves to make the implicit inference described above, but we also regard ourselves as *rightfully* doing so, seeing that we all accept that $A = A$ is known with absolute certainty. Furthermore, we so regard ourselves in full awareness of the fact that there is no other authority that could demonstrate to us that the inference is a legitimate one. In short, we declare *our rightful authority* to assert that $A = A$. Consequently, when we assert that $A = A$ is known with absolute certainty – and thereby implicitly assert, according to Fichte, that if A exists, then A exists – we perform an act of normative self-assertion. But the activity of normative self-assertion is what it is to be a self-positing I. Fichte has thus established the existence of the self-positing I.

As Fichte says repeatedly, the I posits itself absolutely, which is to say, among other things, that the activity of normative self-assertion is utterly ungrounded. The I posits itself as what it is because it posits itself as what it is, which is to say that the I just posits itself. In other words, the self-positing activity of the I is the very essence of the I. For Fichte, this is the fundamental sense of the primacy of practical reason in the *Wissenschaftslehre*. The self-positing I is a continuous act of normative self-assertion. As of yet, though, this activity has no determinate content, for Fichte is not yet laying out the particular modes of the activity of the self-positing I.

As we saw above, before and after the publication of the 1794/95 *Foundations*, Fichte regards the I as a form of intellectual intuition. He expresses the same view in the 1794/95 *Foundations* in different language: the I is both the agent that acts and the product of that activity (Fichte 1982 [1794/95]: 97) or, somewhat more pithily, a subject-object (*ibid.*: 99n.4). Fichte credits Kant with having shown that the first principle of the *Wissenschaftslehre* – namely, that the I posits itself absolutely – is the first principle of all knowledge. He adds, perhaps wistfully, that Kant never explicitly declared it to be the absolute first principle (*ibid.*: 100).

Because the subject matter of the *Wissenschaftslehre* is the entirety of human knowledge, Fichte's first principle cannot be the endpoint of our philosophical reflections. So far we have only dealt with what is in effect a particular kind of self-knowledge, but human knowledge consists of more than self-knowledge. That is, the kind of knowledge described by Fichte's first principle, despite its overwhelming significance, is not sufficient for fulfilling his stated purpose of systematizing the entirety of human knowledge. Consequently, our philosophical principles must somehow take into account the fact that human knowledge cannot simply be identified with the activity of an I that posits itself absolutely. Fichte's second and third principles push us beyond the limitations of self-knowledge and towards the entirety of human knowledge.

Unfortunately, the relationship between Fichte's first principle and his second and third principles is unclear. His second and third principles seem to depend on the first one, yet the nature of that dependence is not easy to fathom. All that can be said at this point is that Fichte does not regard the latter two principles as logical consequences of the first one. So how are we to make further progress in our reading of Fichte's text? The best thing to do is to follow Fichte's advice of attempting to think the *Wissenschaftslehre* for ourselves. The text may be tangled, but the thought behind it can be made intelligible with a little interpretive work on our part.

Fichte commences the discussion of his second principle in a familiar fashion: he says that everyone accepts that $\sim A$ is not equal to A, and also that everyone accepts this proposition as certain even though no one demands a proof of it (Fichte 1982 [1794/95]: 102). Once again, according to Fichte, we are dealing with a fact of empirical consciousness that provides some minimal common ground for the argument to follow.

We cannot deduce the new proposition that $\sim A$ is not equal to A from the proposition that $A = A$. Furthermore, since $A = A$ is the only other logical proposition so far acknowledged by the *Wissenschaftslehre*, we cannot attempt to deduce our new proposition from anything else. Therefore, says Fichte, in so far as we posit $\sim A$, we posit it absolutely in opposition to A when we grant that $\sim A$ is not equal to A (Fichte 1982 [1794/95]: 103).

What does the conclusion of the previous paragraph mean? First of all, we must recognize that Fichte is no longer only talking about self-positing. The self-positing activity of the I is a special form of self-reflection, as we saw earlier. For Fichte, not only can the I take itself to be the object of its own mental activity, but it can also take other things besides itself to be the objects of its mental activity. To use his language, not only can the I posit itself, but it can also posit other things as well. That is, the I may take objects to exist or not exist and to have this or that attribute.

If an existing $\sim A$ is opposed to an existing A, then, of course, both $\sim A$ and A exist, and we understand the former as the negation of the latter. In such a case we could then justifiably assert that $\sim A$ is posited in opposition to A. But at this stage of Fichte's argument only the self-positing I has been established as existing. Since $\sim A$ cannot be deduced from A, nothing about logic itself forces us to move beyond the self-positing I to its negation, which Fichte simply labels the not-I. Logically speaking, that is, given our philosophical starting-point, the self-positing I could be all that there is.

Yet Fichte says that $\sim A$ is posited absolutely in opposition to A. It seems that he wishes to assert the existence of $\sim A$ when he speaks of its being posited absolutely in opposition to A (and thus that he is not merely spelling out the content of an implicit inference as he did at the beginning of the discussion of his first principle). But since the existence of $\sim A$ cannot be logically inferred from the existence of A, the only other way to justify the assertion that $\sim A$ exists is to appeal to our experience of $\sim A$. That is, we *discover* the existence of $\sim A$, and at this stage of Fichte's argument the only thing that we can possibly discover in this fashion is the not-I, whatever it may be.

The foregoing line of reasoning yields Fichte's second principle: the not-I is posited absolutely in opposition to the self-positing I (Fichte 1982 [1794/95]: 104). Although he does not express his second principle in these exact words, this is the principle at work in what follows in the rest of the 1794/95 *Foundations*. To posit something absolutely means, at the very least, to assert its existence on our own authority and in the absence of a logical demonstration of its existence. Not only does the self-positing I posit itself absolutely, as we saw earlier, it also posits absolutely the not-I in opposition to itself.

All is not well, however, for, according to Fichte, the *Wissenschaftslehre* is now threatened with the possibility that its claims are fatally contradictory. For how can the not-I be reconciled with the self-positing I, given the manner in which the two are posited in Fichte's first two principles? That is, the I initially posits itself in an absolute fashion, which seems to imply, among other things, that it posits itself as independent and unrestricted. Yet it then posits the not-I in absolute opposition to itself, which seems to imply that the not-I somehow constrains the I in ways – as yet unspecified – that contradict its initial self-positing as independent and unrestricted. Something similar is true of the not-I as well: it is posited as wholly different from the I, but since it is posited absolutely, the positing of the not-I seems to leave no existential room, so to speak, for the I. In short, the simultaneous positing of the I and the not-I seems to entail their mutual destruction (Fichte 1982 [1794/95]: 106–8).

Fichte's third principle is supposed to address this dilemma, which, as we shall see, is not completely resolved until the end of the 1794/95 *Foundations*. Fichte says that we must continue our experiment; therefore, we must propose a solution and then see what work it will do for us. In this case, Fichte proposes that the I and the not-I mutually limit each other (Fichte 1982 [1794/95]: 108). He then employs the concept of divisibility in further elucidation of this initial proposal, leading him to the proposition that the I and the not-I are posited as divisible in so far as they are regarded as mutually limiting each other.

What Fichte has in mind is not obvious, but perhaps a military metaphor can help us to capture the dynamics of mutual limitation. Fichte's first two principles posit the I and the not-I, as we already know; his third principle, we might say, pits the I and the not-I against each other in a struggle in which neither is ever the complete victor over the other. Since the I and the not-I are posited as divisible, each has aspects capable of interacting with those of its opponent. Therefore, in so far as the clash between the I and the not-I waxes and wanes, various elements of the I advance and retreat, as do various elements of the not-I. The I and not-I are thus comparable to two battling armies. The forces of one side advance and retreat along a line of engagement while the opposing side does the same, but neither combatant vanquishes the other. One side, however, may steadily gain the upper hand. As we shall see, Fichte claims that the I makes progress in its struggle against the not-I, but also never fully subdues it.

When Fichte finally formulates his third principle, he does so in a rather awkward fashion: I oppose in the I a divisible not-I to the divisible I (Fichte 1982 [1794/95]: 110). This is just one instance among many in which Fichte speaks of positing as occurring *in* the I. This seems to be more than just another way of saying that the I is the agent responsible for the act of positing. Because the nature of Fichte's idealism is addressed in the final section of this chapter, a discussion of what it means for something to be posited in the I shall be deferred until then. For now, though, we can simply regard the third principle as Fichte's means of expressing the interaction between the I and the not-I.

In Parts II and III Fichte takes up the chief philosophical issue raised by his third principle, that is, the mutual limitation of the I and the not-I. What are the conditions of its possibility? Successfully answering this question, according to Fichte, is tantamount to distinguishing between theoretical and practical reason (Fichte 1982 [1794/95]: 122–3). In so far as the I posits itself as limited by the not-I, we are in the realm of theoretical knowledge. The foundation thereof is the subject matter of Part II. In so far as the I posits the not-I as limited by the I, we are in the realm of practical knowledge. The foundation thereof is the subject matter of Part III. What follows in Parts II and III is a continuation of the experimental method practised in Part I and takes the form of greater clarification of Fichte's three principles as well as their further application to the basic issues of the *Wissenschaftslehre*.

Because representation is the foundation of theoretical knowledge, Fichte devotes many pages in Part II to various ways of understanding its possibility. The most significant moment of this discussion appears towards the end of Part

II when Fichte introduces the *Anstoss* (Fichte 1982 [1794/95]: 189). Fichte scholars usually translate the German term as "check". Quite simply put, the *Anstoss* is a check on the activity of the I. The I encounters the *Anstoss* and pulls up short, as it were, because it has run into something that is not its own creation. The *Anstoss* is thus understood as a consequence of the "outward-striving activity" of the I (*ibid*.: 191).

The *Anstoss* should not be identified with the not-I, because Fichte clearly states that the *Anstoss* is a product of the activity of the I. Whatever the not-I may be, it is not a product of the activity of the I. The *Anstoss* is the manner in which the not-I manifests itself in our experience. Representation is not a free-for-all. There is a recalcitrant element in representation that is imposed on us, but it is also one that we usually integrate into our experience. We are all familiar with the difference between perception and imagination. The former essentially depends on some given element lacking in the latter. The *Anstoss* is similar to that recalcitrant aspect of perception that is not up to us, yet Fichte does not say whether or not we should identify the *Anstoss* with sensation.

It follows, though, that the *Anstoss* is not merely a check on the activity of the I. It is also an incitement to further activity. We might try to capture the dual nature of the *Anstoss* as both check and incitement by thinking of it as an *irritant* to the I. A speck of dust blurs our vision, leading us to remove it in order to restore our sight. We can think of the *Anstoss* in similar terms, although the analogy with vision is admittedly an imperfect one. Something foreign to the I appears in the I. The activity of the I usually succeeds in incorporating it into our experience; however, there is no guarantee that the I will always be able to do this.

The discussion of Part II shows, according to Fichte, that representation is possible only on the assumption that a foreign element manifests itself in our experience. But this is another way of expressing the contradiction that worried us at the very end of our discussion of Fichte's second principle. How can we plausibly claim that the I posits itself absolutely if representation must be understood as Part II indicates? The answer is to be found in Part III.

Part III contains many formulations of the basic contradiction that requires resolution: how can the I consistently posit itself first as infinite and unlimited and then as finite and limited? The only way to eliminate the contradiction, says Fichte, lies in more accurately determining the propositions that are at variance (Fichte 1982 [1794/95]: 226). That is, we must more precisely specify the different ways in which the I can be said to be infinite and finite, unlimited and limited.

Fichte's doctrine of striving provides the solution. The I is infinite and unlimited in so far as it never ceases attempting to impose its normative standards.

It is finite and limited in so far as these efforts encounter resistance and are influenced by the counter-activity of the not-I. All that can justifiably be said about the not-I is that it is the negation of the I, and that it stands in opposition to the activity of the I. The *Wissenschaftslehre* is still too general at this stage of Fichte's exposition to say anything more determinate about the not-I.

The I attempts to impose rationality on all that surrounds it, because it charges itself with the task of making all else rational. The I demands that the object conform to it, as Fichte puts it; and this demand, he tells us, is Kant's categorical imperative (Fichte 1982 [1794/95]: 230). The insistence on conformity gradually transforms the world into a realm of ever greater rationality. This task is not undertaken in vain, but it is an endless one; hence the *infinite* striving of the I. All reality, says Fichte, should be posited through the I, but there is no guarantee that such a state of affairs will ever come to pass (*ibid.*: 231–2).

The demand that everything should conform to the I is practical reason at its most general (Fichte 1982 [1794/95]: 232). Initially, the I posits itself as independent and unrestricted. We saw earlier in the discussion of Part II that the I discovers a foreign element in its experience that is an essential aspect of the possibility of representation. In the realm of practical reason, says Fichte, there is also something alien. It is not derivable from the I itself; instead, it is confirmed by our own experience (*ibid.*: 233). Here too, in other words, there is an *Anstoss* (*ibid.*: 242–3). We posit ourselves as free but encounter resistance. We then set out to achieve the independence that is posited at the beginning of our philosophical reflections. We succeed in so far as we make everything conform to the standards that the I lays down in its continuous act of normative self-assertion.

As the obstacles to the successful use of reason are progressively overcome by the activity of the I, the realm of freedom becomes ever larger. Every small step forwards contributes to greater freedom for the I, because it is the nature of obstacles to be such only in so far as they thwart our purposes. Consequently, as they are removed in accordance with the rational activity of the I, the realm of our freedom is enlarged. We become ever more independent, slowly approaching, although never actually attaining, the goal that we posited for ourselves at the very beginning of the *Wissenschaftslehre*.

Experimental conclusions

After Fichte concludes the discussion of Part III, the 1794/95 *Foundations* abruptly stops. In the absence of a conclusion from Fichte's own hand, we must produce one on our own. But we must first deal with several issues mentioned in passing in the earlier sections of this chapter. Only then will we have a more complete idea of how we are to evaluate Fichte's experiment.

Fichte has often been interpreted as advocating a metaphysics of the I in which the self-positing activity of the I brings the very world into existence. He sometimes speaks of the self-positing of the I as a form of self-creation and of everything else as being posited in the I; and when this view is coupled with Fichte's rejection of the thing-in-itself, it seems as if there can be nothing but the I and the objects posited in it. Therefore, it might seem to some readers as if Fichte advocates a radical subjectivism that renders the world completely mind-dependent.

On 28 October 1794 Friedrich Schiller wrote the following about Fichte in a letter to Johann Wolfgang Goethe: "To him the world is just a ball that the I has flung and catches again in reflection!" (Hahn 1968: II, 13). This is only one sentence, of course, but it seems to embody the interpretation of Fichte's idealism found in the previous paragraph. Schiller was certainly no fool, and we know that he discussed the *Wissenschaftslehre* with Fichte. Consequently, we must conclude that Fichte is at least partly responsible for Schiller's interpretation.

Although Fichte's language sometimes points in such a direction, the *Wissenschaftslehre* is better interpreted as an epistemology of human subjectivity. According to Fichte, the manner in which philosophers explain the conditions for the possibility of representation is the key to deciding whether or not their results are to be deemed a form of idealism or a form of realism (Fichte 1982 [1794/95]: 147). Idealism, Fichte says, attempts to ground representation in the activity of the I. A thoroughgoing idealism reduces the objects of experience to the status of mind-dependent entities, thereby explaining representation *solely* in terms of the activity of the I. Fichte rejects such an explanation of the possibility of representation, which he calls dogmatic idealism (*ibid.*: 147, 247). Realism, he says, attempts to ground representation in the influence of the object on the I. Dogmatic realism, which Fichte also rejects, regards subjectivity as a *mere* by-product of the activity of the material world (*ibid.*: 146, 160, 164). That is, dogmatic realism admits no role for the normative activity of the I in any explanation of representation. (We might think of dogmatic realism, in more contemporary terms, as a form of naturalism.) For Fichte, the supreme example of dogmatic realism is Spinozism, which he considers a form of materialism (*ibid.*: 101–2, 117–18, 146–7).

The *Wissenschaftslehre* is the middle route between dogmatic idealism and dogmatic realism. It is, as Fichte puts it, critical idealism (Fichte 1982 [1794/95]: 147, 164, 170–71, 247). On the one hand, because the *Wissenschaftslehre* is a form of idealism, critical idealism explains representation in terms of the activity of the I. On the other hand, because the *Wissenschaftslehre* assigns an essential role to the *Anstoss*, there is an aspect of representation that is not a product of the activity of the I, although, as we saw earlier, the I works to incorporate the *Anstoss* into its experience. Therefore, and this might come as a surprise to many, there is an inescapable element of realism in the *Wissenschaftslehre* (*ibid*.: 189, 246–7).[9]

In another surprise Fichte asserts that his critical idealism has a place for the thing-in-itself, assuming that this notion is understood in a manner appropriate to the *Wissenschaftslehre*. Fichte still rejects the thing-in-itself in the sense that was discussed earlier in this chapter, that is, as the unthinkable object that exists apart from our experience. It is sometimes said that Kant regards the thing-in-itself as the transcendent cause of the given element of our representations. As we saw earlier, Schulze interprets Reinhold in this way. Fichte certainly rejects this view, which he would characterize as a form of transcendent realism. His system, he says, despite its realism, is still transcendental in nature (Fichte 1982 [1794/95]: 246–7). That is, the *Wissenschaftslehre* explains consciousness entirely with reference to the activity of the self-positing I, all the while acknowledging that there is an alien element in its experience.

In this sense, therefore, according to Fichte, there is a thing-in-itself in our experience, but since it is *in* the I, it can be subordinated to the activity of the I, even though it is not the direct product of that activity. That is, as we saw earlier, it can be incorporated into our experience. But, as Fichte stresses, *it ought not to be in the I* (Fichte 1982 [1794/95]: 249). Consequently, the I gives itself the task of eliminating the thing-in-itself. Because the I must strive endlessly to do so, the thing-in-itself remains a permanent feature of consciousness that can never be eliminated entirely. Without it, says Fichte, there can be no finite minds.[10]

We see, therefore, that we cannot reject the *Wissenschaftslehre* on the supposition that it argues in favour of a radical subjectivism that is no longer taken seriously. To be posited in the I is not to be created by the I out of whole cloth. Instead, it is to be made an object of the activity of the I, to be worked over, as it were, by the I. Whatever is posited in the I is subjected to its standards. That is, the I attempts to make sense of it in theoretical or practical terms, depending on the particular case at hand.

But Fichte still makes ambitious claims. Consider what his arguments imply with regard to two important issues. First, because his system is grounded in the activity of the self-positing I, Fichte must be read as claiming that the *Wissenschaftslehre* successfully demonstrates the unity of theoretical and practical reason. The argumentative structure of the 1794/95 *Foundations* forces this conclusion upon his readers, since, after all, it purports to derive the foundations of theoretical and practical reason from a single source.

Secondly, Fichte must also be read as offering a practical rejoinder to scepticism. Because he regards reason as fundamentally practical, belief in the external world, as he sees it, is justified as a condition for the possibility of moral action.[11] As we saw above in "The background to the *Wissenschaftslehre*", the *Wissenschaftslehre* is influenced by various sceptical considerations, but it should not be read as endorsing sceptical conclusions. Fichte's response to scepticism reveals the continued influence of the thinking that motivated Kant's moral theology, but suitably transformed to mesh with the purposes of the *Wissenschaftslehre*.

What is our provisional assessment of Fichte's experiment? Recall the two questions raised earlier at the end of "The methodology of the *Wissenschaftslehre*": (i) how can we know that we have constructed a system that adequately accounts for the entirety of human knowledge; and (ii) is the *Wissenschaftslehre* entirely neutral with respect to the non-philosophical sciences? The answers to these two questions are more modest than we might expect.

As regards the first question, we must realize that Fichte never claims that his experiment has been completed. He hopes that he has not made any mistakes in his reasoning, but since he knows that he is fallible, he can never assert that his presentation of the *Wissenschaftslehre* is flawless (Fichte 1988b [1794b]: 129–30). Therefore, his experiment must be regarded as open-ended. As the *Wissenschaftslehre* is applied to the various areas of human knowledge – the 1794/95 *Foundations* discusses only their foundations, as we have seen – we may discover the need for further corrections and revisions.

The type of certainty with which the absolute first principle of the *Wissenschaftslehre* is said to be known is affected by Fichte's experimental method. We might call it a pragmatic certainty. That is, in so far as our use of this principle does not lead us into error, then we may continue to use it in our efforts to systematize the entirety of human knowledge. But if it should ever be shown that it is leading us astray, then we would have to choose another principle. A new philosophical postulate would then take its place as the starting-point of our system, and our experiment would have to begin anew. We can never know in advance that our chosen principle will enable us to complete our experiment, and we may only use it as long as it does not fail us.

As regards the second question, we cannot be certain in advance that the *Wissenschaftslehre* will not clash with any of the non-philosophical sciences. It seems unlikely that it will, if only because a philosophical view of the nature of rational agency – in this case, Fichte's theory of the self-positing I – seems removed enough from the concerns of the non-philosophical sciences as to leave their conclusions untouched. But only the future results of our experiment can decide the matter for us.

Fichte famously writes that most people can more easily take themselves to be a piece of lava on the moon than to make the free choice that stands at the beginning of the *Wissenschaftslehre* (Fichte 1982 [1794/95]: 162n.2). Those who deny a role to reason in the formation of our theoretical and practical beliefs can never see themselves in terms of Fichte's theory of the self-positing I (or, for that matter, in terms of any theory that assigns normativity an essential role in understanding human subjectivity). If they are incapable of seeing themselves as a self-positing I, then, as far as Fichte is concerned, they are outside the circle of philosophy. Fichte recognizes no obligation to argue with them; therefore, he is indifferent as to whether or not their views, whatever they may be, contradict the deliverances of the *Wissenschaftslehre*.[12]

Because Fichte has begun to set out the basic features of rationality with some persuasiveness, he can at least hope that a satisfactory theory of human subjectivity will result from a fully developed *Wissenschaftslehre*. Perhaps an experimental result will emerge that will lead us to question the viability of the *Wissenschaftslehre*. Then again, perhaps not. All that we can do is to remain optimistic as we continue experimenting with the self-positing I.[13]

Notes

1. For further discussion of Kant's moral theology and Fichte's views on revelation, see C. Bowman, "Fichte, Jacobi, and the Atheism Controversy", in *New Essays on Fichte's Later Jena Wissenschaftslehre*, D. Breazeale & T. Rockmore (eds), 279–98 (Evanston, IL: Northwestern University Press, 2002), 281–4.
2. For an excerpt from Schulze's *Aenesidemus*, see G. Di Giovanni & H. S. Harris (eds), *Between Kant and Hegel: Texts in the Development of Post-Kantian Idealism* (Indianapolis, IN: Hackett, 2000), 105–35.
3. For an excerpt from Reinhold's *The Foundation of Philosophical Knowledge*, a methodological work published in 1791, see Di Giovanni and Harris, *Between Kant and Hegel*, 51–103.
4. For extended discussions of the influence of Reinhold and Schulze on the origins of the *Wissenschaftslehre*, see D. Breazeale, "Fichte's Aenesidemus Review and the Transformation of German Idealism", *Review of Metaphysics* 34 (1981), 545–68, and "Between Kant and Fichte: Karl Leonhard Reinhold's 'Elementary Philosophy'", *Review of Metaphysics* 35 (1982), 785–821.
5. I have slightly modified the translation found in Di Giovanni and Harris, *Between Kant and Hegel*, 70.
6. Fichte realizes, of course, that there are empirical sciences whose findings are not known with certainty. How they fit into the account of science briefly summarized in this chapter is too complex a matter to discuss here. Interested readers should consult W. M. Martin, *Idealism and Objectivity: Understanding Fichte's Jena Project* (Stanford, CA: Stanford University Press, 1997), 11–29.

7. P. Heath & J. Lachs (ed. and trans.), *The Science of Knowledge* (Cambridge: Cambridge University Press, 1982) usually translate *"Ich"* as "self". Throughout this chapter I refer exclusively to "the I".

8. That is, all human consciousness. Beings possessing less-developed forms of consciousness are outside the scope of Fichte's investigations.

9. For an extended discussion of Fichte's brand of realism, see D. Breazeale, "Fichte's Abstract Realism", in *The Emergence of German Idealism*, M. Baur & D. O. Dahlstrom (eds), 95–115 (Washington, DC: The Catholic University of America Press, 1999).

10. For further discussion of the place of the thing-in-itself in the *Wissenschaftslehre*, see F. C. Beiser, *German Idealism: The Struggle Against Subjectivism, 1781–1801* (Cambridge, MA: Harvard University Press, 2002), 269–72, 316–19.

11. I am indebted to Beiser, *German Idealism*, 232, for my formulation of this point.

12. For a detailed discussion of the issues raised by this paragraph, see D. Breazeale, "How to Make an Idealist: Fichte's 'Refutation of Dogmatism' and the Problem of the Starting Point of the Wissenschaftslehre", *The Philosophical Forum* **19** (1987–88), 97–123.

13. I should like to thank Laura Eaton, Yolanda Estes, Paul Guyer, Jeff Kinlaw and John Shand for their comments on various drafts of this chapter. My thanks also extend to the three anonymous readers who provided helpful remarks about the penultimate draft.

Bibliography

Baur, M. & D. O. Dahlstrom (eds) 1999. *The Emergence of German Idealism*. Washington, DC: The Catholic University of America Press.

Beiser, F. C. 2002. *German Idealism: The Struggle Against Subjectivism, 1781–1801*. Cambridge, MA: Harvard University Press.

Bowman, C. 2002. "Fichte, Jacobi, and the Atheism Controversy". In *New Essays on Fichte's Later Jena Wissenschaftslehre*, D. Breazeale & T. Rockmore (eds), 279–98. Evanston, IL: Northwestern University Press.

Breazeale, D. 1981. "Fichte's *Aenesidemus* Review and the Transformation of German Idealism". *Review of Metaphysics* **34**, 545–68.

Breazeale, D. 1982. "Between Kant and Fichte: Karl Leonhard Reinhold's 'Elementary Philosophy'". *Review of Metaphysics* **35**, 785–821.

Breazeale, D. 1987–88. "How to Make an Idealist: Fichte's 'Refutation of Dogmatism' and the Problem of the Starting Point of the *Wissenschaftslehre*". *The Philosophical Forum* **19**, 97–123.

Breazeale, D. (ed. and trans.) 1988. *Fichte: Early Philosophical Writings*. Ithaca, NY: Cornell University Press.

Breazeale, D. (ed. and trans.) 1994. *Introductions to the Wissenschaftslehre and Other Writings (1797–1800)*. Indianapolis, IN: Hackett.

Breazeale, D. 1999. "Fichte's Abstract Realism". In *The Emergence of German Idealism*, M. Baur & D. O. Dahlstrom (eds), 95–115. Washington, DC: The Catholic University of America Press.

Breazeale, D. & T. Rockmore (eds) 2001. *New Essays in Fichte's Foundation of the Entire Doctrine of Scientific Knowledge*. Amherst, NY: Humanity Books.

Breazeale, D. & T. Rockmore (eds) 2002. *New Essays on Fichte's Later Jena Wissenschaftslehre*. Evanston, IL: Northwestern University Press.

Di Giovanni, G. & H. S. Harris (eds) 2000. *Between Kant and Hegel: Texts in the Development of Post-Kantian Idealism*. Indianapolis, IN: Hackett.

Fichte, J. G. 1978 [1792¹, 1793²]. *Attempt at a Critique of All Revelation*, G. Green (trans.). Cambridge: Cambridge University Press.

Fichte, J. G. 1982 [1794/95]. *Foundations of the Entire Science of Knowledge*. In *The Science of Knowledge*, P. Heath & J. Lachs (ed. and trans.), 89–286. Cambridge: Cambridge University Press.

Fichte, J. G. 1988a [1794a]. "Review of *Aenesidemus*". In *Fichte: Early Philosophical Writings*, D. Breazeale (ed. and trans.), 59–77. Ithaca, NY: Cornell University Press.

Fichte, J. G. 1988b [1794b]. "Concerning the Concept of the *Wissenschaftslehre*". In *Fichte: Early Philosophical Writings*, D. Breazeale (ed. and trans.), 94–135. Ithaca, NY: Cornell University Press.

Fichte, J. G. 1994 [1797/98]. *An Attempt at a New Presentation of the Wissenschaftslehre*. In *Introductions to the Wissenschaftslehre and Other Writings (1797–1800)*, D. Breazeale (ed. and trans.), 1–118. Indianapolis, IN: Hackett.

Hahn, K.-H. (ed.) 1968. *Schillers Briefe*, 2 vols. Berlin and Weimar: Aufbau-Verlag.

Heath, P. & J. Lachs (ed. and trans.) 1982. *The Science of Knowledge*. Cambridge: Cambridge University Press.

La Vopa, A. J. 2001. *Fichte: The Self and the Calling of Philosophy, 1762–1799*. Cambridge: Cambridge University Press.

Martin, W. M. 1997. *Idealism and Objectivity: Understanding Fichte's Jena Project*. Stanford, CA: Stanford University Press.

Neuhouser, F. 1990. *Fichte's Theory of Subjectivity*. Cambridge: Cambridge University Press.

Seidel, G. J. 1993. *Fichte's Wissenschaftslehre of 1794: A Commentary on Part I*. West Lafayette, IN: Purdue University Press.

Zöller, G. 1998. *Fichte's Transcendental Philosophy: The Original Duplicity of Intelligence and Will*. Cambridge: Cambridge University Press.

Further reading

Fichte (1982) is currently the only worthwhile translation of the 1794/95 *Foundations*. Any earlier translation should be avoided. Breazeale (1988: 1–49) provides an excellent historical overview of Fichte's Jena period, and Breazeale (1981) and Breazeale (1982) are especially helpful for understanding Schulze's and Reinhold's influence on Fichte's thinking in the early 1790s. Seidel (1993) is intended as an introduction to the 1794/95 *Foundations*, in particular to the complex arguments of Part I. More advanced readers are advised to consult Martin (1997) and Beiser (2002: 217–345) for sophisticated discussions of much of the metaphysics and epistemology of the Jena *Wissenschaftslehre*.

3

G. W. F. Hegel
Phenomenology of Spirit

Michael Inwood

At the beginning of the nineteenth century Germany was in turmoil. The French Revolution and the Enlightenment that inspired it were still sending shock waves throughout Europe. Germany in particular – the scene of several of Napoleon's battles and the beneficiary of many Napoleonic reforms – was undergoing a profound transformation of its political, religious and cultural life. Poets such as Goethe and Schiller were creating for Germany a great national literature. The religious beliefs to which most Germans were, even in this enlightened age, still deeply attached, were in turn attacked, defended and reinterpreted. History itself was often given a theological significance, seen as the gradual realization of divine providence or at least as an education of the human race that will eventually lead to its perfection. Kant's "critical" philosophy had generated an intense intellectual ferment. It challenged our pretension to know the ultimate nature of reality, even in the distant future, and it cast doubt on traditional religious beliefs. It presented a rational foundation for an individualistic morality that demanded single-minded devotion to duty. It placed aesthetics, the contemplation of beauty, at the centre of philosophy. Younger philosophers, notably Fichte and Hegel's friend Schelling, were inspired by Kant's writings to produce philosophical systems of their own, developing themes in Kant's work. Fichte made morality the central focus of his system, while Schelling turned to art. Both of them rejected Kant's limitation of human knowledge to perceptible phenomena, arguing that we can have knowledge of the "absolute", of ultimate reality, and of the process by which the absolute generates the perceptible world.

This was the context in which Georg Wilhelm Friedrich Hegel, then a lecturer at Jena University, wrote his first major work, the *Phenomenology of Spirit*, which was to be published in 1807. (He had by then left Jena, since Napoleon had, after the Battle of Jena, closed the university, as well as abolishing the Holy Roman Empire.) It was not the last of Hegel's books – he went on to write works on logic, on philosophy of nature and on politics – but it is perhaps the greatest of them and it overshadows the writings of Fichte and Schelling, although not those of Kant himself. It draws together into a coherent narrative the main intellectual currents of the age. It presents an inspiring vision of humanity's advance towards "absolute knowledge". It offers insights into the whole range of philosophical problems. Yet although one of the greatest books ever written, it is also one of the most difficult. It therefore needs, as well as deserves, the introduction that this essay is intended to provide.

Can we know the absolute?

The *Phenomenology of Spirit*[1] opens with a preface, setting the work in the context of its age. Hegel wrote the preface after he had completed the work, so it is better to begin with the "Introduction", which follows the preface. This introduces a view of "cognition" or knowledge common in Hegel's day. Our cognitive equipment is conceived as an "instrument" or a "medium", through which we receive messages from the "absolute", from reality as it is independently of ourselves. The messages may be garbled by the instrument or medium through which they pass and therefore give an inaccurate picture of the absolute. We can represent what Hegel has in mind by supposing (anachronistically) that the self is equipped with something like a camera with which it takes photographs of a reality independent both of itself and of its camera. Consider first an ordinary camera. The pictures it takes may distort the reality (trees, houses, mountains, etc.) they purport to show. The pictures are, in any case, only two-dimensional representations of a three-dimensional reality. How can we tell from the photographs what the trees, houses and mountains are really like? Ordinary photographers have access to the objects photographed as well as to the photographs of them. They can compare the objects with the photographs, see what distortion the photographs involve and with this information correct for the distortion on future occasions and tell what an object is like from its photograph without looking at the object itself. Now suppose that we are not simply partial and occasional photographers, but permanent and global photographers, whose whole cognitive equipment is a quasi-camera providing us with pictures of reality but with no direct access to the reality they portray.

Then we cannot compare our pictures of the absolute with the absolute itself, to eliminate the distortion. For example, our pictures of the absolute are invariably spatial and temporal. Trees, mountains, houses are in space and time. We can imagine, however, that the absolute itself is not in space and time, space and time being effects of the distorting lenses of our quasi-camera. But we could not know that this was so from inspection of our pictures of the absolute. We could never check the accuracy of our pictures by comparing them directly with the absolute. Pictures, with all their possible distortions, are all that we could ever have. On this account, we have no reliable access to the absolute, direct or indirect.

The scepticism that this model implies is not the scepticism of Descartes. This sceptic does not doubt our knowledge of the spatiotemporal world of physics or the everyday world of trees, mountains and houses. What is in doubt is whether such knowledge amounts to knowledge of the absolute: of mind-independent reality. It is the scepticism that results from Kant's *Critique of Pure Reason*, the belief that what we know are only phenomena, things as they appear to us, not things as they are "in themselves", not the absolute.

Hegel believes that the camera model of cognition entails such scepticism. But he rejects both the model and the scepticism. The camera model assumes that the photographer and the camera are quite distinct from the reality they photograph: that we ourselves and our cognition are distinct from the absolute and come to it from outside. But this is incoherent. We and our knowledge cannot be entirely separate from the absolute. We must be a product of the absolute, a spin-off from it. The absolute, whatever else it may be, must be such as to generate knowers and their knowledge. We can endorse this requirement and we perhaps could, with some ingenuity, devise a model of cognition that satisfies it. It would not follow, however, that the knowledge generated by the absolute presents an accurate picture of it. Lunatics and ignoramuses are as much a product of the absolute as anyone else. But it does not follow that they know the absolute. The knowers generated by the absolute may all be blinkered and their knowledge distorted or restricted. So Hegel needs to say more to dispose of the camera model and camera-scepticism.

Secondly, then, the camera model conceives the self as a single individual: as "I" rather than "we". But this is not how knowledge works. A human being belongs to a network of human beings, inheriting knowledge from their forebears, sharing their knowledge with each other and bequeathing it to their successors. An isolated human being would, if it knew anything at all, know only a fraction of what "we" know. How can the camera model accommodate this? Do we each have our own camera and gain access to others only by photographing them? Or do we all peer through the same camera? The camera model will need considerable modification to allow for this communality of knowledge. Perhaps camera-sceptics will agree that we have far more relatively "direct" knowledge than they originally allowed. We know about past and present human beings, what they have said, done and believed. We know the language and customs of our own society and perhaps of others too. But, the sceptic may insist, while we may know the knowers and the knowledge generated by the absolute, their interrelations and their products, the absolute itself still eludes us. The problem has shifted from the "I" to the "we". What *we* know may be as remote from the absolute as what *I* know.

Thirdly, however, as a camera-sceptic I am not simply a photographer. I also claim to know that I am a photographer. How do I know this? Do I have a second camera that I use to photograph myself and my camera, as well as the reality I purport to photograph? This threatens to introduce an infinite series of cameras, each of which photographs the next. Or do I use a single camera to photograph not only the absolute, but also myself, the camera and its relationship to the absolute? If so, why do I trust the camera to produce an accurate picture of my cognitive situation, when I do not trust its photographs of the absolute? I divide into two selves, one mistrustful of my cognitive powers, the other entirely confident of the nature and limits of these powers. (Consider, analogously, those who argue from the complexity of the human brain and its processes that our picture of the world is largely the product of our brains and is unlikely to represent with much accuracy the world itself. Why are they so confident of their view of the brain?)

Forms of consciousness

The camera model is flawed. But is there an alternative? Hegel has an alternative, namely, that the absolute, far from being alien and hidden, is the logical structure of the world, a logical structure that also forms the core of the human mind. But there are many alternatives to the camera model, besides Hegel's own. There are, or have been, many "shapes" or "forms" of consciousness, and the camera-model is only one of the more recent ones. (Hegel associates "the unknowable *absolute Being*" with the Enlightenment (*PS* 296, cf. 348ff.)). Instead of responding directly to the camera model with his own alternative, Hegel considers these forms of consciousness, the various ways in which we (or I) have tried to apprehend the world around us. All but the most global of sceptics will allow that we can at least describe with some accuracy these forms of consciousness. So Hegel can examine the forms of consciousness with an easy conscience. But in doing so, is he not evading the sceptic's question? That question is: can we know the absolute? Hegel raises an apparently different question: what conceptions of the absolute have we had? What bearing can this second question have on the first? It is conceivable that none of our conceptions of the absolute get to the bottom of it. However, Hegel has several reasons for his approach. First, he is alive to another sceptical difficulty, besides the supposed remoteness of the absolute from ourselves. There are alternative forms of consciousness, alternative conceptions of the absolute. How are we to tell which is right? The very possibility of a coherent alternative view threatens the credibility of Hegel's own view. Hegel's reply to this is that every form of consciousness, apart from his own, is internally incoherent and its incoherence can be seen and acknowledged not only by Hegel and his readers, but also by the form of consciousness itself. The self-refutation of other forms of consciousness does not, of course, guarantee the correctness of Hegel's own view, unless *all* other forms of consciousness are refuted, unless, that is, Hegel can guarantee the completeness of the array of forms of consciousness presented to us. Without such a guarantee the correct form of consciousness may have escaped his notice. Hegel is confident that his method provides such a guarantee. His confidence is unjustified.[2] But he may be granted that the refutation of alternative views is a necessary condition of the confirmation of his own view, even if it is not a sufficient condition.

Secondly, it is not the case that each form of consciousness is simply an alternative to every other form of consciousness and therefore to Hegel's own view. The forms of consciousness are arrayed in ascending order, a logical (and sometimes historical) order, such that as each form collapses, the kernel of truth in it is absorbed into its successor. The forms of consciousness bear some resemblance to the fly swallowed by a lady, which was then eaten by a spider, which was eaten by a bird and so on, except that the process does not terminate in the death of mankind or of Hegel, but in a stable philosophical system that presupposes the unstable forms of consciousness that it has absorbed. This is another reason why Hegel examines other forms of consciousness before introducing his own alternative. Hegel's system presupposes and absorbs other forms of consciousness and cannot be fully understood without them.

Thirdly, because the forms of consciousness are in order of increasing complexity and because they lead up to Hegel's own system, a journey through them is an appropriate introduction to Hegel's system. To understand Hegel's system is almost as difficult as swallowing a horse. So beginners are to start with a fly and work their way up to less digestible things. Everyone can understand the first form of consciousness: "sense-certainty". It is entirely simple and, even if we are not ourselves sense-certain, we can understand it because it is involved in and presupposed by our more complex way of viewing things. As we follow Hegel on his journey through the forms of consciousness, we are "recollecting" past phases of human consciousness.

Fourthly, even apart from its intrinsic difficulty, Hegel's system is not intelligible to all people at all times. There is even a sense in which it is not true for all people at all times. Roughly speaking, Hegel believes that the absolute is identical with the mind. But the mind is not static; it develops over time. The mind of someone who is merely sense-certain, of someone who simply gestures towards perceptible entities, is not identical with the absolute. As the forms of consciousness proceed, not only do the forms themselves become richer and more complex, but so too does the self or mind. The mind is not a free-floating observer that remains the same whatever objects it is conscious of and whatever experiences it undergoes. It develops along with its conception of objects, of itself and of its relation to its objects. The mind thus undergoes a sort of education or purification, and eventually, but not immediately, it converges with the absolute. This process of purification is undergone by the mind over the course of human history. But Hegel's readers need something of it too; they are submitted to a briefer version of the course that their forebears have undergone over centuries. This explains in part the title of Hegel's work. It is literally the study of the appearance(s) of the mind (or "spirit"), and this means, among other things, the study of the *emergence* of the mind or spirit, of its appearance on the scene.

Finally, as we saw earlier, the absolute, whatever else it may be, cannot be entirely distinct from us knowers and our ways of knowing. The mind that is purified by Hegel's system and its way of knowing converges with the absolute. But even the less adequate forms of consciousness that precede Hegel's own, although not identical with the absolute, cannot be simply distinct from it. The absolute must generate not only adequate knowledge of itself, but also the sequence of more or less inadequate ways of knowing it. Half-truths and errors not only lead up to the truth, but are, as existent phenomena, just as real as truths and must, therefore, be produced by the absolute. So the forms of consciousness are themselves an aspect of the absolute's manifestation of itself.

It does not follow from this, however, that to know all our forms of consciousness, all our ways of approaching the absolute, amounts to knowing the absolute. The forms of our consciousness, although generated by the absolute, may be among its less significant products, providing no more direct insight into the depths of reality than do trees, birds or butterflies. Hegel believes that this is not so. Our urge to know the absolute is not unreciprocated. Rather, the absolute itself has an essential urge to be known by us. It is not, like Descartes's *malin genie*, knowledge-resistant, ingeniously frustrating all our attempts to know it. Nor is it simply knowledge-indifferent, neither resisting nor assisting our attempts to know it. The absolute is knowledge-friendly, positively assisting our cognitive endeavours by meeting them halfway. Hegel finds this view expressed in a pictorial, unphilosophical form in "revealed religion", Christianity, the theme of the last section of the penultimate chapter of the work, "Religion". Christianity is revealed religion not in the sense that it is known by inspiration or by supernatural means in contrast to rational argument or inference from natural phenomena. It is revealed, in Hegel's sense, because it ascribes to the absolute an intrinsic urge to be known, whatever the means by which such knowledge is obtained. In Christianity the absolute reveals itself in human form; it emerges from its hiddenness and presents itself to our cognition. Our successive forms of consciousness, the stages of our journey of discovery, are, as it were, the rungs of a ladder thrown down to us by the absolute. Moreover, we ourselves cannot be distinct from the absolute; we are products of it. So in being known by us, the absolute is in a way known by itself. The absolute's urge to be known is an urge to know itself.

We are, however, getting ahead of ourselves. When we reach the top of the ladder we shall see that all this is so, we shall see the necessity and the significance of the journey we have undertaken. But initially we do not see this. Or rather, the form of consciousness under consideration does not see it. Hegel sees it, because he has lectured on this subject before and knows how the journey is going to end. We, Hegel's readers, are less well-informed than Hegel, but we see more than do most of the forms of consciousness we consider, since we have a richer, more complex form of consciousness. But a form of consciousness itself is aware only of itself. It cannot compare itself to a higher form of consciousness and judge itself to be inadequate by contrast. Nor can we criticize a form of consciousness by comparing it unfavourably to a higher form, to our own for example. This would, first, be an ineffectual type of criticism. It would just be our word against the word of the form of consciousness under attack. And, secondly, it could not represent the way in which human beings over history, or students in a lecture hall, advance from one form of consciousness to the next. They do not advance solely by being confronted with a higher form of consciousness than their own. They advance, initially, by discovering for themselves the inadequacy of their current form of consciousness. So it is with each form of consciousness that Hegel considers. Hegel lets us see how each form of consciousness contains an internal incoherence that the form of consciousness can discover for itself, without help from Hegel or from any higher form of consciousness.

Consciousness

The overall structure of the *Phenomenology* is this. It initially focuses on the object of consciousness. It then turns to the subject of consciousness. The subject of consciousness then attempts to close the gulf between itself and the object by imposing reason on (or discerning reason in) the world. With this achieved, humanity undertakes its long historical journey from the Greek city-state to the French Revolution. Finally, consciousness soars above the world to the realm of religion, a viewpoint from which it can survey its whole journey and the necessity of the stages through which it passed.

What keeps consciousness on the move? How does it get from one stage to the next? Consciousness has, at any given stage, a "concept", a general view of what the absolute is. But when it tries to work this out in detail, it finds that it cannot do it; it cannot meet the standard it has set itself. Hence each form of consciousness is a variety of scepticism. Consciousness thought it had hold of the absolute, but the absolute eludes its grasp. It has not done what it set out to do. It has not done *nothing*. What it does often exceeds its expectations. And what it does forms the basis of the next form of consciousness. A closer look at the work will illustrate this.

The first main section, "A. Consciousness", considers three successive ways in which consciousness deals with objects around it. These three forms of consciousness have no specific historical location and are forms of the consciousness of a single individual. (History requires more people and greater self-awareness than consciousness yet commands.) Hegel begins with "sense-certainty", just focusing on and indicating features of one's surroundings. He does so because it is the simplest form of consciousness, and is an ingredient in any higher form of consciousness, not because people in the remote past were exclusively sense-certain. In fact, Hegel denies that anyone, whether in the past or the present, is exclusively sense-certain, although he does allude to philosophers who *believe* that we know things immediately, without arguments or conceptual detours; we might call them "intuitionists" or "naive realists".

"Consciousness" contrasts with "self-consciousness". But this does not mean that consciousness has no self-awareness. Each form of consciousness has a conception of itself as well as of its objects: "consciousness is, on the one hand, consciousness of the object, and on the other, consciousness of itself; consciousness of what for it is the True, and consciousness of its knowledge of the True" (*PS*: 54). Consciousness needs this if it is to test its type of knowledge as a whole. Consciousness is not yet self-conscious, however. The conscious self is harnessed to a specific type of object, an object that, moreover, is not a self, not a consciousness. The self views itself in terms of its specific type of object. Sometimes it sees itself and its object as similar in nature, running parallel to each other. Sometimes it sees itself and the object as performing complementary roles, like a key and a lock. But in either case it is geared to its own range of objects. That is one reason why a form of consciousness is unaware of its own origins, of its emergence from another form of consciousness. The form of consciousness that has emerged from, say, sense-certainty, cannot look back on sense-certainty and its objects. It has undergone a complete overhaul along with its objects and it is now harnessed to its new objects as tightly and as exclusively as sense-certainty was harnessed to its objects.

Such a self is unsatisfactory. A fully developed self is not on a par with its objects, as long as these objects are not selves. Nor is it restricted to a specific range of objects. Neither we nor Hegel are so blinkered. We consider various types of object as we proceed through the *Phenomenology* and imaginatively identify with each form of consciousness as it comes along. So *we* are not restricted to a specific range of objects. Hence section A cannot be giving an adequate view of the self, not, at least, the kind of self that can write or read the *Phenomenology*. But we cannot appeal to this fact to criticize these opening forms of consciousness, saying: "This form of consciousness must be an inadequate version of the self because such a form of consciousness could not do what I am doing, could not look at itself in the way I am looking at it". That may be true, but to use it to move to a higher form of consciousness would violate Hegel's strategy. We must allow the form of consciousness to discover its own inadequacy, or at least show how, from its own resources, it could discover its own inadequacy. We cannot just appeal to our own superior capacities to refute a form of consciousness. It has to do it for itself.

Sense-certainty

In A, then, I am restricted to a specific range of objects and view myself in terms of these objects. So I am just conscious, not self-conscious. When in B I become self-conscious, I detach myself from any and every specific external object and try to find out what I myself am. But before that, I begin with sense-certainty. I am immediately aware of my sensory surroundings. I refer to some particular item as "this". Why refer to an individual object at all? Why not just drowsily absorb my surroundings without focusing on anything in particular? Hegel does not say. Perhaps if I am so drowsy I am not worth bothering with. But it is noticeable that when sense-certainty refers to *this* object, it also regards itself as *this* I or ego as the counterpart to *this* object. I must focus on a definite object to be an I or self. When I inattentively absorb my surroundings, I am absorbed in my surroundings. I do not distinguish myself, as an I, a subject, from my surroundings as an object. To detach myself from my surroundings I have to attend to something, and then I think of it as *this*. Then there are two *thises*, the I and the object, one knowing the other.

The I and the object are now parallel to each other. But they are not of equal status. Initially the object is the essential thing, the active party. The object would exist, if it were not known by me, even if I did not exist. I know the object *because of* what the object is. The object is not as it is *because* I know it. But which object? The word "this" and other words I use to pick out objects – "here", "now", "here and now" – are universal terms, terms that can be applied to anything, and so do not enable me to pick out unambiguously anything in particular.[3] Any object can in appropriate circumstances be referred to as "this", any time as "now" and any place as "here". It is unclear whether the conclusion Hegel draws from this is:

1. Sense-certainty cannot pick out an individual object, only a universal.

or:

2. Sense-certainty can pick out an individual object only by way of a universal.

Either way, sense-certainty is thwarted. If it cannot pick out an individual object, it cannot get at the objects it supposed it could, but only at universals; the object does not meet the standard that sense-certainty set itself. If it can pick out individual objects only by universals, its knowledge does not meet the standard set for it. It is mediated knowledge, not direct or immediate knowledge.

Sense-certainty responds by reversing the relationship between the I and the object. The I is now the essential, active party and the object is passive. Sense-certainty can now refer to itself as a way of picking out the object, saying: "It's the one *I* mean". But then it finds that the term "I" is also universal. It can be used by anyone to refer to themselves. So it cannot be used to pick out anyone in particular, and cannot be used to pick out any object in particular. Again, it is unclear whether Hegel wants to infer:

1a. I cannot refer to my individual self, only a universal self.

or:

2a. I can refer to my individual self only by way of a universal.

Inference 1a is mistaken. The fact that anyone can refer to themselves as "I" does not entail that no one can. "I" differs from "this", "here" and "now". Once we know who is using the word "this", we still may not know what is referred to. But once we know who is using the word "I", we know who is referred to. Still 2a alone is enough to foil sense-certainty. It implies that an individual object is known only indirectly, by way of the universal "I".

The I and the object are now on a par. Neither is more essential than the other. I can only refer to an object by referring to myself. Conversely, I can only refer to myself by referring to a *this*. So I point at something, indicating it as here and now. Pointing brings the I into play more explicitly than speaking. But a new problem arises. The scope of the words "here" and "now" is indeterminate. If I point at my desk, it is unclear whether I mean here where my finger touches the desk, or here on the desk, or here in this room, or here in Oxford, and so on. If I say "now", it is unclear whether I mean now at 2.20, or now during this lecture, or now during this week, and so on. A narrowly focused Here can be expanded indefinitely into a larger Here. A large Here can be divided indefinitely into smaller Heres. A small precise Now can be indefinitely expanded and a large Now indefinitely divided. This divisible Here and divisible Now are, Hegel says, "universals". Sense-certainty again fails to pick out the individual directly, only, if at all, by way of universals.

Perception

Consciousness now mutates into perception. Perception too has no specific historical location. The difficulty it has in reconciling the unity of the thing with the plurality of its properties reminds us of Locke and Kant, and also of some Greek philosophers, but not of primitive peoples. The German *wahrnehmen* ("perceive") is (Hegel believes) a compound of *wahr* ("true") and *nehmen* ("take"). Sense-certainty took things to be immediate and individual when, in truth, they are universal. Perception takes things as they truly are: as universal. Both the perceiver and the perceived are universal. But perception initially assumes that what is essential is the object. The object exists whether or not it is perceived. A lump of sugar, for example, has several properties. It is white, sweet, rough and cubical. Each property is universal, because it can belong to other things too. These properties do not exclude or conflict with each other. Sweetness and whiteness are, unlike sweetness and bitterness, mutually "indifferent". The lump is sweet and white right the way through. It is a medium or community in which the properties lie. This medium, too, is universal, because it accommodates a variety of properties. So it is just "thinghood", not yet a "thing". But the lump has definite properties, properties that contrast with other properties and with things having other properties, with white, bitter salt and with sweet, brown chocolate. So the sugar lump is not just thinghood: not just a universal medium accommodating any and every property. It excludes some properties and the things that have them. It is one thing among other things distinct from itself.

The thing now has two conflicting aspects. It is a universal medium, accommodating several properties. Yet it is also a unity, contrasting with other unified things. The perceiving subject may help. For the subject has the same dual structure as the object. The subject has several senses, by which it perceives different properties of a thing: whiteness by sight, sweetness by taste, roughness by touch. So the subject is a medium accommodating different types of sensation. Yet it is also a unified self, a single I aware that the sugar lump is white, sweet, rough and cubical, not a collection of I's each perceiving a different property of the thing. This dual structure of the I suggests a solution to the problem about the thing. We can unload one of the conflicting aspects of the thing on to the I. Perhaps the thing is *really* just a unity. It looks like a universal medium because our different senses fragment it into diverse properties.

Now new problems arise. Why does the lump appear white, sweet and rough rather than, say, black, pungent and smooth? The properties must be *somehow* in the thing, if we are to account for the different ways in which different things are perceived. Again, the subject has now become a universal medium, the meeting-place of various sensations. But the subject is also a unity. Has the conflict within the thing simply been transferred to the subject? It was, in any case, arbitrary of us to unload the thing's *diversity* on to the subject. We could just as well say that the thing is really just a medium for different properties, with no unity of its own, but derives its unity from the subject. So that is perception's next move: to leave the thing its diversity and unload its unity on to the subject.

This also raises problems. The thing was initially seen as a unity because it has properties that contrast with and exclude the properties of other things. If we leave the thing its properties, we leave it what distinguishes it from other things. The unity cannot easily be detached from the properties and just be imposed by the subject. It is also in the nature of the thing. Again, the conflict within the object has been transferred to the subject. The subject must be a unity if it imposes unity on the thing. But it must also involve diversity if it perceives the diverse properties that it is to unify. Still, we can unload the subject's diversity on to the thing. The subject is really just a unity. Its diversity is derived from the thing.

We have reversed our earlier solution. We first attributed unity to the thing alone and diversity to the subject alone. Now we assign unity to the subject alone and diversity to the thing alone. Neither of these assignments is preferable to the other. We have two items, the self and the thing, or, as Hegel now suggests, just one thing and another thing. Each is both a unity and a diversity.

But neither can be *both* a unity *and* a diversity at once. So each unloads one of its aspects on to the other. Perception says that a thing is *in itself* a unity, but a diversity *for another*, owing to its relations with other things. Or it says that the thing's *essence* is to be a unity, while its diversity is *inessential*, although it is *necessary* because of its relations to other things. None of these manoeuvres works. The thing must be both a unity and a diversity. But these two aspects contradict each other. So perception collapses.

Forces and laws

So far the subject and the object have behaved like dancing partners. Sometimes they do the same steps. When this gets too difficult, they do different but complementary steps. The subject is a unity and confers its unity on to the diverse object. Then the subject is diverse and confers its diversity on to the unified object. The subject, however, did more work than the object. It is the choreographer, deciding which steps the partners are to perform. The *subject* keeps changing its way of looking at the object; the *object* does not change at all. But the subject, consciousness, does not notice this. It lacks the resources to see that it is doing most of the work and is thus quite different from the object. It persists in attributing its own moves to the object.

The next form – force and understanding – has a more definite historical location. The idea that beneath the variety of perceptible things there are simpler, more fundamental stuffs and forces is an ancient idea, proposed by the first philosophers. But Hegel refers primarily to early modern scientific ideas, such as Newton's laws of motion, gravity, electricity and magnetism. In its attempt to ignore its own role and to attribute the changes to the object, consciousness now regards the object as a *force*. This reconciles the contradictory aspects of the thing. The inner force of the object is its unity. But the force manifests, expresses, itself as the diverse properties of the thing: its whiteness, sweetness, roughness. Unity and diversity are both located in the thing. Consciousness is now "understanding", not perception, because it penetrates the perceptible surface of the thing to its inner nature.

A force is sometimes dormant, sometimes manifest. It expresses itself when stimulated or "solicited" by another force. Force 1 is solicited by Force 2, and Force 2 is solicited by Force 1. (Force 2 may be solicited by another, Force 3, but two forces are easier to handle.) They are like two heavenly bodies, each affecting the other's movement by its gravitational force, or like two boxers, each soliciting the other into offensive and defensive moves, parrying blows or exploiting an opening to get in a punch.

Each force accounts for the expression of the other. But what accounts for the whole show, the interplay of forces? Not the forces themselves, the forces withdrawn into themselves and unexpressed. The withdrawal of a force into itself has to be solicited by another force just as much as its expression does. The withdrawal of a boxer into his corner, as much as his aggressive advance, is solicited by the other. Withdrawal is itself an expression of the force and cannot account for the whole show. What accounts for this interplay of forces is the "inner" underlying it. The play of forces is now the realm of "appearance", flanked on one side by the "inner", on the other by the understanding. The inner, the "supersensory world", is a "motionless realm of laws", laws governing appearance, the interplay of forces.

Among these laws is Galileo's law of freely falling bodies: the distance traversed by a body is related to the time for which it has been falling as the square to the root. Then there is electricity, in two forms, which we arbitrarily label "negative" and "positive": two bodies with the same charge repel each other, two bodies with different charges attract each other.[4] These laws involve a distinction between two factors, between time and distance, between positive and negative electricity, and so on. This distinction within the law restores, in the supersensory world, the distinction that disappeared in the realm of appearance. We began with two forces, one actively soliciting, the other passively solicited. Then we realized that each force solicits the other, and each expresses itself, because dormancy is itself an expression of the force. But while difference has vanished in appearance, it has re-emerged in law.

So a static, supersensory inner, the realm of laws, governs the realm of appearance. This involves problems. A law does not fully account for a phenomenon: it only explains what happens given certain initial conditions. The multiplicity of laws also makes it difficult to explain a phenomenon: how are we to know the relative effects of the laws? Newton tried to unify the law of falling bodies and the laws of planetary motion. However, this results (according to Hegel) in not a determinate law, but simply the concept of a law, a declaration that movement is law-governed, with no precise information as to what the law is. The main problem, however, is this. Underlying each law is a force. Not a particular force such as we initially encountered in appearance, but a general force: gravity, electricity and so on. Each force divides in two: distance and time, positive and negative. (Hegel perversely assimilates gravity to electricity, whereas gravity only attracts, never repels.) Why does the single force divide?

Magnetism and inversion

The answer lies in magnetism. Like electricity (whose connection with it was discovered only in the 1820s), magnetism is a polar force: like poles repel, unlike poles attract. But while a body can be electrically charged in one way alone – and cannot be charged in both ways – a magnet invariably has both a north and a south pole. Magnetism fulfils requirements that other forces do not. The distinction is intrinsic to the law: there cannot be one pole without the other. Again, other, static, laws hardly account for change and movement. *We* do it by "explanation", a movement of the mind, a movement in us, not in the law. But magnetism essentially involves movement: if it exists at all, then poles repel their like and attract their unlike. (Hegel exaggerates his case. Monopolar magnets do not exist, but they are imaginable, magnetism being a non-polar force, like gravity. Magnetic polarity is no more self-explanatory than the "distinction" in other laws. Again, if there existed only one magnet, we could not tell the difference between its poles. If there were no other metal for it to attract, we could not even tell that it was a magnet. Movement is essential to our detection of magnetism. But equally a solitary body would not manifest its gravitational force. In both cases movement is needed for us detect the law or force.)

Magnetism involves inversion. A north pole repels a north pole, repels itself, thus becoming unlike itself: a south pole. A north pole attracts a south pole, attracts what is unlike itself, so becoming unlike itself: a south pole. Underlying this apparent sophism is the fact that north and south poles differ only in their behaviour towards each other. If all north poles became south poles and all south poles became north poles, we would detect no difference, as long as they continued to repel and attract as they do now. Hegel exploits the idea of polar inversion to postulate a world that is the inverse of our world of appearance, a world where not only are south poles north poles and vice versa, but whatever, in our world, has one of two opposite qualities has, in this inverted world, the opposite quality: "Fair is foul, and foul is fair". This inverted world would be discernibly different from our own. A north–south switch may be undetectable, but a black–white switch would not: black print on white paper looks different from white print on black paper. The inversion is extended to punishment. In the first world punishment "destroys and disgraces", but in the inversion punishment becomes the pardon that preserves one's "essential being" (*PS*: 97) This echoes the Sermon on the Mount, with its exaltation of the lowly, who will presumably notice their changed condition.

Hegel's next step is to deny that our world and its inversion are two distinct worlds. There is just one world, constituted by the interplay between opposites. Within this world inversion already occurs. Opposites do not always turn into each other, but opposites often require, and sometimes engender, each other. A bisected magnet becomes two magnets each with two poles. Hegel assimilates this to inversion: since a south pole essentially requires a north pole; the essence or intrinsic nature of a south pole is a north pole. Not all opposites are like this. A black object need have no white in it. Everything might be black, although then there would be nothing to discern its blackness. Still, the world is, on this view, a system of mutually dependent opposites, each pair involving something like inversion.

This view of the world is more or less Hegel's own. He does not criticize it in the way he criticized earlier forms of consciousness. It is his response to Schelling, who postulated a simple neutral "absolute" and then wondered how it generates a diverse world, in particular how it divides into nature and mind. This problem arose with Kant's view that the world of empirical phenomena stems from interaction between the I and things-in-themselves. The I is not just an appearance; it is what phenomena appear *to*. So the I is a thing-in-itself, existing as much as other things-in-themselves. Reality divides into two realms: the I and the reality with which the I interacts to produce appearances. Why does reality divide into the I and the non-I? We need to explain this if we are to explain the world of phenomena. Kant was happy to leave it unexplained. But Schelling grappled with the problem of the absolute's division into mind and nature. And here is Hegel's suggestion. The absolute is not the "night in which all cows are black" (*PS*: 9). It is more like a magnet, essentially dividing into two poles, the self and the non-self. The self is no longer inessential as it was in earlier forms of consciousness. It is one pole of the magnet. The other pole is the inner nature of things, the mirror-image of the self. In between is the world of appearance. Without the self, there would be no inner nature, and thus no realm of appearance.

Self-consciousness

The remainder of the *Phenomenology* may be surveyed more cursorily. Hegel's overall strategy is this. The magnet model implies that the self is the mirror image of, if not identical to, the inner nature of things. But if this is to be more than an empty declaration, the self must actively establish its convergence with the nature of things. To do this, it must change itself. The boundary between the self and what is other than the self expands as the *Phenomenology* proceeds. This happens in three main stages. In "Self-consciousness", the individual establishes itself in distinction from the external world. Then the self cultivates the world both cognitively and practically, to become "spirit", the collective sociopolitical self. Finally, it transcends the sociopolitical world in religion.

Sense-certainty, perception and understanding tried to come to terms with the *object* of consciousness, assigning a subdued and subordinate role to the *subject* of consciousness, the self. In the next main section, "B. Self-consciousness", the self becomes the central focus of attention and, rather than conforming to the external world, enters into opposition to it. It eats it, fights it, enslaves it. It retreats into itself away from the world, as a Stoic. It denies its reality, as a Sceptic. Finally, it rises above the world to a remote God as "unhappy consciousness". The German word for "self-conscious" ordinarily means "self-assured", not, like its English counterpart, "embarrassed". But Hegel has a deeper reason for postulating conflict between the self and the world. To understand an object properly, we must not be wholly absorbed in it. We must withdraw from the object, take our distance from it, to bring it into focus. We must even enter into opposition to the object, distinguish ourselves from it and develop ourselves independently of it. A child is contentedly absorbed in its surroundings, but in adolescence we enter into opposition to the world. Only so can we develop into rational adult selves with a rational, objective view of the world, to which we later become reconciled.[5] So too with the human being in the state of nature with which this section opens. It has a sort of self-consciousness, aware of itself as an I or ego, but (like a child) regards itself as the centre of things and looks for confirmation of this in the world around it. It begins by desiring living things and eating them, but finds that unsatisfying and monotonous. It then encounters another self-consciousness also looking for confirmation of its identity. They fight each other in order to display their selfhood and to confirm it by gaining recognition. One wins and enslaves the other, although the loser, who is subjected to discipline and made to produce things for the master to consume, benefits from servitude, while the master derives little satisfaction from recognition, since it is recognition by a slave. The next stage, now a stage in a historical as well as a logical sequence, is Stoicism, a doctrine advocating indifference to pains and pleasures, which originated in Greece but became popular among the upper classes in the Roman Empire. It is an appropriate sequel to the master–slave episode, since one Stoic philosopher, Epictetus, was a slave, although later liberated, while another, Marcus Aurelius, was an emperor. Scepticism, another Greek invention that persisted into the Roman Empire and beyond, is the next stage. It is an even more radical retreat into one's inner self than Stoicism. The Stoic cultivates indifference to misfortunes, such as enslavement. The sceptic doubts that the misfortune has occurred. At the final stage of this section "unhappy" consciousness projects the master–slave relationship on to the religious plane. It abases itself before a distant God. It attributes to God all its merits and achievements, and regards itself as worthless, deriving such value as it has from its relationship to God. This represents early and/or medieval

Christianity, thus continuing and concluding the historical sequence. It is apparently quite different from Hegel's Christianity, which involves elevation to God, not abasement before God.

Reason and spirit

Nevertheless, belief in a God, a remote God, extricates us from the phenomenal world, detaches us from our surroundings. It deepens our understanding of ourselves, since God is a sort of mirror image of the self. Then we come back to the world and master it, exploring it in science, cultivating it with gardens and cities, and constructing social and political institutions. Christianity does not let us remain absorbed in this remote God or oscillate between God and a godless world. The Christian God himself descends into the world and masters it. And this symbolizes what we ourselves do. We return from our elevated detachment from the world and come back to master it, in science, philosophy and social organization generally. Accordingly, the next section, "C. Reason", brings the self and the world together again. "Reason" is not the same as the "understanding" of section A. Understanding distinguishes and separates. It distinguishes itself from its object. Reason brings the subject and the object together. "Reason is the certainty of consciousness that it is all reality" (*PS*: 140). Reason imposes its own thoughts on the world, subjecting it to scientific and moral order. Section C involves a "repetition" of A and B, since what we bring into order are the objects of consciousness and our own selves. It does not follow a historical sequence. It presents and criticizes various theories current in Hegel's own time. First he looks at "observing reason", which deals with the description and explanation of nature and also of human psychology. The climax of observing reason is Hegel's critique of two theories fashionable at the time: physiognomy, the doctrine that you can tell a person's character from the structure of the face; and phrenology or craniology, the doctrine that a person's faculties and character correspond to the bumps on the skull. (An apt reply to a physiognomist, Hegel suggests, is to punch him on the nose to show him that changing the structure of his face does not change his character.) Since "observing reason" has hopelessly failed to comprehend the self, we turn to practical or moral reason for the "actualisation of self-consciousness through its own activity" (*PS*: 211). This section shows the inadequacy of individualistic morality, especially, although not exclusively, in Kant's version of it. A single individual cannot cope morally with an amoral world, with a world that lacks a shared moral code embodied in laws and institutions. In particular, the individual's reason, as Kant views it, is not able to propose or to test moral laws. A stable social order requires not only *Moralität*, an individual's personal "morality", but also *Sittlichkeit*, a shared "ethical life" or social morality embodied in institutions. (It is mainly the moral and political sections of the *Phenomenology* that involve a plurality of subjects and display historical development. Hegel does not stress that *observing* reason is a collective enterprise with a history of its own.)

How does ethical life arise? Hegel does not say. He quotes Antigone's claim that the unwritten laws of the gods "are not of yesterday or today, but everlasting, Though where they came from none of us can tell" (*PS*: 261). In the next main section, "Spirit", history begins again, not in the state of nature as in B, but in the Greek city-state. The German *Geist* ("spirit"), often refers to the individual "mind". But spirit here is not the individual mind. It is the "ethical life of a nation" (*PS*: 265): "an I that is We and We that is I" (*PS*: 110). Reason's mastery of nature has resulted in an orderly, civilized world imbued with spirit. The individual subject no longer confronts an object alien to itself. The surrounding world is imbued with the same spirit as the individual. The ethical world of the city-state is comparable to the innocent contentment of childhood. But conflict lurks beneath its surface harmony. Hegel illustrates this with his favourite play, Sophocles' *Antigone*. Antigone's brother has been killed after the defeat of his rebellion. The king, Creon, forbids the burial of slaughtered rebels. Antigone disobeys and buries her brother. Hegel regards this as a conflict not just between two individuals or between an individual and the state but between two sets of values: the values of the family, maintained by women and underwritten by the gods of the underworld, and the values of the state, maintained by men and underwritten by the gods of the upper world. Antigone and Creon are each in the right and each in the wrong. Each champions one set of values, but violates another set of values. So each of them is guilty. "Not even a child is innocent. Only the inactivity of a stone is free of guilt".[6]

Such conflicts of value led to individualism, to the separation of the individual from the spirit, from ethical life, the shared values of the city-state, and to the dispersal of citizens into their private realm under the Roman Empire, where everyone is just an individual, a property-owning person, separate from every other person. So now we move away from "true spirit" of Greece to "alienated spirit" and to education or "culture". The education in question is initially the education of the Germanic tribes that overran the Roman Empire, an education that "alienated" them from their native language and customs. But Hegel traces the development of European culture, primarily in France, the centre of the medieval world, down to the French Revolution. This development too is driven by the conflictual interplay between different values: between the nobility and the monarch, between the state and the rich, and later between religious faith and the intellectual sophistication of the nobility. This culminates in revolution, a quest for "absolute freedom", overturning any institution or organization seen as an obstacle to the will of the people, which is now once again just a mass of distinct individuals. Finally, Hegel turns again to individualistic morality and the idea of conscience, which he sees as the moral underpinning of the French Revolution. The conscientious individual is detached from society and its values, whittled down to a bare, featureless ego. Like the sceptic in B, the individual resolves its isolation by turning to God.

Religion

With this abrupt transition Hegel introduces the penultimate section, "Religion". Now his account of history begins yet again. This time it goes back beyond the Greeks to "natural religion", the religions of Persia, India and Egypt, in which God or the absolute remains remote from the world and cannot find adequate embodiment in it. It proceeds to the "religion of art", Greek religion, although Hegel takes this opportunity to survey the whole of Greek art and its connection with Greek life. The Greek gods are embedded in the world and harmoniously portrayed in art. "Revealed religion", Christianity, emerging from the ruins of ancient religion, is the consummation of both natural religion and Greek religion. God is initially remote, but descends into the world to transfigure it. Long before Nietzsche, Hegel declares that "God is dead", referring both to the decay of religion in the Roman Empire (*PS*: 455) and to the death of Christ (*PS*: 476). Christ's death symbolizes (among other things) the death of the remote, abstract God of the unhappy consciousness and is followed by the descent of the Holy Spirit, which represents the elevation of humanity above their natural condition: the convergence of humanity and deity. Christianity, even as Hegel describes it, is philosophically defective; it presents in pictorial imagery what should strictly be presented in terms of prosaic thought. So "Religion" is followed by a short concluding chapter on "Absolute Knowledge", which sums up the whole work and gives a brief account of "science", of Hegel's own philosophy to which the *Phenomenology* was originally intended as an introduction.

Religion is not, in Hegel's view, a peripheral and optional enterprise. It plays a crucial part in the emergence and development of the human mind. Differences between cultures and societies are rooted in religious differences. (It does not, of course, follow that every human individual is explicitly religious, any more than the fact that man is a tool-using animal entails that everyone uses all the tools available.) Christianity in particular opens up the world to our moral and cognitive endeavours. It makes the world morally and cognitively manageable.[7] Especially in its Lutheran version, it fosters and sanctifies the organized individualism characteristic of modernity.[8] The individual is no longer wholly absorbed in society, like the Greek, nor simply a detached property owner, like the Roman. Like Christ – humanity's representative – the human individual has intrinsic value, not just the value of an element in a system. The value and freedom of the individual is not incompatible with a stable social order. In Hegel's view, the inner depth of the individual requires, and is required by, the structured liberal societies emerging from the debris of revolution. This is what, among other things, Hegel means by saying: "everything turns on grasping and expressing the True, not only as *Substance*, but equally as *Subject*" (PS: 10).

A second function of Christianity is this. A lower form of consciousness is blinkered, restricted in its vision to itself and its own objects. Some higher forms of consciousness are also blinkered. A Greek, for example, was too deeply embedded in "ethical spirit" to be able to assess society and its laws from outside. In general, Hegel believes that properly to understand a level of consciousness, *n*, one has to rise to a higher level, *n + 1*. But to where can one rise to survey, as Hegel does, the whole course of history? To God! But how can one then descend again to consider the details of history and to participate in the life of one's own community? Christianity supplies the model for that in the incarnation. Christ forms a bridge between the elevated position from which we survey the whole and the worldly situation of the engaged citizen.

The Christian God is not, however, just a bridge between worldly forms of consciousness and a standpoint outside them. It also prescribes the forms of consciousness we are to pass through. God needs to be known by us. God is like an author in search of readers, who produces a series of drafts, each adapted to our current stage of development, in the hope that eventually we shall understand. That is another meaning of the incarnation.

Hegel does not mean that Christianity guarantees the *correctness* of our beliefs, conduct and institutions. What it does is rather to explain how we came to form certain types of belief, engage in certain types of conduct, and establish certain institutions in the first place. He is trying to answer such questions as "How is human consciousness possible?", "How is science possible?" and "How is the modern liberal state possible?", and not simply "How can we know that our beliefs, theories, and institutions are correct?" (His conviction that Christianity is especially favourable, perhaps even necessary, for the growth of science is not invalidated by occasional conflicts between Christians and scientists, any more than occasional conflicts between politicians and scientists show that science could have arisen and developed outside a stable political order.)

What do we find when we reach the final draft? Do we find God? Or the absolute? Or do we just discover the necessity of all the drafts we have read? God is not, in Hegel's view, an entity that exists unchanging in its own right, regardless of how human beings think and act. God is a sort of projection of humanity on a higher plane. What God is corresponds to the nature of the human beings whose projection it is. Egyptians, Greeks and Christians differ in their view of God. Which of them is right? There is no answer to that question if it is taken to mean: which of these views, if any, fits the fact of the matter? Each of them has the god or gods that suit their stage of development. Does this mean that God and gods do not exist at all? Not according to Hegel. After all, a human society or a state is a projection of human beings. It is not something over and above the human beings who make it up, their thoughts and their deeds. A segment of humanity, a people, has a society and a state corresponding to its nature. But this does not mean that societies and states do not exist. Why should it be different with God? However, the transcendent God is, Hegel tells us, "dead". The claim is not that such a God never has existed, but that he has been killed off by, among other things, Martin Luther's reformation. Luther made the state thoroughly secular.[9] Hegel wrote the transcendent God's obituary: God is no more distinct from the forms of consciousness by which we reach him than Oxford University is distinct from Oxford colleges.[10]

Has Hegel solved the epistemological problem with which he began? The absolute was initially conceived as "in itself", in contrast to "for us", as a mind-independent reality to which our "concept" needs to be adapted if we are to find the "truth". But the expression "in itself" has, for Hegel, another meaning. What is "in itself" is merely potential, in contrast to "actual". It is like a seed that has not yet grown into a tree. It is not yet "true". It does not measure up to its own "concept". What it needs, therefore, is not just to be investigated, but to be developed up to its concept, developed by "us", although we shall in the process also develop ourselves. Analogously, if in a moment of despair I ask "Who am I?", I shall not find the answer simply by investigating my present state. That is just a mess. The answer is to be found by developing myself: by fulfilling my "concept". That is why the absolute needs to be known. "In itself" it is like a potential author, an author without readers. It needs to become "for us" and, since we are not distinct from the absolute, that means that it must become "for itself", that is, in Hegel's usage, "actual". Hegel does not strictly believe in such an author. Perhaps he is an atheist. But if so, it is an atheism made possible by Christianity. Hegel's atheism is a gift from God.

Notes

1. In my references to this work, I cite the pagination of *Phenomenology of Spirit*, A. V. Miller (trans.) (Oxford: Clarendon Press, 1977).
2. Michael Forster, in his *Hegel and Skepticism* (Cambridge, MA: Harvard University Press, 1989), argues that the circularity of Hegel's account, the fact, that is, that the end of the *Phenomenology* returns to the first form of consciousness, guarantees the completeness of the forms of consciousness Hegel examines. But even if the circularity is genuine, it remains possible that Hegel has skipped over a form of consciousness and/ or that there are forms of consciousness outside Hegel's circle.
3. Such words are now usually called "token-reflexive" rather than "universal". But this does not affect Hegel's argument.
4. According to Coulomb's law, the force with which charged bodies repel or attract each other is inversely proportional to the square of the distance between them.
5. For Hegel's account of this, see his *Philosophy of Mind*, W. Wallace and A. V. Miller (trans.) (Oxford: Clarendon Press, 1971), 55–64.
6. This is my translation. Miller has: "Innocence, therefore, is merely non-action, like the mere being of a stone, not even that of a child" (*PS*: 282).
7. See, for example, Hegel's *Philosophy of Mind*, 44–5.
8. Cf. William James, *Principles of Psychology* (New York: Dover, 1950), vol. I, 316: "The impulse to pray is a necessary consequence of the fact that whilst the innermost of the empirical selves of a man is a Self of the *social* sort, it yet can find its only adequate *Socius* in an ideal world."
9. Cf. J. N. Figgis, *Studies of Political Thought: From Gerson to Grotius, 1414–1625* (Bristol: Thoemmes, 1998), 65: "When Luther burnt the *Corpus Juris Canonici*, he symbolised and intended to symbolise the entire abolition of all claims, not only to superiority, but even to any kind of coercive or inherent jurisdiction in the Church. He destroyed, in fact, the metaphor of the two swords; henceforth there should be but one, wielded by a rightly advised and godly prince."
10. I borrow this analogy from Chapter 1 of Gilbert Ryle's *The Concept of Mind* (London: Hutchinson, 1949).

Further reading

Hegel is often his own best commentator. Thus *Hegel's Philosophy of Mind*, W. Wallace and A. Miller (trans.) (Oxford: Clarendon Press, 1971), the third part of his *Encyclopaedia of the Philosophical Sciences* (1830), covers some of the same ground as the *Phenomenology of Spirit*, often in a more digestible form. His *Elements of the Philosophy of Right*, H. Nisbet (trans.), A. Wood (ed.) (Cambridge: Cambridge University Press, 1991) similarly sheds light on the ethical parts of the *Phenomenology*. His views on such matters as gravity, electricity and magnetism are expounded at length in *Hegel's Philosophy of Nature*, A. V. Miller (trans.) (Oxford: Clarendon Press, 1970), the second part of his *Encyclopaedia*. His *Lectures on the Philosophy of Religion*, E. Speirs and J. Sanderson (trans.) (London: Routledge, 1895), and also P. Hodgson and R. Brown (trans.) (Berkeley, CA: University of California Press, 1984–6), are the best source for Hegel's views on religion. His account of the relationship between religion and art is presented in his *Introductory Lectures on Aesthetics*, B. Bosanquet (trans.), M. Inwood (ed.) (Harmondsworth: Penguin, 1993).

There are several good books on Hegel's thought in general. Shorter works include: E. Caird, *Hegel* (Edinburgh and London: Blackwood, 1883); F. Copleston, *Fichte to Hegel* (New York: Doubleday, 1965); G. Mure, *The Philosophy of Hegel* (Oxford: Clarendon Press, 1965); P. Singer, *Hegel* (Oxford: Clarendon Press, 1983); and S. Houlgate, *An Introduction to Hegel: Freedom, Truth and History*, 2nd edn (Oxford: Blackwell, 2005). Longer works are: W. Stace, *The Philosophy of Hegel: A Systematic Exposition* (London: Macmillan, 1924); J. N. Findlay, *Hegel: A Re-examination* (London: Allen & Unwin, 1958); W. Kaufmann, *Hegel: Reinterpretation, Texts, Commentary* (New York: Doubleday, 1965); C. Taylor, *Hegel* (Cambridge: Cambridge University Press, 1975); and M. Inwood, *Hegel*, 2nd edn London: Routledge, 2002). The essays in F. Beiser (ed.) *The Cambridge Companion to Hegel* (Cambridge: Cambridge University Press, 1993) cover the whole range of Hegel's thought. There are also several fine books devoted to the *Phenomenology of Spirit* in particular, including: R. Norman, *Hegel's Phenomenology: A Philosophical Introduction* (Brighton: Harvester, 1976); R. Solomon, *In the Spirit of Hegel* (New York: Oxford University Press, 1983); T. Pinkard, *Hegel's Phenomenology: The Sociality of Reason* (Cambridge: Cambridge University Press, 1994); M. Forster, *Hegel's Idea of a Phenomenology of Spirit* (Chicago, IL: University of Chicago Press, 1998); R. Stern, *Hegel and the Phenomenology of Spirit* (London: Routledge, 2002); and H. S. Harris, *Hegel's Ladder* (Indianapolis, IN: Hackett, 1997). Among the many good accounts of Hegel's ethical philosophy, A. Wood, *Hegel's Ethical Thought* (Cambridge: Cambridge University Press, 1990) and M. Hardimon, *The Project of Reconciliation: Hegel's Social Philosophy* (Cambridge: Cambridge University Press, 1994), can be especially recommended.

4

Arthur Schopenhauer
The World as Will and Representation

Dale Jacquette

Author, text and context

Arthur Schopenhauer is one of the most remarkable, yet iconoclastic and uncharacteristic, of the great thinkers of nineteenth-century German idealism. A post-Kantian philosopher who disassociated himself from the mainstream post-Kantians, Hegel, Fichte and Schelling, Schopenhauer weaves together the natural science of his day with transcendental metaphysics inspired especially by the writings of Plato and Kant, and the mysticism and compassionate ethics of Asian religious philosophy in Buddhist and Hindu traditions.

Schopenhauer's masterwork, *Die Welt als Wille und Vorstellung*, was published as a single volume in 1818, and reissued in a revised and expanded two-volume second edition in 1844, followed by a third edition in 1859, the year before his death. In its English translations as *The World as Will and Idea* or *The World as Will and Representation*, the book's title indicates a division of the world into two metaphysical aspects. Schopenhauer distinguishes between the world as it is represented to thought, known to common sense and empirical science, and as it exists independently of thought as Kantian thing-in-itself. He further identifies thing-in-itself, in what he claims is his unique philosophical discovery, as the transcendental Will.

The first edition of Schopenhauer's text is divided into four books. The same four books also appear in the second and third editions in revised and updated form as the first of two volumes. They are divided into the following topics.

- First Book: The world considered as consisting of representations, thoughts and perceptions, which can be explained through the fourfold root of the principle of sufficient reason. (The World as Representation. First Aspect)
- Second Book: The world considered as thing-in-itself, identified with Will. The existence of thing-in-itself is established by abstract transcendental reasoning, and its character as Will is described. Thing-in-itself is objectified as distinct representations for, which is to say experienced by, representing subjects. Representations in turn exemplify Platonic Ideas, interpreted by Schopenhauer as grades of the Will's objectification in the world as representation. (The World as Will. First Aspect)
- Third Book: Platonic Ideas exemplified in the world as representation, considered abstractly as independent of the principle of sufficient reason, are examined for further insight into the world as representation. The Ideas are described as embodied in art and nature, passively experienced and actively communicated by artists of aesthetic genius. (The World as Representation. Second Aspect)
- Fourth Book: The world as representation is characterized as endless striving in Schopenhauer's concept of the individual or empirical phenomenal will to life. Schopenhauer develops the philosophical basis for an outlook of moral pessimism. He addresses the problems of death, freedom, ethics and salvation from the cycle of suffering that stems from the endless demands of phenomenal willing through denial and suppression or transcendence of the will to life. (The World as Will. Second Aspect)
- Appendix: "Criticism of the Kantian Philosophy".

The second volume supplements the second and third editions. It contains fifty essays presenting Schopenhauer's elaborations and later discoveries of scientific and historical evidence to illustrate and lend further justification to the philosophical system set forth in the first volume. These are arranged as additions in four parts corresponding to each of the four books in the first volume, bearing such generally self-explanatory titles as "On the Fundamental View of Idealism", "On Man's Need for Metaphysics" and "On the Possibility of Knowing the Thing-in-Itself".

The World as Will and Representation is Schopenhauer's third book. In 1813 he completed and, as was customary at the time, published at his own expense the doctoral dissertation he had begun at the University of Berlin, the degree for which was later awarded *in absentia* from the University of Jena. The dissertation investigates the scope and limits of knowledge, and lays the groundwork for Schopenhauer's subsequent philosophy. *On the Fourfold Root of the Principle of Sufficient Reason* is a brilliant, penetrating and well-argued enquiry that is still widely read and much admired even among philosophers who otherwise have little sympathy for Schopenhauer's metaphysics.[1] Afterwards, from 1814 to 1818, Schopenhauer lived in Dresden with his mother Joanna, a popular novelist, in whose literary salon he met many interesting personalities, including Goethe. Schopenhauer corresponded with Goethe, whose *Farbenlehre* [*Theory of Colors*] inspired Schopenhauer to write his second book in 1816, *On Vision and Colors: An Essay*. It was also during this early fruitful period that Schopenhauer completed the first edition of *The World as Will and Representation*.[2]

Schopenhauer then returned to Berlin, where he hoped to obtain a professorship in philosophy, an effort in which he was disappointed, although he was granted a provisional lectureship. Apparently through a combination of hubris and supreme contempt for his well-established philosophical rival, Schopenhauer scheduled his *Privatdozent* lectures for fee-paying students at precisely the same time as Hegel's, assuming that Hegel's students would defect from Hegel and flock instead to Schopenhauer's podium. In the event, the exact opposite happened, and Schopenhauer lost whatever small handful of students had first attended his course out of curiosity. It was a professional embarrassment from which Schopenhauer never personally recovered, costing him the possibility of a professional academic career as a university philosopher. It only served to deepen his already bitter animosity toward what he considered to be Hegel's undeserved reputation.[3] Relying instead on a modest inheritance from his father, a merchant with commercial interests who may have committed suicide in 1805, Schopenhauer was able to pursue independent philosophical studies outside the university, a prospect that offered him greater intellectual freedom while at the same time guaranteeing him virtual obscurity throughout most of his life. As a result, his ideas did not receive sufficient attention at the time, his books were not reviewed, and he remained an outsider with respect to the most active philosophical movements at the time, when philosophy was only beginning to become professionalized. He left Berlin once again in 1831 during the cholera epidemic that claimed the life of Hegel, residing in Frankfurt for the remainder of his life, writing and revising the later works that amplify the central ideas of *The World as Will and Representation*.

Throughout his writings, Schopenhauer describes his philosophical system as the development and exploration of the consequences of a single thought (*WWR* 1: xii; xv–xvi). That thought, as the title of his most important work indicates, is that the world has two aspects, and can only be understood from the standpoint of its fundamental duality. The world has an empirical side, which Schopenhauer refers to as the world as representation (*Vorstellung*), that we experience perceptually by means of the senses, and that we can in principle adequately explain by proper application of the natural sciences. If we take a superficial view of reality, then, Schopenhauer would say, we might suppose that the scientifically known world as representation is all that exists. As a reflection of his intellectual debt to Plato and Kant, Schopenhauer maintains that there is also another side to the world, which he follows Kant in referring to as thing-in-itself (*Ding an sich*). Thing-in-itself is the world as it exists in itself, independently of all thought and all concepts and categories of mind. Knowledge of thing-in-itself necessarily lies beyond perception and explanation. Schopenhauer regards his most significant contribution to metaphysics, the sense in which he believes that he has gone far beyond Kant and the entire previous history of philosophy, as offering insight into the hidden nature of thing-in-itself as Will (*der Wille*).

Metaphysics of *The World as Will and Representation*

The primary distinction in Schopenhauer's philosophy involves his dualistic conception of the world as mind-dependent representation, reality as it appears to thought, and as mind-independent thing-in-itself. The fourfold root of the principle of sufficient reason, which provides the basis for Schopenhauer's theory of knowledge, divides all explanations for any and every occurrence exclusively within the world as representation into lawlike generalizations concerning logical, mathematical, causal and moral or motivational phenomena. It thus serves as a criterion delimiting the explainable facts that constitute the represented world, and thing-in-itself as that which cannot be explained because it exists entirely outside all thought, and is not subject to the principle of individuation (*principium individuationis*) into objects, parts or moments.

Schopenhauer maintains that the suffering and turmoil resulting from competition among persons and groups is inherently unavoidable because it is a reflection in the world as representation of the irresolvable internal conflicts in Will as thing-in-itself. For rational beings such as ourselves in search of answers to life's problems, Schopenhauer believes that there are just two paths leading to salvation from this suffering, both of which involve a renunciation of the individual will to life (*der Wille zum Leben*) that we all experience phenomenologically as the ultimately insatiable psychological cravings for this or that among the empirical objects of desire. Thus, for Schopenhauer, life is a succession of episodes of striving to fulfil desires, followed by dissatisfaction and ennui, striving and ennui, terminated only by death. Disavowing suicide as offering any sort of philosophical answer in the quest for relief from the torments of the will, Schopenhauer recommends, first, the saintly practice of ascetic abstinence and profound indifference to life and death, and, secondly, the transcendence of self that occurs when aesthetic or philosophical genius is so enraptured in contemplation that it becomes identified with and absorbed into a perceived object of beauty or the sublime in nature or art, during which it passively receives knowledge of the Platonic Forms or Ideas instantiated in the world as representation. Schopenhauer regards knowledge and individual willing as eternally opposed, and hence interprets the ways of salvation as the redirection in one way or another away from the objects of willing toward objects of knowledge.

In his theory of the world as representation, Schopenhauer adopts an extreme form of transcendental idealism.[4] He believes that the physical world experienced in sensation exists entirely in thought, which is to say in each thinker's mind. He claims that on reflection everyone already knows this, and that the world begins with the awakening to consciousness of each individual mind and ends with each thinking being's death. Introducing his philosophical system, Schopenhauer opens the first volume of the book with the startling pronouncement that:

> The world is my representation: this is a truth valid with reference to every living and knowing being, although man alone can bring it into reflective, abstract consciousness. If he really does so, philosophical discernment has dawned on him. It then becomes clear and certain to him that he does not know a sun and an earth, but only an eye that sees a sun, a hand that feels an earth; that the world around him is there only as representation, in other words, only in reference to another thing, namely that which represents, and this is himself.
>
> (*WWR* 1: 3)

Schopenhauer's idealism is formulated in the first person when he declares, as each individual mind could equally say of itself, that the world is *my* representation. What each of us is supposed to know without further demonstration is that the world belongs to me and resides within my mind as a feature of my personal subjectivity.

The same knowledge of the physical world's dependence on individual thought is supposed to be equally available to every thinking subject. If the world is not only my personal representation, but is identical to each thinking subject's distinct representation, existing in each individual's thoughts, then it appears at first as though the world for Schopenhauer cannot be one single unitary thing. Instead, there must presumably be as many different distinct worlds as there are thinking subjects that represent the world. For there are differences in individual perspectives whereby the world is somewhat differently represented in the thoughts of each representing thinker. Idealism is the philosophical thesis that the world consists of perceptual ideas and as such exists within the mind. Schopenhauer embraces idealism in this sense, agreeing that the world as representation is dependent on thought, while insisting that the subjectivity implied by the world as representation is philosophically unobjectionable.

The problem of multiplying worlds within the minds of all perceivers is only one conspicuous challenge to idealism, but it is a problem that does not arise in opposing and arguably more common-sense theories of metaphysical realism. The standard, sometimes patronizingly designated "naive", view concerning the nature of reality is that there is a unified external physical world that exists objectively outside the mind independently of thought of which different perceiving subjects can have different ideas, and that can be represented in their thoughts subjectively in different ways. Schopenhauer's commitment to radical idealism is unequivocal:

> Therefore no truth is more certain, more independent of all others, and less in need of proof than this, namely that everything that exists for knowledge, and hence the whole of this world, is only object in relation to the subject, perception of the perceiver, in a word, representation. Naturally this holds good of the present as well as of the past and future, of what is remotest as well as of what is nearest; for it holds good of time and space themselves, in which alone all these distinctions arise. Everything that in any way belongs and can belong to the world is inevitably associated with this being-conditioned by the subject, and it exists only for the subject. The world is representation. (WWR 1: 3)

Although he espouses an extreme form of idealism in characterizing the world as representation, Schopenhauer acknowledges that different thinking subjects are born at different times, that they become conscious at different times and that some die while others are left alive. He also admits, in agreement with common sense and the findings of natural science, that the world existed at a time before there were any conscious beings, that there were planets and stars and non-thinking entities such as rocks and trees on our own planet, before there were even the simplest thinking subjects. We can further project a future time when all consciousness might be extinguished, in which no thinking world-representing subjects survive, but for which we naturally and reasonably expect there to exist a non-thinking world of planets and stars and rocks and trees that by hypothesis is not represented by any existent thinking subject. Schopenhauer argues that the existence of the physical world depends on at least the opening of a first eye, in effect, the first psychological occurrence of an act of perception or representation, even, as he colourfully says, if it is only the eye of a lowly sentient creature.

As a result, there appears to be a kind of paradox bordering on contradiction in Schopenhauer's espousal of these two points that he must eventually satisfactorily resolve. The world, he says, exists only through perception, while at the same time the world existed in some sense prior to the existence of perceivers as a result of the processes by which perceivers biologically emerge. We would say today that thinking beings *evolve* from a pre-existing non-thinking world, although Schopenhauer's system predates and does not try to anticipate Darwin's theory. Instead, he reasons:

> Thus animals existed before men, fishes before land animals, planets before fishes, and the inorganic before that which is organic; consequently the original mass had to go through a long series of changes before the first eye could be opened. And yet the existence of this whole world remains for ever dependent on that first eye that opened, were it even that of an insect. For such an eye necessarily brings about knowledge for which and in which alone the whole world is, and without which it is not even conceivable. The world is entirely representation, and as such requires the knowing subject as the supporter of its existence. (*WWR* 1: 30)

The solution to the riddle of how the existence of the physical world can possibly depend on and await the opening of a first physical eye lies in part in the fact that for Schopenhauer there can be no world as representation except in so far as it is actually represented. Schopenhauer criticizes metaphysical systems, reductive materialisms and subjectivisms like Fichte's, that entail a distinct ontic separation of perceived object and perceiving subject. He regards subject and object as conceptually interpresuppositional, in the sense that one cannot possibly exist without the other. Whereas Schopenhauer accepts a radical form of idealism with respect to the physical world, treating it entirely as the perceptual contents of each individual mind in experiencing the world as representation, he further requires that the world importantly is also something more. The world consists not only of its represented aspect, but possesses as well a non-representational aspect. This is the world as it is in itself, independently of all thought and of all concepts and categories of mind. It is the world, so to speak, as it would be even if no thinking representing subjects whatsoever happened to exist; it is the hidden world, which Kant in the *Critique of Pure Reason* refers to as thing-in-itself (Kant 1965: A19–B73, B67–68 and *passim*).

What saves Schopenhauer's transcendental idealism from logical absurdity is his conclusion that the world is not only representation, but also Kantian thing-in-itself. The mind-independence of thing-in-itself makes it possible for Schopenhauer to argue that thing-in-itself exists outside the mind and is differently represented to different minds but is not fragmented into as many different worlds as a plurality of mind-dependent subjective realities. He describes these as objects for a subject in an interpresuppositional subject–object relation whereby the existence of a thinking subject presupposes the existence of a perceived object, and conversely. Thing-in-itself, according to Schopenhauer, is not subject to the *principium individuationis*, which on the contrary, he maintains, applies only to the world as representation. As a consequence, thing-in-itself cannot be differentiated into individual objects, parts or moments existing in different minds as different thought sequences. If the world were only representation, then the existence of many different representing subjects would have the immediate paradoxical conclusion that there are as many worlds as there are thinkers capable of representing reality in their thoughts, rather than a single differently represented world. The world in reality and in the only sense in which it could be understood would then be purely subjective. The Kantian thing-in-itself, which Schopenhauer also accepts, avoids the subjectivity of the world in reality except in so far as it exists as representation (*WWR* 1: 7–8).

Identification of thing-in-itself as Will

Schopenhauer agrees with Kant that thing-in-itself is representationally unknowable. Rejecting Kant's proof for the existence of thing-in-itself as the *cause* of the world as representation, he proposes to go beyond the limits of Kant's critical idealism by demonstrating in a different way that not only the existence but the nature and character of thing-in-itself can be non-representationally known (Atwell 1990: 32–43, 1995: 132–4, 163).

He accordingly argues for the existence of thing-in-itself in a different way from Kant. He refuses to say that thing-in-itself could be the cause of representations, because causal explanation applies only within the world as representation. Instead, he holds that the existence of thing-in-itself alone accounts for the objectified representations of something that is not itself a representation. He further maintains that the limitations of the principle of sufficient reason to explain all deeper aspects of the world as representation point to the existence of something beyond the empirical appearances of the world known to experience, as the transcendental ground without which there could be no representations.

In acknowledging the representational unknowability of thing-in-itself, Kant refers to it as "noumenal", meaning that its existence is merely conceivable to the mind, while none of its properties can possibly be known. Building on Kant's distinction between the phenomenal world or world as representation and noumenal thing-in-itself, Schopenhauer believes that he has discovered a new and previously unrecognized way of gaining insight into thing-in-itself, which he designates as Will. He develops two arguments to prove that thing-in-itself is Will. Where Kant categorizes thing-in-itself as "noumenon". Schopenhauer, in light of his identification of thing-in-itself as Will, dispenses with Kant's phenomenal–noumenal terminology, and speaks only of appearances (*Erscheinungen*) or representations (*Vorstellungen*) in contrast with the transcendental thing-in-itself (*Ding an sich*).

Schopenhauer's proofs to show that thing-in-itself is Will appear in the first and second volumes of *The World as Will and Representation*. This fact is not likely to be a mere historical coincidence, but strongly suggests that in the intervening twenty-six years between the first two editions Schopenhauer may have changed his mind or at least rethought how best to present his reasoning, possibly reconsidering what would provide the most acceptable basis for the position he wants to defend.

The first edition argument trades on what Schopenhauer describes merely as an analogy between individual empirical willing and his interpretation of thing-in-itself as Will. He distinguishes between the double – internal and external – knowledge of the body. External knowledge is gained through perception in representations of the body experienced in sensation, of what we can see, hear, feel, smell and taste of the body, just as we can of any other physical entity in the world as representation. The inner or internal knowledge we have of our own bodies in contrast is acquired through first-person experience of willing and acts of will in action, directing the movements of the body from within through volitional decision and resolve. Schopenhauer asks:

> What is this world of perception besides being my representation? Is that of which I am conscious only as representation just the same as my own body, of which I am doubly conscious, on the one hand as *representation*, on the other as *will*?   (*WWR* 1: 18)

Later, Schopenhauer maintains that the dual nature of our bodies, and corresponding to it our dual knowledge of its dual nature, through representation and the lived-through experience of will, suggests the same two ways of understanding the world at large. If the world as a whole has both an inner and external side, if we can know about its external representational side through perception, then, as we become aware of the limitations of exploring and theorizing about the phenomenal world, we may increasingly feel the need to graduate from natural science to transcendental metaphysics. When we do so, we shall have nowhere else to turn except to consider the inner knowledge we have of our bodies in acts of will as a key to the world's hidden inner nature. By analogy, if the inner knowledge of our bodies reveals individual will in contrast with external knowledge of its parts and qualities by perception, then insight into or understanding of the hidden inner nature of the world as thing-in-itself as contrasted with external knowledge of the world as representation acquired by means of the senses can also be appropriately referred to as Will (*WWR* 1: 100).

The second edition argument for the identification of thing-in-itself as Will appears in the significantly titled Chapter XVIII, "On the Possibility of Knowing the Thing-in-Itself". There Schopenhauer offers an importantly different argument, or at least a different way of presenting the original argument. Schopenhauer's second edition proof explains the relation between the knowing subject's individual will and thing-in-itself as Will not merely as an analogy, but as a strict identity. He states:

> I have stressed that … we are not merely the *knowing subject*, but that *we ourselves* are also among those realities or entities we require to know, that *we ourselves are the thing-in-itself*. Consequently, a way *from within* stands open to us to that real inner nature of things to which we cannot penetrate *from without*. It is, so to speak, a subterranean passage, a secret alliance, which, as if by treachery, places us all at once in the fortress that could not be taken by attack from without. Precisely as such, the *thing-in-itself* can come into consciousness only quite directly, namely by *it itself being conscious of itself*; to try to know it objectively is to desire something contradictory. (*WWR* 2: 195)

Schopenhauer does not believe that each act of will in the ordinary sense, as when we desire a drink of water, is identical with thing-in-itself. Rather, in the desire for a drink of water, Will as thing-in-itself can be discovered at the foundation of any of the episodes of willing that we experience phenomenologically. We can find it there by thinking away all of its external trappings to reveal naked pure willing as satisfying the theoretical requirements of the Kantian thing-in-itself.

The pure willing or Will that underlies our willing is not a mere analogue or something similar or corresponding to thing-in-itself, but is instead, so to speak, thing-in-itself itself. It is non-representational, non-individualizable, and, as a further sign of this, not subject in any way to the fourfold root of the principle of sufficient reason. Schopenhauer argues that there is Will or pure willing rather than merely superficial psychological will or what he also calls will to life deep within every individual subjective act of willing. It is the fact about our empirical willing that we need only properly recognize in order to understand that as willing subjects we are already beyond the boundary limiting the world as representation. We are already inside the fortress, as Schopenhauer likes to say, and have no need to continue futilely circling and chipping away at its walls.[5]

The pure willing that underlies any individual act of will is recognized by means of a philosophical thought experiment. Consider any act of will, such as desiring a drink of water. Schopenhauer instructs us to ask a specific series of questions. We start out with introspective representational recognition of willing to drink and ask why we will to drink. The answer could be this or that, depending on the circumstances, since a representing willing subject could have any number of reasons for wanting to drink some water. Perhaps the reason why one wills to have a drink of water is to quench one's thirst, to swallow a pill, or any number of other possibilities. The exact reason does not so much matter as the fact that as an event in the world as representation the psychological act of willing to drink water implies that there exists some kind of motivation for the fact of will. This much is already assumed by the facts of the world of representation falling under the fourfold root of the principle of sufficient reason. Suppose in a given case that the reason is to quench thirst. Then we can ask regressively, for a while at least, why does one will to quench one's thirst? If the answer is that we will to quench our thirst because we will something else again, to avoid pain and an unpleasant sensation in the throat, perhaps, then we can continue to ask: why do we will these things? If Schopenhauer is right, then there is always a good motivational reason to explain why we will each of these things at each step regressively in turn, in a complete account of the motivation for the willing subject's willing to drink.

Schopenhauer claims that the regress of motivations can proceed indefinitely. Eventually and often quite quickly, however, we reach a point where we choose to ask a slightly different question – and clearly nothing prevents us from asking this right away and without further ado at the very outset – which is: why does one (simply) will? We will to drink because we are thirsty. We may be thirsty for any of a number of complex reasons. But why do we will? Why is it that we will anything at all, as opposed to not willing or to willing this or that? Schopenhauer insists that this apparently legitimate question has no correct answer. This is because in a certain sense we simply *are* (identical with) Will. The fact that one wills is a fact to be deduced from the fact that one wills this or that, a drink of water or to own a Rolls Royce. When one wills this or that, one always does so for a reason, which is to say for a particular cause, aimed at a particular object, and with a particular motivation. Since motivational explanation is one of the four roots of the principle of sufficient reason, it follows for Schopenhauer that a subject's willing this or that is always explainable.

In contrast, there is no correct answer to the general question of why we will at all, or why there exists such a thing as willing, as opposed to why we may happen to will this or that. Pure willing as such is beyond the reach of explanation governed by the fourfold root. If we reach back far enough, to the point where it no longer makes sense to enquire into the motivations generally for willing anything whatsoever, as opposed to willing this or that, then Schopenhauer holds that we have moved beyond the purview of the fourfold root, and have crossed over to thing-in-itself. It is precisely then that our reflections should be met with the feeling or recognition of unmotivated willing that lies deep within us, at the heart of every act of ordinary willing. Pure, undirected, objectless and unmotivated willing is not the willing of any particular object by any particular willing subject for any particular reason. It is just pure willing, plain and simple. If we know how to look for it, we can find it on the ground floor of any act of ordinary willing, when we dig deep enough and think away the objects and reasons for willing in order to arrive at willing in its purest form, which Schopenhauer refers to as Will. It is because pure willing or Will is unmotivated, undirected toward any objects, unindividualizable and inexplicable by any of the modes of explanation available under the fourfold root of the principle of sufficient reason, that Schopenhauer regards it as satisfying the theoretical requirements of thing-in-itself.

Platonic ideas as grades of the Will's objectification in the world as representation

Schopenhauer interprets abstract timeless or eternal and unchanging Platonic Ideas within his system as distinct grades of the Will's objectification manifested in the world as representation. What he means by this is that there is a mapping of different degrees of the Will's objectification onto all of the separate kinds of perceivable objects that inhabit the phenomenal world. The grades of the Will's objectification in turn are measured for Schopenhauer by the extent to which individual instantiations of an Idea are more or less alike. A low grade of the Will's objectification is found in the case of primitive substances and forces of nature, up through the plants and animals that are increasingly distinct from one another, until we arrive at the height of this pyramid or great chain of being, where human beings reside as more individualized and distinct from one another than any other kind, class or category of entity. As we move up higher in the ranking of grades of the Will's represented objectifications, the instantiations of Platonic Ideas in the world as representation are increasingly individualistic. This is why the pyramid of representations is supposed to be capped by human beings as the most highly individualized of all instantiations of Ideas.

Just as Plato in his later dialogues holds that all the many different individuals and breeds of dogs in the world of Becoming exemplify or participate in the real world of Being as the Form or Idea of Dog, so Schopenhauer maintains that the world as Will manifests itself in many different ways in the world as representation, and that the types or kinds of things in which its manifestations occur can be understood as different degrees of the Will's objectification. Schopenhauer argues that there exists a specific grade of the Will's objectification, its translation, so to speak, into the objects for subjects in the world as representation. The grades of the Will's objectification correspond, for example, to Plato's Idea of Dog, dogness or doghood, which is the universal property of being a dog in its most general terms. It is in relation to this Idea that all individual dogs are instantiations, particular objectifications of thing-in-itself as Will in the world as representation.

Where Plato describes the Forms or Ideas as real abstract entities, sometimes metaphorically characterized as hovering, so to speak, in Platonic heaven, or on display in an ethereal Platonic museum, Schopenhauer speaks with similar effect, in what he believes correctly interprets Plato's original conception, of a specific grade of the Will's objectification exemplified in the empirical world as representation. Thus, Plato posits the archetype Dog in which all individual dogs and kinds of dogs participate, or which they imitate or instantiate, which Schopenhauer regards mathematically as a specific degree of the way in which Will as thing-in-itself is objectified in the world as representation corresponding to the general concept of Dog. The Will's objectification in the world as representation is the translation of blind urging or undirected striving into the world experienced by thinking subjects as individual things, including the plurality of individuated represented things distributed in space and time, among which are to be found all individual dogs and types and breeds of dogs.

The Platonic hierarchy of Ideas in turn suggests an ordering of Ideas by degrees, which Schopenhauer characterizes as grades of the Will's objectification.

The suggestion is not that the world as Will does anything to cause or bring about its appearances in the world as representation, but simply that Will is objectified as a manifold of distinct represented objects for representing subjects. The physical presupposition for such representing, the brain and nervous system of sensing and intelligent beings such as but not limited to ourselves, is itself just another uniquely graded objectification of the world as Will. Schopenhauer also, at least apparently in opposition to Plato, offers a significantly different hierarchy of Ideas interpreted as distinct grades of the Will's objectification in the world as representation. He regards our species of rational thinking human beings as occupying the pinnacle within the hierarchy of Platonic Ideas, rather than the impersonal Platonic Idea of the Good as explained in Plato's dialogue the *Republic*. Schopenhauer's ordering of Platonic Ideas as grades of the Will's objectification is reminiscent of pre-Darwinian conceptions of the animal kingdom arranged in a strictly linear rather than branching order, beginning with the simplest most primitive life forms and proceeding upward teleologically to humankind as the glory of creation.[6]

Plato, finally, describes a separate realm, the real world of abstract Ideas, popularly portrayed as a Platonic heaven or museum of archetypes, that is specifically made a part of his theory in order to accommodate the Ideas. There is the real world of Being consisting of the Ideas, according to Plato, at least as his theory is usually interpreted, and the unreal world of appearance or Becoming in which particular individual things participate or imitate or instantiate the Ideas in a many–one relation. Plato's theory of Ideas gives rise to many difficult and unanswered questions. Plato was aware of some of these problems, but there is no doubt within his theory as to where the Ideas are supposed to be situated. At least, again, as Plato's theory is usually understood, the Ideas do not exist in the changing spatiotemporal world of appearance or Becoming, but in the abstract eternal and immutable order of Being, designated specifically as the realm of Ideas. Schopenhauer for his part does not have the luxury of appealing to a separate dedicated order of Platonic Ideas. As a result, he invites a kind of dilemma that does not affect Plato's theory, except in the guise of a counterpart difficulty concerning the habitation of the immortal soul once it departs from the body. Since the soul is not itself an Idea, but undergoes changes of thought and attitude, it cannot easily be said to return to the world of Being once it leaves the body behind in the world of Becoming. Schopenhauer's parallel difficulty is to locate the Platonic Ideas and explain within his system where they are supposed to reside in either the world as Will or as representation.

There are only two possibilities, neither of which is entirely satisfactory, especially as literal interpretations of Plato's original concept of the Ideas. Platonic Ideas for Schopenhauer cannot reasonably be set down as belonging to thing-in-itself construed as Will, because the Ideas are distinct from one another and hence in some sense subject to the *principium individuationis*. Nor, however, does it appear likely at first thought that Platonic Ideas can be located in Schopenhauer's world as representation. The Ideas as such are supposed to be not spatiotemporal, but abstract, and are usually assumed, at least in Plato's sketchy presentation of the theory, as general entities that the individual things in the world of appearance only imperfectly "imitate" or "strive", metaphorically speaking, to become as much like the archetypes to which they belong as possible, or in which they "participate". Since these are the only two aspects of Schopenhauer's one and only two-sided world as representation and thing-in-itself, there is no clear-cut metaphysical realm or ontic category to which he can plausibly assign the Platonic Ideas, no place to which he can attribute them as belonging without doing violence to the way in which the Platonic Ideas are usually conceived (Plato, *Republic*, 509d5–511e6, 514a–b4, 595a–602b).

Schopenhauer solves the problem in the only way possible, given his division between the world as Will and representation. He declares that the Platonic Ideas are aspatiotemporal, unsusceptible to alteration or change of any kind, and existing eternally rather than involved in any process of becoming. These are exactly the attributes by which Plato distinguishes the Ideas from the concrete physical spatiotemporal things that instantiate, imitate or participate in the Ideas. "Accordingly," Schopenhauer says, "what follows ... has already impressed itself as a matter of course on every student of Plato ... Those different grades of the will's objectification, expressed in innumerable individuals, exist as the unattained patterns of these, or as the eternal forms of things" (*WWR* 1: 129). Significantly, he then adds: "Not themselves entering into time and space, the medium of individuals, [the Ideas] remain fixed, subject to no change, always being, never having become. The particular things, however, arise and pass away; they are always becoming and never are" (*WWR* 1: 129). Schopenhauer holds that the Ideas, by virtue of constituting grades of the Will's objectification, are nevertheless perceivable properties of experienceable objects in the world as representation.

A noteworthy application of this concept of Platonic Ideas is in Schopenhauer's philosophy of art, in which the artistic genius is described as capable of passively receiving the Platonic Ideas in will-suppressed moments of aesthetic transport, in which desire is overcome for the sake of knowledge and an appreciation of beauty and the sublime. Schopenhauer exploits the identification of

Platonic Ideas with grades of the Will's objectification in hierarchical ordering as a framework for considering the relative significance of the arts. Architecture is ranked at the lowest end, because it has primarily to do with such low-level grades of the Will's objectivity as gravity, mass and space. He proceeds thereafter through the other arts finally to music, which Schopenhauer remarkably interprets not as imitating other objects in the world as representation, but, like the natural world, as itself the direct objectification of thing-in-itself in the world as Will. Within each level, Schopenhauer further maintains that art having to do with the distinctive high-order individuality of human beings is always the most interesting and aesthetically valuable. Schopenhauer's interpretation of Platonic Ideas as grades of the Will's objectification is also among the most controversial parts of his philosophy because of its proposition that Platonic Ideas are perceivable in the world of representation. In spite of but in partial concession to such objections, Schopenhauer insists that his account is correct, not only philosophically, but as an historical exposition of Plato's original views, and that it is only as abstract degrees of the ways in which Will is objectified in the world as representation that Plato's theory of Ideas can be properly understood.[7]

Moral pessimism: the hungry Will, suffering, salvation and saintly denial of the Will to life

The Will, Schopenhauer maintains, is hungry. There is nothing in existence besides the Will as thing-in-itself and its objectifications in the world as representation. As a consequence, the transcendental Will can only feed on itself through its representational objectifications. The restless blind urging of Will as thing-in-itself is what keeps the physical universe in motion. It is the hidden inner force of gravity, electromagnetism, the principles of crystal growth, vegetation, nutrition, the reproductive urge and all other natural phenomena. In a revealing passage Schopenhauer writes:

> By virtue of such necessity, man needs the animals for his support, the animals in their grades need one another, and also the plants, which again need soil, water, chemical elements and their combinations, the planet, the sun, rotation and motion round the sun, the obliquity of the ecliptic, and so on. At bottom, this springs from the fact that the will must live on itself, since nothing exists besides it, and it is a hungry will. Hence arise pursuit, hunting, anxiety, and suffering. (*WWR* 1: 154)

The only field of action where the Will can feed on itself is within the world as representation. It is the arena where individual objectifications of Will face each other in harsh competition for resources, and ultimately, as Schopenhauer says, for the most precious commodities of space and time. The strife and conflict necessitated by the character of the true nature of the world as Will manifesting its undirected, objectless and subjectless pure desire is the irremediable cause of all the suffering the world has known, and from which there is ultimately no escape.

The fact that there is no prospect for attaining lasting peace or satisfaction of the Will's endless demands for gratification is the basis for Schopenhauer's notorious moral pessimism. There is no philosophical justification for expecting the misery in the world ever to be meaningfully alleviated once and for all, because the world in reality, thing-in-itself as Will, is insatiable in its blind needs. It is perpetually caught in a never-ending cycle of suffering want, frustration in its brutal confrontations with others, and boredom and dissatisfaction when it momentarily attains its desires. Schopenhauer describes a pathetic pattern of desire, want and lack, satiety, surfeit and ennui, as the inevitable pattern of human suffering even for the most fortunate willing subjects in the firm grip of the will to life. In all of philosophical literature there is no more uncompromisingly negative perspective than Schopenhauer offers on the prospects of existence.

Thus for Schopenhauer, as for the Buddha, and enshrined in the first of the Four Noble Truths of Buddhism, life is suffering and existence a sin. "For this reason," Schopenhauer explains:

> we wish to consider in *human existence* the inner and essential destiny of the will. Everyone will readily find the same thing once more in the life of the animal, only more feebly expressed in various degrees. He can also sufficiently convince himself in the suffering animal world how essentially *all life is suffering*.　　(WWR 1: 310)

The inevitable suffering for all willing beings comes about in Schopenhauer's metaphysics and moral philosophy because of the necessity of the Will's feeding on itself, setting itself in eternal opposition to itself through its objectifications in the world as representation (WWR 1: 146–7). All living things either feed on other living things or else at least compete with them for possession and use of the inorganic world of substances. There is no avoiding the endless aggression and vying for advantage that determines the place of each objectification of Will in the world's mammoth food chain. This is true not only in nature, in Schopenhauer's view, but even and especially in the most advanced human cultures and civilizations.

We are all a part of the struggle for existence, like it or not, as predator or prey. We are in that regard the inevitable helpless creatures of the world as Will objectified here in the world as representation. The inner character of thing-in-itself is revealed in Schopenhauer's philosophy as the grim law of eat or be eaten, and in the end, no matter what, ultimately to be eaten, at least by bacteria or worms, or consumed by fire or another destructive element, as yet another objectification of the insatiably hungry Will. "Thus the will-to-live generally feasts on itself," Schopenhauer explains, "and is in different forms its own nourishment, till finally the human race, because it subdues all the others, regards nature as manufactured for its own use" (*WWR* 1: 147). What sustains each individual subject in the struggle for existence against all other objectifications of thing-in-itself as Will, according to Schopenhauer, is the Will's most immediate objectification known only inwardly in the guise of individual willing, which Schopenhauer interprets in all of its activities as the will to life.

Thing-in-itself, the hungry Will, feeding on itself in every imaginable way in the world as representation, leaves in its path a wake of carnage and misery. With his eyes attuned to the suffering in the world, Schopenhauer can see little else, only momentary reprieves and temporary islands from the general pattern of pain, unfulfilled but tormenting desires and bitter disappointments, as the only reward for when we do happen to succeed at obtaining whatever it is we tell ourselves we need and want. At the end, taunting us at every step, is the spectre of death as something that threatens to take away whatever it is we might otherwise have achieved. It is death that, despite being nothing real, as the closure of both representing subject and represented object, and hence of the entire world as representation, haunts us with dread. The only release from the fear of dying lies in attaining the rare form of philosophical wisdom that Schopenhauer offers as a corollary to his idealism. It involves emulating certain types of religious saints who thoroughly renounce the will to life and thereby inadvertently bring about their own deaths by starvation. What Schopenhauer admires in such practices is the ascetic's denial of the will to life and supreme indifference to all matters of life and death (*WWR* 1: 275–382, and *passim*).

The cause of suffering is not accidental or avoidable, according to Schopenhauer, but constitutes the world's most essential feature. We might imagine that suffering happens to some persons who are unlucky or who make bad decisions. There is no need for anyone to suffer if they choose wisely in life, if they are born with good health and sound genes, raised in a supportive and sufficiently affluent family and community, and then proceed to judge correctly about how to live their lives, and how to conduct themselves in following life's path wherever it leads. This, together with a little bit of good luck, we may like to think, is all one needs to avoid unnecessary suffering. As moral optimists, we may still recognize that misfortune is always possible, and if we look about we might see many people who seem to be living just such happy and satisfying personal lives. If there are also dangers and diseases and reversals of happiness, on the whole, we may assume that these are not necessarily the lot of every person, and that a good life within its natural limits is possible in principle for all, at the end of which there is the possibility of an eternal reward and the soul's salvation in an afterlife. Then, perhaps, the trials and tribulations of the present existence will be left behind and our spirits will remain active and content in a higher plane of existence removed from all strife.

Schopenhauer admits none of this. He interprets all of life as nothing but a parade of uninterrupted suffering from which there is no possibility of relief in this world or in a life after death. What we ordinarily think of as happiness is for Schopenhauer merely the relative cessation or alleviation of suffering. This is a controversial idea, because although a pleasant day can be ruined by the pain caused by a bee sting, we ordinarily do not think of our happiness consisting in part in our not having been stung by a bee. Schopenhauer's pessimism consists in the fact that he regards thing-in-itself, the reality that lies hidden behind or beneath the world as representation in which our struggles occur, as Will in perpetual self-conflict. Suffering is the inevitable result of the fact that the Will's objectifications are ceaselessly involved in competitions of every kind, ultimately for matter understood as causality, space and time, which in one way or another pit every represented object against every other. From plants seizing precious space to root on stony ground, competing for water, light and soil, predator and prey, nourishment, attraction of a mate and the raising of offspring, sibling rivalries, dog-eat-dog business struggles and the battle of the sexes to world wars and the planetary push and pull of gravitational forces across vast distances of space, the world as representation for Schopenhauer is pervaded by conflict, a monstrous coliseum in which every existent entity, living or non-living, struggles like a gladiator to defeat every other existent entity. It must be so, moreover, if Schopenhauer is right, because the world in reality, thing-in-itself, reveals its character in the world as conflict, and is eternal and unchanging in its self-opposition. The world as Will endlessly consumes itself in the only way it can, according to Schopenhauer, objectifying itself in the world as representation where every entity inevitably tries to consume every other (Copleston 1946: 91; Murdoch 1992: 57–80).

Whether he is right in viewing the world so pessimistically, it is clear that Schopenhauer has fully anticipated the objection to be raised from the standpoint of those who see the world more positively. Schopenhauer will say that such persons have simply not lived long enough or looked deeply enough into the sufferings that surround them on every side, if only they would open their eyes. What optimists misinterpret as the bright future or highest potential for the world and the prospects for human life within it Schopenhauer maintains is at best only a momentary respite from an overall pattern of the devouring of one objectification of the insatiably hungry Will by another. As such, it is nothing positive but purely negative, like the non-occurrence of a bee sting that would have spoiled a pleasant day if it had occurred. If the true nature of thing-in-itself, the world as Will, is to cannibalize itself by proxy through its objectifications in the world as representation, then there must be give and take, times of eating for some and of being eaten for others, although eventually all in one form or another must suffer the same destructive fate.

An optimist, lacking the proper metaphysical foundation for understanding the world as representation, in Schopenhauer's opinion, adopts an unbalanced attitude. The optimist is focused almost exclusively on those who are momentarily privileged to be eating rather than eaten, and mistakes these limited one-sided occurrences as typical for all of life. What optimists fail to appreciate is that for every objectification of Will that is temporarily thriving, there are countless others that must pay the price. If human life in a particular historical period is good for many persons, the pleasure that occurs requires the desolation of many other objectifications of Will that are sacrificed in the process. For every successful happy individual there must be many more suffering exploited individuals who are used and consumed conditionally to benefit those whose good fortune deprives others of the necessities of life and finally of life itself. In the end, more importantly, the satisfaction of desires produces its own intense dissatisfaction, at the end of which death and often poverty, humiliation and debility are waiting even for those who appear in the course of life to have succeeded temporarily in gratifying their individual wills.

Schopenhauer identifies the strivings of will as the source of all suffering. To live is to will, to will is to strive and to strive is to suffer, even and especially when the will temporarily succeeds in achieving that for which it strives. The pain of the world is therefore owing entirely to will, and ultimately to Will. Since the world in reality, thing-in-itself, is Will, there is no possibility of escaping altogether from strife, misery and conflict. The only relief from the world's suffering, according to Schopenhauer, is to follow one of two paths of salvation, both of which involve renouncing or transcending the individual will to life. These are the life of saintly asceticism and of aesthetic loss of self in the contemplation of beauty and the sublime in nature and great works of art, typified in the work of aesthetic genius. Although Schopenhauer is no Christian or philosophical advocate of Christianity, he makes occasional references to the life of Christian saints, and to the ascetic practices of the Asian religions of Buddhism and Hinduism, as indicating an imperfect grasp of this philosophical truth. He is interested in the positive analogies between the concepts of asceticism found in extreme forms among these religious traditions, in which he claims to see a common unspoken recognition of the same underlying need to avoid the sufferings of will by denying the will to life. Schopenhauer is also concerned to distinguish his philosophy from similar but he believes importantly different philosophical systems, such as Stoicism and Epicureanism, that have also approved a course of practical life that proposes in one way or another to avoid suffering (*WWR* 1: 388–9).

The alternative pathway to salvation is the life of aesthetic genius. Of course, we cannot simply choose to be geniuses. We are either gifted in this way or not. Schopenhauer insists that the average person has as much possibility of interacting with true genius, say, Leonardo da Vinci, Michelangelo or Ludwig van Beethoven, as in sharing the company of princes. Yet he also claims that to a limited extent virtually everyone is capable to at least some degree of enjoying the momentary release from the striving of the individual will to life that comes from the partial absorption of self and freedom from desire in experiencing beauty or the sublime in nature or art. The difficulty in this way of salvation from suffering is that of achieving complete transcendence of self lasting for more than a few precious moments at a time, even if we consciously cultivate aesthetic experience as an occasional holiday from the stressful demands of willing. Schopenhauer admits that even the aesthetic genius, after passively receiving the Platonic Ideas in episodes of silencing the will, must act wilfully thereafter in order to produce great art, choosing a subject and controlling the use of media to create a statue, poem, painting or sonata.

The obvious implication of pessimistically renouncing the will to life is to make terms philosophically and emotionally with the inevitability of death. If Schopenhauer is correct in his assumptions and inferences, he proves that death is not an event, and hence altogether something unreal. Although dying slowly or quickly is a real phenomenal occurrence, death itself is not an occurrence in the world as representation, but is rather an endpoint or limit of the world as representation, and, in particular, in the first-person formulation, as *my* representation. The world as representation begins and ends with the consciousness of the individual representing subject, which at death comes to an immediate abrupt end, after which there remains only thing-in-itself. An individual's death, accordingly, is not something that occurs in or as any part of the world as representation. Nor can death possibly be in or a part of the world as thing-in-itself or Will, since there are no events or individuated occurrences, nothing happening in space or time for thing-in-itself, and in particular no progressive transition from life to death or from consciousness to unconsciousness. If we assume with Schopenhauer that there exists only the world as representation and as thing-in-itself interpreted as Will, then there is no place on either side of the great divide for death, no possibility for the existence or reality of death (*WWR* 1: 280).

The individual will, by virtue of being a manifestation of the world as Will, has a dual nature. It is at once the ephemeral subject of life and death, and the expression in the world as representation of the real world or thing-in-itself, the world as Will, blind urging or aimless undirected desire. "There is something in us, however," Schopenhauer observes, "which tells us that this is not so, that this is not the end of things, that death is not an absolute annihilation" (*WWR* 1: 324). Schopenhauer's thought at first makes it seem as though he is holding out the possibility for personal survival after death. If death is not absolute annihilation, then some part of a living person must persist through the event of death. This Schopenhauer admits, but only in a limited sense that precludes the possibility of an afterlife for the empirical self. The Will as thing-in-itself, of which each individual will is an expression in the world as representation, cannot be destroyed. This is not the comforting sense of survival by which a particular person with specific memories and expectations continues after the body's death, as projected by popular religions and mind–body dualisms in the philosophy of Plato and Descartes. Schopenhauer offers only the same metaphysical indestructibility to which any non-personal phenomenal entity in the world of appearance is equally fated. The non-finality of death is no more than the persistence of Will as thing-in-itself that "endures", although not within space or time, no matter what happens to the empirical world as representation, and regardless of whether or not it remains inhabited by living intelligent subjects of individual will (*WWR* 1: 282–3). That death is not total annihilation for Schopenhauer is true enough; yet death remains the total annihilation of the self, soul or thinking subject in the psychological sense of the individual will to life or particular empirical personality.[8]

The part of me that survives death, therefore, Schopenhauer believes, the Will that transcends my individual willing, is no different from, but exactly the same as, the Will part of you that survives death. What is immortal in each of us is at most a kind of generic world soul that is not individual or personally individualized, that does not entertain any succession of thoughts, but is simply the Kantian thing-in-itself identified by Schopenhauer as Will. It engages in no psychological episodes as we ordinarily think of them occurring in time. It has no memories of a past embodied life or expectations or ongoing experiences following the body's death. If the Will surviving our death is in any sense a part of us, it is equally the same part of every other thinking representing subject, and not only of human psychological subjects, but of every willing thinker, beginning with the simplest and most primitive life forms. We as thinkers share in thing-in-itself as the immortal part of our willing and representing psychologies with every other thinker. The immortality in which we participate has nothing about it that is individual or empirical. It is uncaused, unmotivated, unexperienced and unexplainable, unindividuated, psychologically contentless and undirected toward any particular intended objects or objectives. The soul's immortality of which Schopenhauer speaks is therefore not like going to heaven and playing a lyre, feasting on ambrosia, or meeting and communing with God or conversing with those who have already gone before us into death (*WWR* 2: 199–200). It is not like anything at all, because it is only the persistence of thing-in-itself outside space and time without the interpresuppositional subject–object objectification in psychology that constitutes the world as representation, and that persists only for as long as the individual representing subject remains conscious.

Schopenhauer's philosophy of sex

Schopenhauer's moral pessimism further provides the basis for an interesting philosophical perspective on the nature of animal and human love and sexuality. Although he is often classified as a "romantic" philosopher in the sense that he emphasizes the sufferings of life and in particular the struggles of the aesthetic genius to perfect creative artistic expression, Schopenhauer, as we might expect from other aspects of his thought, does not offer an especially romantic view of sex and love in the popular sense of the word.

The first edition of *The World as Will and Representation* contains only occasional references to the problems of understanding the sexual impulse. The second volume, in contrast, as part of the supplement to the first volume's fourth book, elaborates on these topics in considerable detail. It is here in the second edition of the text that Schopenhauer devotes the 36 pages of Chapter XLIV to "The Metaphysics of Sexual Love". Schopenhauer's philosophical interest in sexual phenomena can be divided into four parts.

- Explaining the sexual impulse in terms of the metaphysics of the world as Will and representation, and in particular the genitals and sexual behaviour as an objectification, like the survival instinct, of the will to life.
- Understanding the importance empirically of sex in our lives and the particular forms that courtship and mating behaviour can be observed to take, while helping the philosopher to exercise reason in avoiding sexual infatuations at the expense of knowledge.
- Recommending absolute chastity and celibacy in the voluntary resistance

to sexual urges as asceticism's first step in denying the will to life and attaining salvation from the sufferings of the individual will.

• Accounting for pederasty or male homoeroticism as an aberration from what Schopenhauer identifies as its natural function in procreation, the widespread occurrence of which arises as a problem and paradox for the theory that all sexual behaviour is directed toward reproduction.

Schopenhauer's pronouncements about sex combine rare insight and candour with extraordinary naivety, a peculiar touch of Puritanism, and an evident poverty of informed personal experience. It is irresistible to point out that Schopenhauer himself did not marry or raise children, although he is known in his youth to have undergone at least one disastrous love affair. We cannot simply conclude with Nietzsche in *The Genealogy of Morality*, however, that Schopenhauer was beset by a prudish aversion to sex, and that he sought in his concept of aesthetics a kind of escape from sexual desires.[9] Whatever his psychology, Schopenhauer offers a coherent set of philosophical reasons for resisting the sexual impulse as an essential element in attaining salvation by denying the will to life.

Sex is obviously a phenomenon of the world as representation. It cannot be part of the world as Will or thing-in-itself, because thing-in-itself is not subject to the *principium individuationis* or causal explanation under the fourfold root of the principle of sufficient reason. Experiencing sexual desires and engaging in sexual activities is part of our animal nature, of our empirical lives as manifested in the represented world that we share with most living creatures. It is a part of life that is found even in sexually differentiated plants that are altogether incapable of thoughts, desires or attitudes, but whose reproductive organs are nonetheless objectifications of Will manifested in the will to life. Schopenhauer, indeed, declares that sexual reproduction is "life's final end and highest goal" (*WWR* 1: 329), although we must always bear in mind that Schopenhauer's pessimism does not in the first place set a particularly high premium on life. Schopenhauer nevertheless draws on Greek myths and on the authority of Hesiod and Parmenides for evidence of an early belief that eros is the first principle from which all other things proceed (*WWR* 1: 330). Phallus and lingam worship in ancient Greece, Egypt and India additionally support his interpretation of the role of erotic desire of a distinctively male-oriented type. Schopenhauer states:

> Now, as the focus of the will, that is to say, its concentration and highest expression, are the sexual impulse and its satisfaction, it is expressed very significantly and naively in the symbolical language of

nature by the fact that the individualized will, hence man and the animal, makes its entry into the world through the portal of the sexual organs. (*WWR* 2: 571)

There is admittedly much that is peculiar about sex and the intensity of the sexual impulse that stands in need of philosophical explanation. Schopenhauer remarkably asserts that it is a proof of the importance of sex in the objectification of the world as Will within the world as representation that animals including ourselves enter the world by means of openings in the genitals, as though passing through a door.

Genitals themselves are objectifications of the will to life, much as Schopenhauer says that a person's physiognomy is a clear indication of individual character. He even goes so far as to remark on the "naivety" of flowers that display their genitals to public view, while animals to a greater or lesser extent generally conceal them (*WWR* 1: 156). Schopenhauer attaches further significance to the fact that the head and genitals are widely separated on the human body, as a sign that reason as the seat of knowledge is in opposition to desire in the will to life, and that their distance apart reflects the objectification of the Will in the world as representation of a fundamental distinction that separates willing from contemplation. He remarks in this context that sexual reproduction is a primary affirmation of the will to life, which only human beings are able to suppress for the sake of attaining salvation from the cycle of suffering (*WWR* 1: 330).

Schopenhauer regards the preservation of life and sexual reproduction as the fundamental ends of life. We know that some species of animals perish immediately upon conception, or after the laying of eggs, raising of offspring, or upon completion of whatever process is minimally necessary to assure the chances of a future generation of their kind to succeed. It is as though there is no further need for an organism's existence once this vital biological purpose has been fulfilled. Such scenarios foster and at the same time lend scientific support to theories of the "selfish gene", according to which an animal, non-human or human, exists purely or primarily for the sake of propagating more genidentical genes. This contemporary concept, in nineteenth-century terms, is largely presaged by Schopenhauer's philosophy of sex. All the romance of poetry and literature, all of the feelings and physical effort invested in love affairs and mating rituals, the marriage customs and taboos surrounding sexual behaviour, exist, according to Schopenhauer, exclusively for the sake of enabling the species to reproduce. This is in some ways an unsurprising conclusion, but in Schopenhauer's discussion the assumption leads to a number of unexpected implications about the metaphysics of sex.

First, he analyses in some detail the choices people make in sexual partners and the emotional investments they make in their sexual lives. Why, as many persons have observed, do "opposites attract"? Why do tall women often choose short men as sexual partners, and the reverse? Schopenhauer argues that the reason has to do with long-term genetic perfecting of the species. We instinctively turn to individuals who complement our physiological assets and make up for our deficiencies in order to produce offspring that are as near to the perfect archetype of the human species, the Platonic Idea or degree of the Will's objectification in the world as representation, that two individuals having sex together for the purpose of procreation can practically achieve. For the same reason, Schopenhauer remarks, perhaps bitterly, women often do not choose intellectual men as sexual partners, but prefer other qualities that may be more directly related to biological fitness. With due apologies for the gender bias that colours this whole line of reasoning, we find Schopenhauer asserting:

> [T]he woman is generally attracted by the man's qualities of heart or character, as being those which are inherited from the father. The woman is won especially by firmness of will, resoluteness, and courage, perhaps also by honesty and kindness of heart. Intellectual merits, on the other hand, do not exercise any direct and instinctive power over her, just because they are *not* inherited from the father. With women want of understanding does not matter; in fact, extraordinary mental power, or even genius, as something abnormal, might have an unfavourable effect. Hence we often see an ugly, stupid, and coarse fellow get the better of a cultured, clever, and amiable man when dealing with women.   (*WWR* 2: 544)

We are motivated by powerful unseen forces to have sex. We do so exclusively, Schopenhauer believes, in order to propagate the species. We cannot help ourselves in this frenzy, because we are the unwitting pawns of the will to life that drives our behaviour as an objectification of the world as Will. The full spectrum of amorous passion, from flirtation to wooing a potential lover and finding a soul mate, to the heat of lust and even rape, according to Schopenhauer, appearances notwithstanding, are all directed toward the same goal of procreation and in particular of perfecting the species to a greater approximation of its ideal Platonic archetype.

The recognition that we are mortal, and that in a relatively brief time we must leave behind the world as representation, accounts for the urgency with which the will to life compels us to invest an enormous amount of energy and value in our sexual lives, often to the detriment of other rationally more vested interests. Schopenhauer recognizes these subdural factors as determining all erotic tendencies. "[A]ll amorousness is rooted in the sexual impulse alone," he writes, "is in fact absolutely only a more closely determined, specialized, and indeed, in the strictest sense, individualized sexual impulse, however ethereally it may deport itself" (*WWR* 2: 533). Beneath the exterior of romantic notions of love, all the hearts and flowers of sexual interaction, there is only the Will's objectification of the will to life manifested as the compulsion to procreate, to engage in sexual intercourse for the sake of the will to life's projecting itself beyond death into the future as best as it can through the engendering of biological progeny and the perfection of successive generations of each species. It is no wonder, then, that Schopenhauer is often cited as a precursor of Sigmund Freud's theory of the id, ego and superego, the hidden psychological motives having to do with the id's primitive desires, and the neuroses that arise when its wilful urges are not satisfactorily sublimated. Although Freud claimed not to have read Schopenhauer until after he had developed his own theory of the subconscious, Schopenhauer's ideas would have been very much in the air of late-nineteenth- and early-twentieth-century Vienna during Freud's intellectually formative student years.[10]

As such an adamant manifestation of the will to life, the sexual impulse must be thoroughly resisted if knowledge is to triumph over will. Schopenhauer accordingly regards chastity as the first step on the road to asceticism in denying the will to life (*WWR* 1: 380). If the price to be paid for overcoming sexual desire is neurotic behaviour and psychoses of the sort Freud sought clinically to diagnose and resolve, Schopenhauer, lacking any prescience of Freud's conclusions, would presumably regard such unhappy consequences as still worth attaining the goal of freeing the self of its attachments to the will to life for the sake of securing the only meaningful salvation from suffering. Even deep and absorbing contemplation of the beautiful and the sublime enables the individual to suppress and transcend the will to life, and in particular to avoid sexual desire, according to Schopenhauer. He thereby invites Nietzsche's later criticisms of the unhealthy aesthetic escapism from the erotic will to power that Nietzsche castigates as part of Schopenhauer's nihilistic saying "no" to life. If we are to free ourselves from the sufferings imposed by the will to life, Schopenhauer believes that we must first learn to subdue the sexual impulse, which asserts itself insistently in so many areas of our lives.

Finally, let us consider the topic of pederasty. If the real purpose of all of human eroticism is procreation, how are we to explain or explain away homosexuality? Schopenhauer recognizes the phenomenon, but at first dismisses it harshly as an aberration against nature. Later, in the chapter on the metaphysics of sexual love in the final edition of the second volume, he seems to have recognized that the problem is rather more complicated and significant, and he devotes an entire seven-page "Appendix to the Preceding Chapter" specifically on the problem of understanding pederasty. Whether or not homosexuality is unnatural or a "misguided instinct", as Schopenhauer continues to affirm, it represents in any case a serious challenge to his interpretation whereby all eroticism is directed exclusively to the production of ideal progeny and the projection of the will to life into the future beyond the individual's death. Why, to begin with the only category of examples that Schopenhauer explicitly mentions, are some men sexually attracted to other men, and why do they seek to have sexual relations largely or exclusively with persons of their own gender?

Limiting his discussion to pederasty or anal intercourse between males, or even more widely construed as any sort of sexual contact between males, is already an unacceptable restriction. If Schopenhauer's purpose is to reconsider his thesis that all sexuality is directed toward procreation, then he ought to examine every possible counter-instance. This would obviously include female homoeroticism or lesbianism, which Schopenhauer either finds unthinkable or unmentionable in print, or, less likely, of which he has never heard. His attempt to reconcile the existence of pederasty with the theory that all sexuality exists entirely for the sake of the will to life's urge to produce children further assumes, partly on the authority of a passage in Aristotle's *Politics* VII, 16, that pederasty is primarily if not exclusively practised by older men beyond the age of forty-five. Schopenhauer's hypothesis is that the sexual impulse in men of that age requires some sort of outlet, but that if they were to engage in vaginal intercourse with fertile women, their offspring in all probability would be imperfectly formed.

The truth of any of these assertions is open to serious doubt. Men of far more advanced age than forty-five are certainly capable of siring healthy children. Nor, in the first place, is it true that pederasty even in the narrow sense of male–male anal intercourse is a practice limited to men in that age bracket, or to men penetrating younger male partners, as was the socially instituted proclivity especially among aristocratic men in ancient Greece and Rome. The literary evidence as a matter of fact suggests that in these early Mediterranean cultures, pederasts, most of whom were simultaneously involved in heterosexual relations and were often married men with children, courted young boys from the age of thirteen up to the time when the boys' first beard hairs began to darken, but only when they themselves were between the ages of twenty-one and forty-five. To be chasing boys at the gymnasium for sexual liaisons after the age of forty-five in that culture would have earned an otherwise respectable pederast in ancient Greece an abusive term of social disapproval, ridicule and opprobrium.[11]

All in all, it must be said that Schopenhauer does not do a very creditable job of defending his philosophy of sex against the obvious objection that many aspects of sexual desire and sexual behaviour are not even indirectly related to procreation.[12] People seem to have sex in a wide variety of ways for a wide variety of reasons, all of which may equally deserve to be considered as natural, and many of which might in the end be reflections of the will to life, as Schopenhauer needs in some sense to say, but not all of which can be plausibly associated with individual willing as a deliberate or subconscious urge to reproduce.

Significance of Schopenhauer's philosophy

We have only had the opportunity to look into a few aspects of Schopenhauer's complex philosophical system. Schopenhauer offers penetrating insights into some of philosophy's deepest problems. He divides all fields of study into specific categories based on his fundamental metaphysical distinction between the world as Will and representation. In its time his book bearing the same title made an enormous impact on philosophy and the theory and practice of music and the fine arts.

Schopenhauer is most often associated with his extreme moral pessimism. He maintains that all willing subjects in the world as representation are condemned to perpetual suffering. His conclusion is not merely the reflection of a sour personality, but follows as a logical implication of the thesis that thing-in-itself is Will, and that its character as revealed in the perceived world is one of implacable conflict and strife. He touches a nerve for many thoughtful persons. When we consider the antagonisms that prevail at every level of social and political interaction throughout the world, and extend the same concept also to the inanimate order as a competition for space and time among all physical entities in motion, then we begin to appreciate the extent to which Schopenhauer may have understood more than philosophers before or since his day about the nature of the human condition as a manifestation of still larger forces at work everywhere throughout the universe.

In the end, we must acknowledge that Schopenhauer deserves the mantle of being Western philosophy's greatest pessimist. He is nonetheless no misanthrope, for he places human beings at the height of existence as the most individualistic, and he regards the Platonic Idea of humanity as the highest grade of the Will's objectification in the world as representation. He is concerned throughout his lifework, moreover, with finding ways to salvation from suffering for all willing subjects, even if these are available in practice to their full extent only to a select few. What is clear on almost every page of *The World as Will and Representation* is Schopenhauer's powerful intellect grappling with the philosophical difficulties about the nature of the world and the meaning of human life in relation to physical and transcendental reality that have preoccupied the greatest minds in philosophy's history. Where Schopenhauer stands out among his predecessors and in all of subsequent metaphysics, ethics and aesthetics, is his combination of natural science and transcendental investigation, his rigorous standards of argument, and his uncompromising avowal of whatever implications emerge in the course of philosophical reasoning.[13]

Notes

1. *WWR* 1: xiv; *FFR*: xxvi. See R. Taylor, "Introduction", in *The Fourfold Root of the Principle of Sufficient Reason*, A. Schopenhauer, E. F. J. Payne (trans.), ix–xviii (LaSalle, IL: Open Court Publishing, 1974), ix–xi, and F. C. White, *On Schopenhauer's Fourfold Root of the Principle of Sufficient Reason* (New York: E. J. Brill, 1992) 1–11, 152–3.
2. Authoritative philosophical biographies include H. Zimmern, *Schopenhauer: His Life and His Philosophy* (London: Allen & Unwin, 1876, rev. 1932); M. Fox, *Schopenhauer: His Philosophical Achievement* (Totowa: Barnes and Noble, 1980); P. Bridgwater, *Arthur Schopenhauer's English Schooling* (New York: Routledge, 1988); A. Hübscher, *The Philosophy of Schopenhauer in its Intellectual Context: Thinker Against the Tide* (Lewiston, NY: Edwin Mellen Press, 1989); R. Safranski, *Schopenhauer and the Wild Years of Philosophy*, E. Osers (trans.) (Cambridge, MA: Harvard University Press, 1990). See also P. Gardiner, *Schopenhauer* (Harmondsworth: Penguin, 1967); D. W. Hamlyn, *Schopenhauer* (London: Routledge & Kegan Paul, 1980); B. Magee, *The Philosophy of Schopenhauer* (Oxford: Clarendon Press, 1983, rev. 1997).
3. The Berlin fiasco is recounted by W. Wallace, *Life of Arthur Schopenhauer* (London: W. Scott, 1890), 149–50. Schopenhauer's later considered opinions on the limitations of academic philosophy are discussed in *PP* 1 ("On Philosophy at the Universities"): 137–97.
4. "Accordingly, true philosophy must at all costs be *idealistic*; indeed, it must be so merely to be honest … It is quite appropriate to the empirical standpoint of all the other sciences to assume the objective world as positively and actually existing; it is not appropriate to the standpoint of philosophy, which has to go back to what is primary and original. *Consciousness* alone is immediately given, hence the basis of philosophy is limited to the facts of consciousness; in other words, philosophy is essentially *idealistic*" (*WWR* 2: 4–5).
5. The difference in Schopenhauer's proofs identifying thing-in-itself as Will in the first and second editions of the text are dramatically illustrated in a comparison of *WWR* 1: 99 with *WWR* 2: 195.

6. A useful discussion of Schopenhauer's analysis of Plato's Ideas is offered by J. Young, *Willing and Unwilling: A Study in the Philosophy of Arthur Schopenhauer* (Dordrecht: Martinus Nijhoff, 1987), 73–5, 85–6, 91–7.
7. Schopenhauer's account of Platonic Ideas is criticized by C. Janaway, *Self and World in Schopenhauer's Philosophy* (Oxford: Clarendon Press, 1989), 9, 27, 277. See J. Young, "The Standpoint of Eternity: Schopenhauer on Art", *Kant-Studien* **78** (1987), 424–41; T. J. Diffey, "Schopenhauer's Account of Aesthetic Experience", *The British Journal of Aesthetics* **30** (1990), 132–42; and the essays on Schopenhauer's aesthetics collected in D. Jacquette (ed.), *Schopenhauer, Philosophy, and the Arts* (Cambridge: Cambridge University Press, 1996).
8. See D. E. Cartwright, "Schopenhauer on Suffering, Death, Guilt, and the Consolation of Metaphysics", in *Schopenhauer: New Essays in Honor of his 200th Birthday*, E. von der Luft (ed.), 51–66 (Lewiston, NY: Edwin Mellen Press, 1988); D. Jacquette, "Schopenhauer on Death", in *The Cambridge Companion to Schopenhauer*, C. Janaway (ed.), 293–317 (Cambridge: Cambridge University Press, 1999), and "Schopenhauer on the Ethics of Suicide", *Continental Philosophy Review* **33** (2000), 43–58.
9. F. Nietzsche, *On the Genealogy of Morality*, M. Clark & A. J. Swenson (trans.) (Indianapolis, IN: Hackett, 1998), 63–73. See I. Murdoch, *Metaphysics as a Guide to Morals* (Harmondsworth: Penguin, 1992), 61–2, 67–70.
10. See W. Bischler, "Schopenhauer and Freud: A Comparison", *Psychoanalytic Quarterly* **8** (1939), 88–97; R. K. Gupta, "Freud and Schopenhauer", *Journal of the History of Ideas* **36** (1975), 721–8. Freud reportedly read Schopenhauer for the first time in 1919, significantly, while working on *Beyond the Pleasure Principle*.
11. "The older male lover (or *erastes*) [pederast], aged between twenty and forty, was expected not only to provide his beloved (or *eromenos*) [catamite], aged between twelve and eighteen, with unstinting affection but to encourage and oversee his development of mind and body and his training in the morals, customs and responsibilities of civic society" (R. Lambert, *Beloved and God: The Story of Hadrian and Antinous* (New York: Viking, 1984), 78). See also R. Flaceliere, *Daily Life in Greece at the Time of Pericles*, P. Green (trans.) (London: Phoenix, 2002), 109–12.
12. An eloquent testimonial to the multiform natural values of romantic love not directed exclusively toward procreation is found in A. Gide, *Corydon*, R. Howard (trans.) (New York: Farrar, Straus, Giroux, 1983).
13. I offer a more complete critical exposition of Schopenhauer's philosophy in D. Jacquette, *The Philosophy of Schopenhauer* (Chesham: Acumen, 2005).

Bibliography

Collected writings

1946–1958. *Schopenhauers sämtliche Schriften*, 7 vols, A. Hübscher (ed.). Wiesbaden: Eberhard Brockhaus Verlag.

Selected works in translation with standard abbreviations

1966. *The World as Will and Representation*, 2 vols, E. F. J. Payne (trans.). New York: Dover Publications [*WWR* 1, 2].

1974. *The Fourfold Root of the Principle of Sufficient Reason*, E. F. J. Payne (trans.). LaSalle, IL: Open Court Publishing [*FFR*].

1974. *Parerga and Paralipomena*, 2 vols, E. F. J. Payne (trans.). Oxford: Clarendon Press [*PP* 1, 2].

Selected secondary philosophical literature

Atwell, J. E. 1990. *Schopenhauer: The Human Character*. Philadelphia, PA: Temple University Press.

Atwell, J. E. 1995. *Schopenhauer on the Character of the World: The Metaphysics of the Will*. Berkeley, CA: University of California Press.

Bischler, W. 1939. "Schopenhauer and Freud: A Comparison". *Psychoanalytic Quarterly* **8**, 88–97.

Bridgwater, P. 1988. *Arthur Schopenhauer's English Schooling*. New York: Routledge.

Cartwright, D. E. 1988. "Schopenhauer on Suffering, Death, Guilt, and the Consolation of Metaphysics". In *Schopenhauer: New Essays in Honor of his 200th Birthday*, E. von der Luft (ed.), 51–66. Lewiston, NY: Edwin Mellen Press.

Copleston, F. 1946. *Schopenhauer: Philosopher of Pessimism*. London: Burns, Oates and Washburne.

Diffey, T. J. 1990. "Schopenhauer's Account of Aesthetic Experience". *The British Journal of Aesthetics* **30**, 132–42.

Flaceliere, R. 2002. *Daily Life in Greece at the Time of Pericles*, P. Green (trans.). London: Phoenix.

Fox, M. 1980. *Schopenhauer: His Philosophical Achievement*. Totowa: Barnes and Noble.

Gardiner, P. 1967. *Schopenhauer*. Harmondsworth: Penguin.

Gide, A. 1983. *Corydon*, R. Howard (trans.). New York: Farrar, Straus, Giroux.

Gupta, R. K. 1975. "Freud and Schopenhauer". *Journal of the History of Ideas* **36**, 721–8.

Hamlyn, D. W. 1980. *Schopenhauer*. London: Routledge & Kegan Paul.

Hübscher, A. 1989. *The Philosophy of Schopenhauer in its Intellectual Context: Thinker Against the Tide*. Lewiston, NY: Edwin Mellen Press.

Jacquette, D. 1992. "Schopenhauer's Circle and the Principle of Sufficient Reason". *Metaphilosophy* **23**, 279–87.

Jacquette, D. 1994. "Schopenhauer on the Antipathy of Aesthetic Genius and the Charming". *History of European Ideas* **18**, 373–85.

Jacquette, D. (ed.) 1996. *Schopenhauer, Philosophy, and the Arts*. Cambridge: Cambridge University Press.

Jacquette, D. 1996. "Schopenhauer's Metaphysics of Appearance and Will in the Philosophy of Art", *Schopenhauer, Philosophy, and the Arts*, D. Jacquette (ed.), 1–36. Cambridge: Cambridge University Press.

Jacquette, D. 1999. "Schopenhauer on Death". In *The Cambridge Companion to Schopenhauer*, C. Janaway (ed.). 293–317. Cambridge: Cambridge University Press.

Jacquette, D. 2000. "Schopenhauer on the Ethics of Suicide". *Continental Philosophy Review* **33**, 43–58.

Jacquette, D. 2005. *The Philosophy of Schopenhauer*. Chesham: Acumen.

Janaway, C. 1989. *Self and World in Schopenhauer's Philosophy*. Oxford: Clarendon Press.

Janaway, C. 1994. *Schopenhauer*. Oxford: Clarendon Press.

Janaway, C. 1998. *Willing and Nothingness: Schopenhauer as Nietzsche's Educator*. Oxford: Clarendon Press.

Janaway, C. (ed.) 1999. *The Cambridge Companion to Schopenhauer*. Cambridge: Cambridge University Press.

Kant, I. 1965. *Critique of Pure Reason*, N. Kemp Smith (trans.). New York: St Martin's Press.

Lambert, R. 1984. *Beloved and God: The Story of Hadrian and Antinous*. New York: Viking.

Magee, B. 1983. *The Philosophy of Schopenhauer*. Oxford: Clarendon Press [revised 1997].

Murdoch, I. 1992. *Metaphysics as a Guide to Morals*. Harmondsworth: Penguin.

Nietzsche, F. 1983. "Schopenhauer as Educator". In *Untimely Meditations*, R. J. Hollingdale (trans.), 125–94. Cambridge: Cambridge University Press.

Nietzsche, F. 1998. *On the Genealogy of Morality*, M. Clark & A. J. Swenson (trans.). Indianapolis, IN: Hackett.

Safranski, R. 1990. *Schopenhauer and the Wild Years of Philosophy*, E. Osers (trans.). Cambridge, MA: Harvard University Press.

Simmel, G. 1986. *Schopenhauer and Nietzsche*, H. Loiskandl, D. Weinstein & M. Weinstein (trans.). Amherst, MA: University of Massachusetts Press.

Tanner, M. 1999. *Schopenhauer*. New York: Routledge.

Taylor, R. 1964. "Schopenhauer". In *A Critical History of Western Philosophy*, D. J. O'Connor (ed.), 365–83. London: Free Press of Glencoe.

Taylor, R. 1974. "Introduction". In *The Fourfold Root of the Principle of Sufficient Reason*, A. Schopenhauer, E. F. J. Payne (trans.), ix–xviii. LaSalle, IL: Open Court Publishing.

Von der Luft, E. (ed.) 1988. *Schopenhauer: New Essays in Honor of his 200th Birthday*. Lewiston, NY: Edwin Mellen Press.

Wallace, W. 1890. *Life of Arthur Schopenhauer*. London: W. Scott.

White, F. C. 1992. *On Schopenhauer's Fourfold Root of the Principle of Sufficient Reason*. New York: E. J. Brill.

Young, J. 1987. "The Standpoint of Eternity: Schopenhauer on Art". *Kant-Studien* **78**, 424–41.

Young, J. 1987. *Willing and Unwilling: A Study in the Philosophy of Arthur Schopenhauer*. Dordrecht: Martinus Nijhoff.

Zimmern, H. 1876. *Schopenhauer: His Life and His Philosophy*. London: Allen & Unwin [revised 1932].

Further reading

The best translation to date of Schopenhauer's main two-volume treatise is Payne (Schopenhauer 1966). Payne has also translated Schopenhauer's other writings, and has remained the standard source for readers in English. Payne was not a philosopher, but a self-taught German linguist and ardent amateur of Schopenhauer's philosophy. Several new, updated translations by Schopenhauer scholars who are also philosophers are currently projected. Among commentaries, Jacquette (2005) offers an overview of all major topics in Schopenhauer's philosophy. See Janaway (1989) for an exposition of Schopenhauer's metaphysics in relation to the self, and the papers in Janaway (1998; 1999) for useful background to many aspects of Schopenhauer's thought. Also highly recommended are the biography by Safranski (1990), and works by White (1992) on Schopenhauer's *Fourfold Root of the Principle of Sufficient Reason*, Atwell (1990; 1995) on the character of Will in the self and phenomenal human willing, and the papers in Jacquette (1996) on Schopenhauer's aesthetics.

5

John Stuart Mill

On Liberty

Jonathan Riley

Introduction

A remarkable aspect of John Stuart Mill's argument in *On Liberty* (1859) is his claim to be defending "one very simple principle": that "the *only* purpose for which power can be rightfully exercised over any member of a civilized community, against his will, is to prevent harm to others. His own good, either physical or moral, is not a sufficient warrant" (*OL* i.9; Mill 1977: 223, emphasis added).[1] Prevention of harm to others is a *necessary* condition for the legitimate exercise of any form of coercion against "human beings in the maturity of their faculties". The implication usually seized upon by commentators, which, however, is not the only possible one, is that any adult ought to be free to do anything that does not harm other people. In other words, a civil society has no legitimate authority to regulate any conduct that does not pose a definite risk of harm to others, and should not even consider regulating it. Mill seems to confirm this interpretive strategy later in the same paragraph: "The *only* part of the conduct of any one, for which he is amenable to society, is that which concerns others. In the part which merely concerns himself, his independence is, *of right, absolute*. Over himself, over his own body and mind, the individual is *sovereign*" (*ibid.*, emphasis added).

Many critics question whether he can possibly mean what he seems to be saying. How can his one allegedly "simple" principle be "entitled to govern absolutely the dealings of society with the individual in the way of compulsion and control, whether the means used be physical force in the form of legal penalties, or the moral coercion of public opinion"? He is not even clear about what he means by "harm", say the critics, and he casually shifts between such phrases as "harms others" and "concerns others" without sufficient explanation. In any event, they insist, where the border ought to be drawn between individual liberty and social authority is far too complex an issue to be settled in this simple-minded way. There is no simple solution that holds for all civil societies. Rather, different civil societies can legitimately draw different borders in accordance with their own particular moral and political standards. Even critics who are in sympathy with his focus on the rights of the individual urge us to dismiss as absurd Mill's claim that one simple principle applies without exception to every civil society.

Nevertheless, Mill repeats in the final chapter of his essay that its "entire doctrine" consists of "two maxims", namely, the one simple maxim of individual liberty together with a complementary maxim that might be called one very simple principle of social authority, according to which society rightfully does have authority to consider employing some type of organized force, including physical force as well as social stigma, to coercively interfere with conduct that is "prejudicial to the interests of others" (*OL* v.2, 292). He appears to be reiterating that the individual is "not accountable to society" for conduct that poses no definite risk of harm to the interests of others, but "is accountable" for conduct that does pose such a risk. With respect to conduct that is harmless to others, "society can justifiably express its dislike or disapprobation" only by means of non-coercive measures, including "advice, instruction, persuasion and avoidance by other people" (*ibid.*). With respect to conduct that risks harm to others, in contrast, society or its political representatives can justifiably consider whether to establish and enforce rules that set out the terms and conditions under which the conduct will be permitted if at all. This does not imply that society must always regulate any conduct that is harmful to other people. If the conduct under consideration also produces social benefits that are reasonably estimated to far outweigh the social harms, for example, society might well forgo exercising its regulatory authority. But society has authority to consider coercive interference with any conduct that poses a definite risk of harm to others, and ought always to consider interfering, even though social decision-makers may reasonably decide sometimes to leave such conduct alone.

I shall argue against the critics that Mill means it, and has good reason to mean it, when he claims that these two simple maxims make up a utilitarian doctrine that (although it is not a complete version of utilitarianism) is applicable to any civil society. This radical doctrine of individual liberty and social authority was far in advance of its time and is still not adequately appreciated in the literature today. Mill apparently expected that few would understand it for some time to come: he suggests that most will conflate it with more familiar defences of certain basic or natural rights of the individual that have appeared in virtually every age (*Auto* vii.20–21; Mill 1981: 259–61). The likelihood of such confusion does not seem to have worried him much, however, so long as the so-called "critical" period in which he lived persisted. By a "critical" period, he meant a period of "criticism and negation, in which mankind lose their old convictions without acquiring any new ones, of a general or authoritative character, except the conviction that the old are false" (*Auto* v.16, 171). During critical periods, when the majority's convictions are unsettled, "people of any mental activity" are eager for "new opinions" and quite ready to permit different individuals to pursue their own good "in innumerable and conflicting directions" (*Auto* vii.20, 259). But any critical period is inevitably followed by an "organic" period, in which "mankind accept with firm conviction some positive creed, claiming jurisdiction over all their actions" (*Auto* v.16, 171). The great danger, as historical experience made clear, Mill insisted, was that the majority would resume its oppressive ways during the next organic period, ceasing to tolerate individual freedom to deviate from its settled opinions and customs: "It is then that the teachings of the *Liberty* will have their greatest value. And it is to be feared that they will retain that value a long time" (*Auto* vii.20, 260).

Like the contemporary French philosophers Claude Henri de Rouvroy Saint-Simon, an advocate of decentralized socialism, and Auguste Comte, a disciple of Saint-Simon before going on to found positivism, Mill was convinced that civilization moved necessarily through a succession of critical periods and organic ones. The prevailing critical period, in which traditional Christian beliefs had lost their sway without anything as yet to replace them, had commenced with the Reformation. His central worry was that this ongoing critical period would be succeeded by an organic period in which the majority's new system of firm beliefs (whatever it turned out to be) failed to include his radical doctrine of individual liberty as an essential component. He hoped that later thinkers would clarify his doctrine and persuade fellow citizens to adopt it in time as part of a larger liberal utilitarian creed, which he labelled a "religion of humanity". Indeed, he "looked forward … to a future which shall unite the best qualities of the critical with the best qualities of the organic periods", that is, an ideal state of society in which the majority is firmly committed to his utilitarian liberalism, a creed that would not require to be "thrown off and replaced by others" (*Auto* v.16, 173). Yet he seems far from optimistic that this ideal state of affairs, in which the historical cycle of critical and organic periods is finally brought to an end, will ever be achieved. Rather, he fears the arrival of new forms of majority tyranny, going well beyond any previous forms of despotism, in which powerful new technologies of mass communication, transportation and so forth are employed by the majority (or those who are accepted as its representatives) to stifle individual variety and impose a uniform way of life on all.

Mill's passionate hopes and fears for the future of mankind are manifested in his writings, not in an exciting and turbulent life. As he describes it, his life was "uneventful" (*Auto* I.1, 5). He was born in London on 20 May 1806, the eldest child of James and Harriet Mill. His father was a charismatic man, whose publications, wit and upstanding character made him a leader of the reform-minded intellectuals who banded together under Jeremy Bentham's standard of utility. James gave his son a remarkable education, during the course of which John was also taught by some of his father's eminent friends, including, among others, Bentham himself, David Ricardo, the leading political economist of the early nineteenth century, John Austin, a pioneer of legal positivism, and George Grote, an accomplished student of ancient Greece who did more than anyone else in his day to revive interest in ancient Athens as a highly civilized form of liberal democratic society. James also arranged for his son's employment at the East India Company beginning in 1823. John worked there for 35 years (in the same office as his father until the latter's death in 1836), retiring only when the company itself was terminated in 1858. As of 1856, he had risen to the same senior position that his father had achieved, namely, Examiner of India Correspondence, and thus was second in the chain of command, under the Secretary.

He was married only once, in 1851, to Harriet Taylor (*née* Hardy), about two years after the death of her first husband, John Taylor. She died just over seven years later, only a few months after his retirement, while they were travelling to Montpellier. Their friendship, the "most valuable" of his life, extended back to 1830, and had given rise to malicious gossip for some time prior to their marriage. After she died, he bought a cottage near her gravesite in Avignon, and spent a good part of each of his 15 remaining years there, usually accompanied by his stepdaughter, Helen Taylor. Mill himself died at Avignon on 7 May 1873, and is buried there with Harriet.

He insisted that his wife helped to create many of his key doctrines, especially the doctrine presented in *On Liberty*. After her death, he devoted himself to refining and publishing their shared ideas on various topics of interest, although the essays on religion and socialism as well as his *Autobiography* were only published after his death by his stepdaughter Helen. From 1865–68, he also served as a Liberal Member of Parliament for Westminster. As an MP, he made parliamentary speeches proposing several far-sighted liberal democratic reforms, including extension of the franchise to women and implementation of Thomas Hare's "single transferable vote" method of electing legislators (a type of proportional representation system). He knew these reforms lacked support yet he expected that they would eventually gain acceptance after more public discussion. Perhaps his most controversial (although, in his view, his best) speeches in the House were made in his capacity as chairman of the extra-parliamentary Jamaica Committee, which sought in vain during 1866–68 to bring Governor Edward John Eyre and his principal subordinates to trial in England for unjustified military violence resulting in the deaths of hundreds of black and mixed race Jamaicans. His Jamaica campaign aroused considerable public animosity, even anonymous threats of assassination, and probably cost him his re-election.[2]

Mill was a noble and brilliant man, and his radical doctrine of individual liberty and social authority deserves, and repays, careful study. But the common depiction of his doctrine, in which he is interpreted as endorsing individual freedom to do what is harmless to others while also endorsing social regulation to prevent harm to others, is inadequate as a reading of his text. Part of the problem is that there are different versions of this common picture, each corresponding to a distinct notion of harm. Yet the common depiction *can* be brought into line with Mill's text if harm is defined as any form of perceptible damage suffered without consent. Unfortunately, influential revisionist commentators such as Fred Berger (1984) and John Gray (1996), among many others, impute to him a different and much more limited idea of harm, namely, damage to certain vital interests that ought to be considered as rights or claims with correlative obligations for other people. That revisionist idea of harm does not bring the common depiction into line with his text. Rather, it merely breeds confusion about the nature of his liberalism. As Mill remarks, "The acts of an individual may be hurtful to others, or wanting in due consideration for their welfare, without going the length of violating any of their constituted rights" (*OL* iv.3, 276).[3]

The self-regarding sphere

Mill divides any person's life and conduct into two distinct parts that he calls the "purely self-regarding" sphere and the "social" sphere. He emphasizes that the self-regarding sphere is "the appropriate region of human liberty":

> It comprises, first, the inward domain of consciousness; demanding liberty of conscience, in the most comprehensive sense; liberty of thought and feeling; absolute freedom of opinion and sentiment on

all subjects, practical or speculative, scientific, moral or theological … Secondly, the [simple] principle [of self-regarding liberty] requires liberty of tastes and pursuits; of framing the plan of our life to suit our own character; of doing as we like, subject to such consequences as may follow; without impediment from our fellow creatures, so long as what we do does not harm them, even though they should think our conduct foolish, perverse, or wrong. Thirdly, from this liberty of each individual, follows the liberty, within the same limits, of combination among individuals; freedom to unite, for any purpose not involving harm to others: the persons combining being supposed to be of full age, and not forced or deceived.

(*OL* i.12, 225–6)

A society can only be considered free, he argues, in so far as it recognizes and respects these self-regarding liberties: "No society in which these liberties are not, on the whole, respected, is free, whatever may be its form of government; and none is completely free in which they do not exist absolute and unqualified" (*OL* i.13, 226).

Remarkably, in sketching the self-regarding sphere, Mill admits that expression is *not* self-regarding conduct: "The liberty of expressing and publishing opinions may seem to fall under a different principle, since it belongs to that part of the conduct of an individual which concerns other people". Yet he decides to treat the liberty of expression as "practically inseparable" from self-regarding liberty: "being almost of as much importance as the liberty of thought itself, and resting in great part on the same reasons, [the liberty of expressing and publishing opinions] is practically inseparable from it" (*OL* i.12, 225). Without further clarification, his move is puzzling and does not alter the fact that, strictly speaking, expression belongs within the social sphere rather than the self-regarding one.

The question arises how Mill distinguishes self-regarding conduct from social (or what commentators have labelled "other-regarding") conduct. When defining self-regarding conduct, he says that it does not *affect* other people unless they want it to: "there is a sphere of action in which society, as distinguished from the individual, has, if any, only an indirect interest; comprehending all that portion of a person's life and conduct which affects only himself, or if it also affects others, only with their free, voluntary, and undeceived consent and participation" (*OL*. i.12, 225). Self-regarding conduct apparently does not harm or benefit other people, unless they willingly join in and thereby create in effect a voluntary association of people who are jointly pursuing their self-regarding affairs. Given that others can freely prevent these injuries or benefits by refusing to cooperate in their production, the distinguishing mark of self-regarding conduct is that it does not perceptibly affect the interests of anyone – the agent or anyone else – *without their consent*. In particular, perceptible injury suffered *willingly* is entirely compatible with it. Thus, if we want to say that self-regarding conduct is harmless to others, then the meaning of harm must be limited to perceptible injury suffered without consent. In short, Mill seems to be endorsing in this context the well-known maxim of justice, *"volenti non fit injuria"* ["that which is done with the consent of the person makes no injury to him"].

Yet, as he makes clear in *Utilitarianism*, Mill does not give his unqualified endorsement to this maxim of justice:

> [T]his maxim is ... an instructive specimen of the loose and irregular manner in which supposed principles of justice grow up. This particular one evidently came into use as a help to the coarse exigencies of courts of law, which are sometimes obliged to be content with very uncertain presumptions, on account of the greater evils which would often arise from any attempt on their part to cut finer. But even courts of law are not able to adhere consistently to the maxim, for they allow voluntary engagements to be set aside on the ground of fraud, and sometimes on that of mere mistake or misinformation.
>
> (*UT* v.28; Mill 1969, 253)

There would be no problem if people were always so competent that they never got fooled and never made mistakes when consenting to injuries to self. But they do get fooled and do make mistakes, sometimes to such an extent that society reasonably decides to set aside contracts, promises and other voluntary agreements in matters that are purely self-regarding for the parties concerned. As Mill points out, for example, society legitimately refuses to enforce slavery contracts (*OL* v.11, 299–300). Society can also justifiably allow one party to retract consent to marriage if the marriage proves very unhappy, he suggests, provided children are not involved. The inescapable conclusion is that, for Mill, harm cannot be limited to just those injuries that a person agrees are too injurious for him to accept. There is an objective element to harm, about which even (at least minimally) competent people can sometimes be fooled or mistaken. If this is right, then harm cannot be equated with perceptible injury suffered against one's wishes, since even competent individuals do not always correctly perceive what is injurious and thus may mistakenly accept (a definite risk of) injuries that they subsequently agree are harms that nobody can reasonably accept.

Strictly speaking, it seems that, for Mill, harm is any perceptible damage to one's interests, suffered willingly or not. There are many forms of perceptible injury but mere dislike or emotional distress unaccompanied by perceptible damage is excluded. On this straightforward empirical understanding of harm, self-regarding conduct can harm others with their consent, but harm is not always correctly perceived by the victims, who consequently may be willing to accept (a definite risk of) it even when it is so damaging that they would deeply regret suffering it because nobody can reasonably accept it. There are virtues to sticking with this reading, especially because it absolves Mill from any reliance on maxims of justice in his definitions of harm and self-regarding conduct. But a drawback is that it renders incorrect the claim that self-regarding conduct is always harmless to others. Given the widespread conviction in the literature that Mill is aiming to protect some type of conduct that is harmless to others (even though much disagreement persists as to just what this harmless conduct consists in because of disagreement over the definition of harm), perhaps a somewhat different reading may be more convenient. Specifically, it may be preferable to return to the idea that harm is limited to perceptible injury suffered without one's consent. This permits us to say that self-regarding conduct is by definition harmless to others, in so far as injuries willingly borne do not count as true injuries or harms as per the "*volenti*" maxim. But it is important to keep in mind that Mill himself never says that self-regarding conduct is harmless to others. Rather, he says that it causes them no perceptible injury unless they genuinely consent to the injury. Since self-regarding conduct never *forces* others to undergo any perceptible injury, society has, "if any, only an indirect interest" in that conduct.

The argument of *On Liberty* is coherent in terms of either of these two readings. If harm is interpreted as any form of perceptible injury suffered willingly or otherwise, then self-regarding conduct may harm others with their consent, and society may legitimately consider whether to regulate it when seeking to prevent harm to others. In effect, society is justified on this reading to check whether individuals have really exercised "free, voluntary and undeceived consent" when choosing to accept any perceptible injury, or to refuse any perceptible benefit, in their self-regarding interactions with others. Once satisfied that the requisite consent is in place, however, society has no further authority to coercively interfere with self-regarding conduct. Rather, its regulatory authority is confined to conduct that poses a definite risk of harm to others without their consent and participation.

Despite the undoubted attractions of this reading, I shall adopt for ease of exposition the somewhat different one that limits the very meaning of harm to any form of perceptible injury suffered without one's consent. With certain caveats to be discussed in a moment, self-regarding conduct as Mill depicts it is harmless to others in this sense. Society has no legitimate authority on this reading to consider coercive interference with such conduct, since it poses no risk of harm to others. In contrast to the other reading, this one effectively assumes that society has already satisfied itself that individuals have exercised genuine consent whenever they accept perceptible damages, or refuse perceptible advantages, in their self-regarding interactions with others. Given that the consent is genuine, society is then held to be justified in applying the *"volenti"* maxim, so that all consensual harms are ignored (i.e. treated as "properly" not harms) because they are viewed as compatible with social justice.

The differences between the two readings are unimportant, provided any civil society can find (as Mill clearly thinks it can) non-coercive ways to ascertain genuine consent. In this regard, public officials may take a number of expedient steps, including: discussing with any individual whether he really knows what he is doing and even attempting to persuade him to abandon potentially self-injurious courses of action; posting signs, product labels and other warnings of potential injuries; and even demanding that he provide formal evidence of his wishes before allowing him to venture on some highly dangerous course of conduct. Moreover, society may reasonably decide that genuine consent is simply impossible in some situations such as slavery contracts or even marriage contracts in perpetuity, in which case it may enact into law its disapproval of such contracts, its refusal to enforce them, and its guarantee that one party will not be permitted to force another to keep to the terms of such contracts. These measures do not imply, however, that practices like voluntary slavery and marriage without possibility of divorce will be completely stamped out. Such practices may well persist, despite society's disapproval, until all individuals learn that they have better ways to manage their self-regarding affairs.

Social procedures to ascertain genuine consent in the context of self-regarding conduct are clearly needed in any civil society. Commentators may object that such procedures inevitably involve coercive interference, which, if true, would make the two readings I have proposed diverge in crucial respects. That objection is swept under the rug, so to speak, by my adoption of the reading that takes for granted that any individual's consent in self-regarding matters really is "free, voluntary and undeceived". Like Mill himself, however, I do believe that social procedures to ascertain genuine consent need not be coercive but rather can be expedient tools to make sure that individuals genuinely choose as they wish in self-regarding matters. If that is right, then the two readings are mutually compatible, and the differences between them negligible.

In any case, Mill emphasizes that self-regarding conduct can and should affect others' feelings towards the agent. Others may feel intense dislike or disgust, for example, at an agent's eccentric religious opinions or homosexual lifestyle. But their intense dislike does not amount to harm to them. Harm is something other than mere dislike, namely, perceptible injury, or, on my adopted reading, perceptible injury suffered involuntarily. (By implication, on my reading, self-harm must be accidental, unintentional or the result of incompetence.) Harm thus understood may appear in myriad forms, including physical injury (not excepting death), physical restraint, financial loss, damage to reputation, disappointment of legitimate expectations raised by contracts, promises, or even other customary activities such as public courting and displays of affection, and so forth.[4]

One important caveat is that society cannot legitimately expand this notion of harm, by establishing (in law or custom) rights not to suffer the mere dislike or disgust that anyone may feel at another's self-regarding conduct. Violation of such established rights would, after all, constitute a type of perceptible injury suffered by the right-holder against his wishes (ignoring cases of forfeiture or voluntary waiver). Unfortunately, even advanced societies have established such rights and correlative duties, Mill suggests, and have thereby hidden truly self-regarding conduct, by transforming it into conduct that violates the rights in question. He insists that a civilized society ought never to coercively interfere with self-regarding conduct by establishing such illiberal rights and duties. Rather, equal rights to absolute liberty of self-regarding conduct ought to be recognized and respected.

Other important caveats flow from Mill's concession that self-regarding conduct may also affect others *indirectly*, without their consent: "When I say [that a person's self-regarding conduct affects] only himself, I mean directly, and in the first instance: for whatever affects himself, may affect others through himself" (*OL* i.12, 223). The idea seems to be that a self-regarding action does not "directly, and in the first instance" injure others without their consent and participation, but that it may do so indirectly, and in the second or third or some more remote instance. In other words, a self-regarding action cannot be validly described such that the action *per se* necessarily implies perceptible injury to others without their consent. Rather, any injury to others against their wishes is contingent on the agent's self-injury to which he has consented.

An "objection" to what can count as purely self-regarding conduct "may be grounded on this contingency", Mill concedes (*OL* i.12, 223). In his view, an agent's intentional self-injury may under certain conditions justify the objection that the conduct is not truly self-regarding. More specifically, he says that, by simultaneously violating moral or legal obligations to others, an agent may transform what would otherwise have been a self-regarding action into a harmful social action that is legitimately subject to social regulation:

I fully admit that the mischief which a person does to himself may seriously affect, both through their sympathies and their interests, those nearly connected with him, and in a minor degree, society at large. When, by conduct of this sort, a person is led to violate a distinct and assignable obligation to any other person or persons, the case is taken out of the self-regarding class, and becomes amenable to moral disapprobation in the proper sense of the term.

(OL iv.10, 281)

He illustrates what he means by referring to three kinds of obligations, discussed more fully in *Utilitarianism* (*UT* v.14–38, 246–59). An agent's self-injury may happen to be inseparable from his violation of an obligation of justice which is correlative to another person's rights, for example, in which case the agent is "deservedly reprobated, and might be justly punished":

If, for example, a man, through intemperance or extravagance, becomes unable to pay his debts, or, having undertaken the moral responsibility of a family, becomes from the same cause incapable of supporting or educating them, he is deservedly reprobated, and might be justly punished; but it is for the breach of duty to his family or creditors, not for the extravagance. If the resources which ought to have been devoted to them, had been diverted from them for the most prudent investment, the moral culpability would have been the same. (<i>OL</i>. iv.10, 281)

Or his self-injury may coincide with his violation of obligations of charity or kindness, which (though owed to others) are not correlative to rights. Again, the agent deserves moral disapproval and might well be punished in this case:

Again, in the frequent case of a man who causes grief to his family by addiction to bad habits, he deserves reproach for his unkindness or ingratitude; but so he may for cultivating habits not in themselves vicious, if they are painful to those with whom he passes his life, or who from personal ties are dependent on him for their comfort. Whoever fails in the consideration generally due to the interests and feelings of others, not being compelled by some more imperative duty, or justified by allowable self-preference, is a subject of moral disapprobation for that failure, but not for the cause of it, nor for the errors, merely personal to himself, which may have remotely led to it. (<i>OL</i> iv.10, 281)

Finally, the agent's self-injury may at the same time be a violation of his duties to the general public:

> In like manner, when a person disables himself, by conduct purely self-regarding, from the performance of some definite duty incumbent on him to the public, he is guilty of a social offence. No person ought to be punished simply for being drunk; but a soldier or a policeman should be punished for being drunk on duty.
>
> (*OL* iv.10, 281–2)

As Mill makes clear, the agent in these examples is deservedly condemned and might be properly punished for violating his obligations to others, not for his self-regarding conduct *per se*. The violation of duty is a type of perceptible injury to others without their consent and, as such, takes the cases out of the self-regarding sphere: "Whenever, in short, there is a definite damage, or a definite risk of damage, either to an individual or to the public, the case is taken out of the province of liberty, and placed in that of morality or law" (*OL* iv.10, 282).

Mill's admission that self-injurious conduct may at times be inseparable from immoral or illegal conduct that is deservedly reprobated, does not imply that he is backing away from his claim that there is a sphere of purely self-regarding conduct which is "the appropriate region of human liberty". Self-regarding conduct is not always or necessarily inseparable from the violation of duty. The intemperate or extravagant man who pays his debts and supports his family, the cocaine addict who is duly generous and kind to others, and the soldier or policeman who confines his drinking to his off-duty hours, are not deservedly castigated or punished, however much others may dislike their self-regarding conduct.

The individual's right to self-regarding liberty

Mill's liberty principle says that every adult has a moral right (and thus ought to have a legal right) to absolute liberty with respect to the purely self-regarding portion of his life and conduct. This remains so even if harm is defined in the straightforward empirical way as any form of perceptible damage suffered willingly or otherwise, provided that society employs non-coercive procedures to ascertain genuine consent in self-regarding matters and then invokes the *"volenti"* maxim of justice whenever consent to self-injury is found to be genuine. On that reading, however, self-regarding conduct may harm others with their consent. For convenience, I have essentially employed a short-circuited version of that approach, by incorporating the *"volenti"* maxim into the very definition of harm such that genuinely consensual injuries to self are ignored.

To understand the liberty principle, the idea of a *right* must not be conflated with the idea of *liberty* to choose as one wishes among self-regarding actions. A right properly understood is a claim on society for protection, where the claim is correlative to obligations for other people. The claimant, or someone (a relative, perhaps, or a public official) acting on his behalf, has the power to demand or waive enforcement of the correlative duties. If enforcement is demanded, the duty-bearers should willingly perform their duties in good conscience. In case they are unwilling, however, society legitimately employs some form of coercion, including legal penalties and social stigma, to enforce the duties.

As distinct from a right, liberty consists in doing as one pleases. An individual has absolute liberty with respect to some possible set of actions provided he can choose as he wishes among all actions in the set. Evidently, an extremely powerful agent might enjoy such complete liberty with respect to some set of actions without possessing a right or even permission to the liberty in question. But Mill argues that every adult has a moral right to choose as he wishes among purely self-regarding actions. Every adult has a claim on society to protect him in the enjoyment of his self-regarding liberty, by enforcing others' obligations not to interfere with his self-regarding choices.

Mill insists that equal rights to absolute self-regarding liberty are justified by general "utility in the largest sense, grounded on the permanent interests of man as a progressive being" (*OL* i.11, 224). Absolute self-regarding liberty is justified to promote *individuality*, or the habitual disposition to act in accord with one's own judgement and inclinations, which is "one of the principal ingredients of human happiness, and quite the chief ingredient of individual and social progress" (*OL* iii.1, 261). In this regard, recall his admission that self-regarding conduct, although it does not directly and immediately injure others' interests without their consent, can and should affect others' feelings of mere like and dislike. He emphasizes that certain "natural penalties" are inseparable from self-regarding liberty because other people have equal rights to freely avoid the company of any adult whose self-regarding conduct displeases them:

> We have a right ... to act upon our unfavourable opinion of any one, not to the oppression of his individuality, but in the exercise of ours. We are not bound, for example, to seek his society; we have a right to avoid it (though not to parade the avoidance), for we have a right

139

to choose the society most acceptable to us. We have a right, and it may be our duty, to caution others against him ... In these various modes, a person may suffer very severe penalties at the hands of others, for faults which directly concern only himself; but he suffers these penalties only in so far as they are the natural, and, as it were, the spontaneous consequences of the faults themselves, not because they are purposely inflicted on him for the sake of punishment.

(*OL* iv.5, 278)

Thus, others' mere dislike of the agent's self-regarding conduct, although it is distinct from any harm to them, does count in Mill's utilitarian form of argument. But such mere dislike never justifies coercive interference with self-regarding liberty. Those who are merely upset by the self-regarding conduct have rights to freely avoid the agent and warn their acquaintances against him. Their liberty to act on their aversion does not injure them without their consent, although it may result in harm to the agent of the self-regarding conduct: "the natural penalties ... cannot be prevented from falling on those who incur the distaste or the contempt of those who know them" (*OL* iv.11, 282).

Mill's utilitarian form of argument for equal rights to absolute self-regarding liberty is far more elaborate than I can adequately discuss here. He recognizes that most members of civil societies may have no desire for individuality, so that reasons other than the promotion of their individuality must be supplied to make the utilitarian case. What social benefits can the many expect if the few who desire it are guaranteed the self-regarding liberty required for self-development? He points to such benefits as: new and better ideas, practices and technologies discovered by the few individuals of "genius" through their "experiments of living"; more effective government as a result of critical advice supplied by the intellectual and moral elite; the encouragement of personal diversity and tolerance as opposed to a totalitarian uniformity; and the prevention of a complete "despotism of custom" such as that found in contemporary China, which he associates with social stagnation and decline (*OL* iii.10–19, 267–75).[5]

Worthy of emphasis is Mill's insistence that a variety of ways of life is necessary for progress and the general welfare. This includes a variety of self-regarding lifestyles within any society, as well as a variety of cultures within any family of nations. (Any voluntary group or society that permits its members to freely exit may be said to have a moral right to self-regarding liberty in its collective or political interactions with others.) Such pluralism exists in so far as people do not share the same circumstances or characters so that they reasonably arrive at different and perhaps conflicting ideas of a good life. The "European family of nations" has been fortunate to possess a degree of pluralism in this sense, he says, because individuals, classes and nations within that family, despite being intolerant "at every period" of others' ways of life, "have rarely had any permanent success" in their attempts to compel the rest to live in accord with some one idea of the good. But this pluralism does not flow from any innate differences in individuals, classes or nations, in his view, so that its existence cannot be taken for granted. Rather, it tends to vanish as "the circumstances which surround different classes and individuals, and shape their characters, [become] more assimilated" (*OL* iii.18, 274). Unfortunately, the forces promoting assimilation are so powerful in advanced societies such as Britain, France and the United States, he fears, that "it is not easy to see how [individuality] can stand its ground" (*OL* iii.19, 275).

The social sphere

Whereas the self-regarding sphere is "the appropriate region of human liberty", the social sphere is the region where social regulation may be appropriately considered. The social sphere consists of that portion of any person's life and conduct that *does* affect other people "directly, and in the first instance", without their genuine consent. In other words, social conduct includes any conduct that directly injures or benefits the interests of others against their wishes, or that poses a definite risk of these unwanted injuries or benefits for them. By forcing others to endure (a definite risk of) some form of perceptible injury without their consent, for example, social conduct harms them even in the technical sense of harm that builds the "*volenti*" maxim into its meaning. Society clearly has legitimate authority under Mill's doctrine to consider regulation of such harmful social conduct.

It may seem that a different approach is required for social conduct that benefits another person without his consent. But this is not so. Harm to others is always involved at the same time in these cases. One person may benefit another without his consent, for example, by forcing him to consume products like medicines for his own good. But such putatively beneficial social conduct constitutes interference with the other's self-regarding liberty, assuming that he is a competent agent who is aware of the potential self-injury associated with failure to take his medicine. The simple liberty principle itself implies that society must take steps to prohibit such meddlesome social conduct since the direct harm of interference with the other's self-regarding liberty outweighs any putative benefit of paternalism.

There are also cases, however, where social conduct that benefits another's interests without his consent does not constitute interference with his self-regarding liberty. One person may benefit another's interests by forcing him to participate in the efficient production of public goods such as national security, a system of justice or public museums. The other's failure to contribute endangers the production of the public good and thus poses a risk of perceptible damage to others by denying them their share of its collective benefits against their wishes. Society rightfully has authority to consider whether to compel contributions in these cases. Moreover, in Mill's view, its political representatives may reasonably exercise legal compulsion in order to prevent the loss of essential public goods. Even so, especially for public goods that are not so important as to be essential, he argues that the government should be reluctant to compel contributions, except as a last resort (*OL* v.16–23, 305–10).

It is worth remarking that, strictly speaking, the self-regarding sphere is embedded within the social sphere in Mill's doctrine as he explains it. Society has legitimate authority to employ non-coercive measures to check whether the individual's consent to the risk of self-injury is genuine in his purely self-regarding conduct. Moreover, if the consent is not really "free, voluntary and undeceived" because the individual is found to be a child or otherwise incompetent, for example, or to be misled by others, then society has authority to interfere with his behaviour. Strictly speaking, this interference is not coercive because the conduct is not truly intended by the agent. Rather, the individual is being forced by others or by his own incompetence to engage in unintentional behaviour that carries a definite risk of harm to self. He does not genuinely wish to engage in such behaviour. Again, I am largely ignoring this aspect of Mill's doctrine for ease of exposition.

Society's authority to regulate social conduct

The principle of self-regarding liberty has no bearing on the social portion of any person's life and conduct. Rather, the principle of social authority applies. When considering how best to exercise its rightful authority to regulate social conduct, Mill suggests, any civil society should again be guided by the standard of general utility "in the largest sense". According to that standard, it seems, society ought to establish and enforce moral and legal rules of social conduct to prevent people from directly causing perceptible injuries to the interests of others without their consent. Society must be "much more cautious" in coercively interfering with an adult's inactions, he remarks, than it needs to be in interfering with his actions. But "there are many cases" where a person "obviously" has a moral duty to act for the benefit of others, and society legitimately enforces the duty in order to prevent harm in the form of the loss

of those benefits: "In all things which regard the external relations of the individual, he is *de jure* amenable to those whose interests are concerned, and if
need be, to society as their protector" (*OL* i.11, 225).

Mill goes on to say that "there are often good reasons" for society not to
employ legal penalties or social stigma to enforce its rules of social conduct:

> but these reasons must arise from the special expediencies of the
> case: either because it is a kind of case in which he is on the whole
> likely to act better, when left to his own discretion, than when con-
> trolled in any way in which society have it in their power to control
> him; or because the attempt to exercise control would produce other
> evils, greater than those which it would prevent.   (*OL* i.11, 225)

When the external enforcement of duty is precluded by such reasons, he
explains, "the conscience of the agent himself should step into the vacant judge-
ment-seat, and protect those interests of others which have no external protection" (*OL* i.11, 225).

A full discussion of Mill's utilitarian theory of social regulation is beyond
the scope of this chapter, but three points deserve emphasis. First, as he
explains in the fifth chapter of *Utilitarianism*, a civil society's most important
moral rules are its rules of justice, which promote the general welfare by regulating social conduct that causes perceptible injuries of an especially *serious*
kind to other people without their consent. To protect any individual from suffering such grievous types of harm, utilitarian rules of justice distribute individual rights and correlative duties backed up by the threat of suitable legal and
social punishment, except when good reasons exist from "the special
expediencies of the case" to rely solely on individual conscience for enforcement. Mill implies that general utility provides a moral criterion for deciding
when a harm is so severe that every individual ought to have a right – a claim
on society – not to suffer it. Thus, individuals ought to have legal rights not to
be killed merely because of their ethnicity, for example, and rights not to be
arbitrarily deprived of the competitive market fruits of their own labour and
saving, among many other rights, given that general rules distributing such
rights and correlative obligations are reasonably expected to promote the
general happiness.

Mill's argument in *On Liberty* is consistent with his account of social justice
in *Utilitarianism*, contrary to the charges of many commentators. In his view,
any coercive interference with the individual's self-regarding liberty is a type of
harm so serious that the individual ought to have a right not to suffer it. Utilitarian rules of justice distribute equal rights to absolute self-regarding liberty

for all adults. To promote the general welfare, every adult must have a legal claim not to be impeded by others when choosing among his self-regarding actions and inactions as he pleases, and others must have correlative duties not to impede him. For Mill, the benefits of self-development through spontaneous self-regarding choice and experimentation always outweigh the mere dislike and emotional distress thereby occasioned for other people, together with any "natural penalties" that flow to the agent from others' dislike and distress. Others are not obstructed in the making of their own choices by feeling mere dislike, as they would be obstructed by experiencing some form of perceptible damage without consent. Anyone who feels mere dislike remains at liberty to avoid the agent of the self-regarding conduct, and thus can continue to freely pursue his own good in his own way without suppressing the individuality of that agent. The natural penalties that flow to the agent are, however, harms to him which his own intentional self-regarding conduct has indirectly caused him to suffer. Again, the agent remains perfectly free to alter his self-regarding conduct if he wishes, in order to remove the cause of others' aversion and avoid the natural penalties that flow from it.

Evidently, Mill is working with a non-standard version of utilitarianism that assigns great weight to rules of justice in its calculations of the general welfare. There may be some similarity in this respect between Mill's utilitarian liberalism and some modern versions of liberalism such as John Rawls's (1993) contractualist liberalism, which assigns absolute priority over other social considerations to rules of justice distributing equal rights and liberties. But modern liberalisms, including the Rawlsian variant, shy away from anything like a right to absolute liberty of self-regarding conduct. At the same time, there is continuing controversy over the precise structure of Mill's utilitarianism. Some commentators are inclined to interpret him as subscribing to a sophisticated act-utilitarian theory such as Richard Hare's (1981), which employs rules as useful devices for most people to adopt but ultimately relies on "higher-level" reasoning about the likely consequences of particular actions and inactions to settle conflicts of rules, frame rules for new situations and so forth. Others see him working with a sophisticated version of rule utilitarianism or, perhaps better, disposition utilitarianism, in the same tradition, more or less, as Richard Brandt (1992) and John Harsanyi (1992). I am inclined to the latter view, which restricts consequentialist reasoning to the selection of an optimal social code, or optimal type of personal character comprising a suitable mixture of self-regarding and social dispositions. But I cannot pursue this any further (for further discussion, see Riley (2000, 2005b,c)).

A second point worth emphasizing is that the self-regarding liberty maxim sets an absolute limit on the scope of social morality and thereby limits the extent to which any civil society can legitimately employ coercion to regulate social conduct under the social authority maxim. Society may, for example, rightfully establish and enforce laws of justice that require business firms to publish accurate information about the products they sell. Such rules are designed to prevent fraudulent market conduct that directly causes severe harm to consumers. Similarly, society may legitimately prevent firms from polluting the environment, compel them to provide safe working conditions for their employees, and force them to collect personal information from the buyers of their products as a condition of sale to facilitate police investigations of any ensuing crimes in which the products are abused to seriously harm other people. But society can *never* rightfully implement rules that *prohibit* the sale of products that can be used without direct harm to others. Social regulation of the sellers cannot properly be extended to a social ban on their sales activities because such a ban would interfere with *the consumer's* self-regarding liberty. The individual consumer has a moral right to buy as he pleases any products that have purely self-regarding uses.

The third point to stress is that society's possession of legitimate authority to consider regulating social conduct does not imply that society should always establish and enforce rules to govern every type of social action or inaction that poses a risk of harm to others. If an individual's social conduct is reasonably expected to yield more (direct and indirect) social benefits than harms to other people, for example, then it is generally expedient for society to adopt a policy of *laissez-faire* rather than of regulation with respect to that type of social conduct. A social policy of "letting people alone" is, with some exceptions, better for the general welfare than a policy of coercive interference is in the cases of both trade and expression, Mill suggests, even though these types of social conduct do pose risks of direct and immediate damage to others without their consent. When some sellers gain market share over their rivals, or when some speakers are preferred to others by an audience, "society admits no right ... in the disappointed competitors, to immunity from this kind of suffering" (*OL* v.3, 293). Indeed, a policy of *laissez-faire* may be utilitarian even if the relevant social conduct is reasonably expected to generate more social harm than benefit. This may happen when the various costs of establishing and running a regulatory regime exceed the net harms to be prevented by regulating the conduct.

The upshot is that any civil society may rightfully permit individuals and voluntary groups (such as business firms) to enjoy liberty with respect to some types of social conduct, even though the moral right to absolute liberty is confined to purely self-regarding conduct. This moral and legal permission to choose among a limited set of social actions is contingent on relevant social benefit–cost estimates, which may vary across different societies or even the same society at different times. Moreover, even if individuals and groups are entrusted with legal rights to perform these social actions, those legal claims are properly qualified in such a way that the right-holder remains obligated to obey society's rules of justice. Sellers who are permitted to freely compete with others in the market remain obliged to obey laws that forbid fraudulent dealing, for example, just as speakers remain obliged to obey laws that forbid malicious libel or incitement to violence. Nobody has a moral right to *absolute liberty* with respect to social conduct.

Given his endorsement of broad (although not unqualified) policies of *laissez-faire* for social conduct such as trade and expression, it is a fatal error to interpret Mill as confining individual liberty to self-regarding conduct. Contrary to an influential reading of his purpose, he is not attempting in *On Liberty* to mark out in detail the boundary between individual liberty and social regulation. The self-regarding sphere is, he implies, a *minimum* sphere of human liberty that ought to be recognized and protected by every civil society as a matter of *justice and right*. He is very clear that individual liberty may also be appropriate in some parts of the sphere of social conduct. The optimal boundary between individual liberty and social regulation does *not* run, therefore, between the self-regarding and social spheres.

Moreover, since he is mainly concerned in *On Liberty* to defend the simple maxim of *self-regarding* liberty, it is hardly surprising that he does not spell out in that essay all of the exceptions that he would build into a broad *laissez-faire* policy for either trade or expression. Trade and expression are types of social conduct, he admits, and thus do not fall within the ambit of the self-regarding liberty principle, even though free speech if not free markets may be "almost of as much importance" as self-regarding liberty itself. In any case, he does list in the final chapter of Book VI of *Principles of Political Economy* (1848; 7th edn 1871) many cases in which he thinks government interference with free markets is justified; and he also discusses in various other writings what he regards as justified exceptions to freedom of expression, including copyright, malicious libel and invasion of privacy, even though he only mentions incitement to violence in *On Liberty*.

The Periclean ideal of character

It emerges that, for Mill, any member of a civilized society ought to develop an ideal personal character in which a "pagan" disposition to choose as one pleases in purely self-regarding matters is combined with a "Christian" or "Platonic" disposition to govern oneself in obedience to moral and legal rules of just social conduct.

> "Pagan self-assertion" is one of the elements of human worth, as well as "Christian self-denial" [quoting from John Sterling's *Essays*]. There is a Greek ideal of self-development, which the Platonic and Christian ideal of self-government blends with, but does not supersede. It may be better to be a John Knox than an Alcibiades, but it is better to be a Pericles than either; nor would a Pericles, if we had one in these days, be without anything good which belonged to John Knox. (*OL* iii.8, 266)

He associates this "ideal of self-development" (or, what is the same thing, this ideal of *individuality*) with Pericles, and thereby draws attention to Pericles' famous funeral oration, delivered during the second year of the Peloponnesian War. In that oration, as reported by Thucydides, the great statesman does hold out to the ancient Athenians an ideal of character, which he saw latent in their traditional customs and way of life, that combines a disposition to tolerate individual spontaneity in certain personal matters with a disposition to comply with rules established and enforced by democratic majorities in social concerns. True, the ancient Greek communities may not have recognized any individual *right* to self-regarding liberty:

> The ancient commonwealths thought themselves entitled to practise, and the ancient philosophers countenanced, the regulation of every part of private conduct by public authority, on the ground that the State had a deep interest in the whole bodily and mental discipline of every one of its citizens. (*OL* i.14, 226)

Yet Athenian society, perhaps alone among the Greek cities and certainly in marked contrast to Sparta, seems to have tolerated individual liberty and diversity in a portion of life regarded as private, with the important caveat that religious belief was not regarded as such.

Mill's reliance on Athens as a model for a free society was apparently inspired by George Grote. In his magisterial *History of Greece* (1846–56), Grote (2000: vol. 5, 74–84) draws a sharp contrast between leading modern societies, which he views as becoming increasingly ossified in their conformity to popular majority opinion, and the apparently vibrant liberal democratic culture of ancient Athens during its Periclean golden age. Mill seems to share Grote's perspective. He fears that modern societies such as Britain, France and the

United States are already in decline, "advancing towards the Chinese ideal of making all people alike" (*OL* iii.18, 274). If modern nations do succumb to the tyranny of majority opinion, in other words, to a "despotism of custom" in which all individuals are strongly pressured to conform to the majority's notions of human excellence and stigmatized for non-conformity, this despotism, he says, will probably take a somewhat different form than "stationariness", the form it has taken in China. The new despotism that threatens modern Europe and America is "not precisely stationariness" but rather endless change "for change's sake": "It proscribes singularity, but it does not preclude change, provided all change together" (*OL* iii.17, 273). Everybody must conform to the majority's wishes even with regard to self-regarding matters such as dress and lifestyle, but majority opinion itself is volatile, restless, insatiable, eager to seize on novel products and services made possible by technological progress in the advanced industrial economy: "We have discarded the fixed costumes of our forefathers; every one must still dress like other people, but the fashion may change once or twice a year" (*OL* iii.17, 273).

Against this ideal of all being alike in their whole life and conduct, Mill defends the Periclean ideal of individuality, whereby the individual is encouraged not only to make his self-regarding choices as he likes, in accord with his own judgement and inclinations, but also to develop his intellectual and moral capacities such that he understands the general utility of reasonable social rules of justice, and thus genuinely consents to obey such rules without the need for social coercion. An ideal society composed of individuals who had developed such ideal Periclean characters would be a liberal democratic "society of equals", in which all adults would have an equal right to assert themselves as they pleased in their self-regarding affairs, all would have an equal opportunity to participate in a democratic political system for enacting laws to regulate social conduct, and all would willingly comply with the laws of social justice duly enacted by elected legislative majorities, with the important caveat that broad freedom to criticize and urge reform of the standing rules must be permanently protected in light of human fallibility. Mill's discussion of such an ideal "society of equals" is scattered across various of his other writings, and is not our main concern. I shall return to it briefly in the conclusion. But first I shall say something about applications of the doctrine of *On Liberty* as I have interpreted it.

Applications

I have already indicated some of the main practical implications of Mill's doctrine for any civil society, but it may be helpful to spell them out. First, an adult has a moral right to engage as he pleases in purely self-regarding conduct. This includes conduct that many others will strongly dislike, such as reading books that question the existence of God, viewing porn movies, listening to raunchy music, selecting a career as a prostitute, having homosexual sex with other consenting adults and buying any products, including alcohol, drugs, guns and poisons, that can be used in such a way that they pose no definite risk of direct injury to others against their wishes. Society may, however, legitimately place special legal restrictions on any individual whose history shows that his consumption of alcohol, drugs or porn poses a risk of serious harm to others by causing him directly to commit violence against them. Society may also rightfully require sellers to record personal information from buyers of guns or poisons to facilitate police investigations of any criminal abuses of those products.

Secondly, society should adopt non-coercive measures and procedures to confirm genuine consent to the risk of self-injury posed by dangerous activities such as crossing an unsafe bridge or skydiving out of an aeroplane.

Thirdly, society should refuse to recognize or enforce contracts in perpetuity, such as selling oneself into slavery, which cannot be consented to by any reasonable person who at all values his liberty and individuality.

Fourthly, society may rightfully consider using force to regulate social conduct that poses a risk of harm to others. But that does not imply that society must always decide to regulate such conduct. Rather, society may legitimately grant extensive but not unlimited individual liberty to engage in social conduct such as trade or expression, even though the conduct directly harms others without their consent. With some exceptions, free trade or free speech is reasonably held to promote the general welfare, either because the conduct produces net social benefits, or because the cost of regulating it exceeds the harm to be prevented through regulation.

Fifthly, society should employ legal coercion only to restrain *unjust* social conduct, that is, conduct that poses a risk of injury to the interests of others which is so *serious* or *grievous* that it ought to be recognized as a violation of legal rights.

A final practical implication is that society cannot rightfully employ any regulatory regime that amounts to a ban on self-regarding activity. Sellers cannot legitimately be prohibited from selling products with self-regarding uses, for example, and speakers cannot legitimately be prevented from communicating messages that can be heard or seen without direct injury to others against their wishes.

I shall not attempt to further illustrate these various practical implications, although I have provided more detailed discussions elsewhere (Riley 1998,

2005a,b). It is, however, important to recognize that many scholars remain dubious about the practical appeal of Mill's doctrine, which they typically view as fraught with internal tensions if not inconsistencies. As Richard Posner, who expressly admires Mill's libertarian spirit, puts it: "Descent to the level of application brings a number of questionable features of Mill's analysis into view" (2003: 202). It is instructive to consider briefly some of these "questionable features", although I do not have space to deal with all of Posner's objections.

Posner complains that Mill provides a superficial and perhaps even incoherent account of liberty of conduct and its limits. He does not go so far as to charge that Mill's "specimens of application" contradict his principles. But he says that Mill makes "only perfunctory and unpersuasive" efforts, if any, to show how a reconciliation can be effected (*ibid*.: 205). There may be some truth in this since Mill's discussion of applications is highly compressed. Yet Posner himself does not appear to have made much effort to see how the applications may be reconciled with the liberty principle and its complement, the social authority maxim. He objects, for example, to "the proposition that people should be forbidden to marry if they lack the means to support any children that the marriage may produce". In his view, "it is difficult to imagine a more obnoxious interference with private conduct than requiring prospective spouses to prove their solvency to the state's satisfaction" (*ibid*.). But he never bothers to explain what is so "obnoxious" about society establishing customs to that effect, enforced by stigma, as opposed to laws enforced by government. More importantly, who can seriously endorse Posner's apparent view that couples should have a right to produce as many children as they like even if they have no means to support or educate the children? Producing children at the expense of other people is certainly not self-regarding conduct.

Posner also claims that "Mill's discussion of polygamy is particularly unsatisfactory" (*ibid*.). He expresses surprise that Mill does not endorse the liberty to engage in polygamous marriage if the parties genuinely consent. But Mill clearly does endorse that self-regarding freedom, provided that adults who disapprove of polygamy are free to exit the community and children receive an education that satisfies basic standards sufficient to enable them to learn to think for themselves as adults. Posner is just mistaken about this. Mill is not endorsing polygamy itself, of course, but rather the *freedom* to engage in it. He is revolted by the fact that in his day many English-speaking persons who "profess to be a kind of Christians" are highly intolerant of this self-regarding activity, which they call "immoral", although it poses no risk of harm to them. These so-called Christians persecuted the Mormons for freely practising polygamy, and were even eager to deploy military force to the remote Utah territory to stamp out what they found so disgusting.

Mill makes it clear that he disapproves of polygamous marriage contracts as being tantamount to the enslavement of women. Posner asks: "But if so, why would it be improper, as he believed, for the US government to seek to extirpate the practice?" (*ibid.*). Yet, as readers of *The Subjection of Women* (1869) are aware, Mill feels the same way about monogamous marriage contracts under the patriarchal laws and customs of contemporary civil societies like Britain and America. He seems to have been bothered in particular by the virtual impossibility of divorce such that, by consenting to (monogamous or polygamous) marriage, a woman effectively resigned for ever her liberty to manage her personal concerns. Any such contract in perpetuity strikes him as patently unreasonable, and he recommends that society should refuse to enforce them. Instead, all marriage contracts ought to contain sunset clauses and thus come up for periodic renegotiation, with complete freedom of divorce if the relevant parties unanimously consent, and some freedom of divorce (under certain conditions) even if the parties do not unanimously consent. Mill does not recommend that society should abolish all types of monogamous marriage contracts, so there is no reason for him to recommend that the government should "extirpate" all polygamous ones.

Posner goes on to argue that Mill's theory "would have required the US government to allow segregated schools in the South, because southern blacks were free to move to the North if they didn't like southern customs" (2003: 206). The idea seems to be that Mill must defend the liberty to practise racial segregation, so long as blacks were free to leave the community, because segregation is analogous to polygamy: "Segregation was a vestige and reminder of slavery, but remember that the fact polygamy was a 'mere riveting of the chains of one half of the community' did not in Mill's view warrant government interference with it, as long as the people affected by it were free to leave" (*ibid.*: 205, quoting Mill in *OL* iv.21, 290). But we must be careful here. It is silly to suggest that blacks consented to segregation in the same way that Mormon women accepted polygamy as part of their culture. After all, the southern states *outlawed* racial integration whereas the Mormon community did not outlaw monogamy in Utah or even in their own community. The Mormons did not force all prospective spouses to practise polygamy but southern racists forced all residents to practise segregation. Segregation was merely a guise for unequal treatment of blacks by whites. By forcing black children to attend separate public schools with far fewer resources than the schools attended by whites, southern state governments sanctioned social conduct that directly injured black children against the wishes of their parents. Evidently, Mill's doctrine says that any civil society may rightfully consider regulating such conduct, and ought to legally prohibit it if (as seems obvious) doing so advances the general welfare as he conceives it.

Posner shows no sign here of understanding the central distinction between self-regarding conduct and social conduct because he ignores the difference between consensual polygamy and non-consensual discrimination against others on the basis of race. A consensual regime of racial segregation is, however, also conceivable. Suppose that blacks and whites mutually consented to segregated schools and adopted measures to ensure that the separate school systems received equal resources on a per student basis. Suppose too that anyone who disapproved of this voluntary segregation regime could freely leave. In this imaginary case, Mill's doctrine implies that the consenting adults have a moral right to freely practise segregation. But so what? As Posner admits, this does not mean that a Millian must view segregation as admirable. Mill emphasizes that self-regarding conduct may well be tasteless and disgusting. Members of other communities have equal rights to freely avoid these segregationists if they cannot be persuaded to abandon the practice. But self-regarding liberty is absolute in Mill's doctrine. It cannot be reduced to some limited liberty to choose *only* that self-regarding conduct of which some majority approves.

This leads us to what Posner calls "the largest objection to Mill's analysis" (2003: 206). Posner agrees with James Fitzjames Stephen that there is "a deep tension in *On Liberty*" because Mill could never make up his mind whether people are "imitative and conformist" or "robustly individualistic":

> On the one hand, Mill thought people extraordinarily submissive to the force of public opinion, to the point where ... just being accused of immorality was likely to have the same coercive force as the law. On the other hand, he thought it feasible to dissuade them from condemning even deeply offensive behavior, such as gambling, drunkenness and prostitution, if it caused them no direct physical or financial harm.
>
> (*Ibid.*: 206)

If people are highly susceptible to "the pressure of public opinion", then "they may be incapable of responsibly exercising the broad liberties that he wanted conferred on them". Drunkenness in the home or pub may lead to the commission of drunken crimes, for example, drunken driving. If people are so individualistic that they can be persuaded to tolerate drunken behaviour (although not crimes) that most people nevertheless find "deeply offensive", however, then "they are unlikely to be as swayed by public opinion as Mill thought" (*ibid.*: 206).

But this is a fake dilemma. There is nothing inconsistent about an enlightened public opinion such that people have learned to respect the individual's freedom to engage in self-regarding conduct of which the majority strongly disapproves. Disapproval does not need to be translated into coercive interference with respect to conduct that poses no risk of injury to others without their consent. People have the moral right to condemn and avoid the individual's gambling, drunkenness or prostitution as they please, and the "natural penalties" that flow from their disapproval cannot be prevented from falling on the individual. But people cannot rightfully employ the *coercive* force of law or of social stigma against the individual, to prevent him from making self-regarding choices as he wishes. They cannot rightfully stigmatize him, for example, by "parading" their contempt for his self-regarding conduct (*OL* iv.5, 278). Society should not permit them to insert public statements of condemnation into the mass media, for example, nor should it permit them to organize public demonstrations demanding that his employment must be terminated or his business boycotted. In this regard, Posner seems blind to the difference between being stigmatized by organized pressure groups and "just being accused of immorality" by a few acquaintances and their circle.

Posner has not, in my view, scored any telling hits against Mill's doctrine. His particular objections are only the tip of the iceberg. But they are fairly representative of what passes for scholarly criticism of the doctrine. Readers will encounter many similar objections in the literature. Such objections tend to expose the typical critic's own presumptions and inattention to the text, I have suggested, rather than any obvious confusions on Mill's part. Registering one's disagreement with his doctrine is one thing. No one is required to be a Millian liberal. But purporting to show "deep tensions" in it is something else. As far as I am aware, nobody has proved that such tensions exist.[6]

Conclusion

In *On Liberty*, Mill provides a radical doctrine of absolute self-regarding liberty that he claims is applicable across all civil societies. Absolute liberty of self-regarding conduct is the minimum extent of individual liberty that is essential, he thinks, for the promotion of individuality as "one of the principal ingredients of human happiness". Individuality, or the habit of choosing in accordance with one's own judgement and inclinations, is also "the chief ingredient of individual and social progress" (*OL* iii.1, 261). By implication, the moral right to self-regarding liberty and individuality is crucial to spur the development of any civil society into an ideal "society of equals". In other words, this right protects the capacity of the individual to develop an ideal Periclean type of character by learning from his own experience and that of others what sorts of personal dispositions bring the most happiness for human beings. Since these dispositions include the disposition to choose as one pleases in self-regarding matters that pose no definite risk of injury to others against their wishes, the cultivation of this ideal type of character by all implies the flourishing of pluralism not only within society but also among societies.

As Mill says in *The Subjection of Women*, his vision of a modern "society of equals" involves extending "the morality of justice" to all. In contrast to ancient Athens, where "the equals were limited to the free male citizens", all adults, including women and resident aliens, would be included as equals:

> the true virtue of human beings is fitness to live together as equals; claiming nothing for themselves but what they as freely concede to everyone else; regarding command of any kind as an exceptional necessity, and in all cases a temporary one; and preferring, whenever possible, the society of those with whom leading and following can be alternate and reciprocal. (*SW* ii.12; Mill 1984, 294)

Temporary political command would rotate regularly among different groups of elected representatives who freely claimed and conceded office in accord with popular sentiments. In addition, society would be composed of myriad smaller unions of equals, such as local communities, economic partnerships and marriages. Command within these various associations would also be temporary and rotating, with different partners taking the lead depending on the tasks to be performed.

Mill's imagined "society of equals" is a grand liberal democratic ideal. Its realization depends on the cultivation of the requisite intellectual and moral capacities within the family, he argues, which in turn presupposes that men and women have learned to love one another as equals within ideal marriages. Although adults should be free to jointly form and dissolve sexual relationships as they please, provided they cause no direct harm to others including their children, he speculates that cultivated human beings will typically choose to practise monogamy in order to develop a profound mutual intimacy. In addition to monogamous marriage, any such ideal society would feature a constitutional democratic government, universal liberal rights and substantial equality of wealth, whether its economy was organized as a cooperative form of capitalism or as a competitive market form of socialism.

Without going further into the character and institutions of ideal liberal democratic societies, the key point is that, for Mill, equal justice, individual liberty and general happiness would all be promoted simultaneously in such a society or family of societies. The members of such a society would be jointly committed to a purely secular utilitarian "religion of humanity" that sacralized not only their particular ideal liberal democracy but also those established by other peoples. If such highly developed adults continued to find attractive some form of theism, it would of a Manichean or Platonic variety that sees mankind working in aid of a good but not omnipotent god, struggling against powerful evil gods or intractable materials to achieve and maintain an earthly ideal for human beings. The doctrine of *On Liberty* is at the heart of this radical liberal utilitarian vision. That doctrine deserves careful attention by anyone who is committed to the ultimate attainment of "the permanent interests of man as a progressive being".

Notes

1. Henceforth, *OL* i.9, 223. An analogous shorthand will be adopted after the initial reference when multiple references are made to any of Mill's other texts, as is the case for his *Autobiography* (*Auto*), *Utilitarianism* (*UT*) and *The Subjection of Women* (*SW*). Mill never altered *On Liberty* after it was first published, preferring to leave the text as it was rather than attempt to revise it without his wife Harriet's help. He says in his *Autobiography* that she provided come of the key ideas, and was in effect the joint author of the essay. Harriet died unexpectedly in 1858, and *On Liberty* is dedicated to her memory.
2. For more detailed discussion of Mill's life, see J. Riley, *Mill on Liberty* (London: Routledge, 1998), 3–36 and N. Capaldi, *John Stuart Mill: A Biography* (Cambridge: Cambridge University Press, 2004), as well as references cited therein.
3. Admittedly, Mill is not as clear as he might have been about his idea of harm. Nevertheless, he is also not as ambiguous as his critics typically allege, referring as he does at multiple points to "perceptible damage", which does not necessarily rise to the level of violations of rights. Unlike the narrow revisionist idea of harm, which he explicitly rejects, the broad idea of harm that I attribute to him makes sense in terms of his textual remarks. But even that broad idea requires some qualification, as I shall spell out in due course.
4. A question that could be posed is: to what extent, and on what grounds, precisely, can a utilitarian deny that dislike or disgust are harms? I answer as follows. A utilitarian can draw a conceptual distinction between mere dislike and perceptible damage, and deny that mere dislike counts as harm at all on these conceptual grounds. This denial that mere dislike counts as harm must not be confounded, however, with a denial that mere dislike counts in Mill's utilitarian calculus. As I explain in the next section, mere dislike does count as a form of disutility but, in contrast to harm, there is no need for society to consider whether to employ coercion to prevent the individual from causing others to experience it. Rather, in Mill's utilitarianism, mere dislike is taken account of by _giving anyone who feels it perfect liberty to avoid what causes him that dislike, warn his friends and acquaintances accordingly, and so forth. Their equal rights to liberty allow all adults to make whatever self-regarding choices seem best to them in terms of their own judgement and desires, including *aversions*. It is not expedient to coercively

interfere with any agent who is causing others to feel mere dislike, by forcing that agent to abandon his self-regarding choices. For further discussion, see Riley, *Mill on Liberty*, 157–65 and *Mill's Radical Liberalism* (London: Routledge, forthcoming), Ch. 3.

5. A utilitarian *can* justify a *universal* right to the liberty of self-regarding actions based on the likely social benefits developed by only a small minority. It would be a mistake to assume that it is possible for society, prior to distributing rights, to ascertain, continuously and without much cost, which particular adults wish to develop their intellectual and moral capacities by making whatever self-regarding choices seem best in terms of their own judgement and inclinations. Under such an assumption, rights to self-regarding liberty might be expediently denied to individuals who consent to forgo them because they do not wish to exercise them at a given time, subject to continuous renegotiation. Since the costs of continuously monitoring people to see if they change their mind about this are obviously prohibitive, however, a utilitarian society must distribute equal rights to liberty and encourage all adults to exercise their rights by making whatever self-regarding choices seem best in terms of their own judgement and inclinations, leaving it to the individual to effectively waive his right altogether if he fails to make any choice of his own but instead blindly imitates other people. It would clearly defeat the whole enterprise if society (or its representatives) had legitimate authority to decide *without his consent* whether any particular individual "capable of rational persuasion" should be permitted self-regarding liberty. That would give some people (perhaps a ruling elite) the blanket authority to harm disfavoured individuals by coercively interfering with any self-regarding choices they might attempt to make. Such authority can hardly be endorsed by any utilitarian like Mill who recognizes the various social benefits to be gained if competent individuals are encouraged to do as they like rather than submit to others in purely personal matters.

6. More powerful objections than Posner's could perhaps be marshalled, but these provide a useful example of how similar objections fail to stand up.

Bibliography

Berger, F. 1984. *Happiness, Justice and Freedom: The Moral and Political Philosophy of John Stuart Mill*. Berkeley, CA: University of California Press.

Brandt, R. B. 1992. *Morality, Utilitarianism, and Rights*. Cambridge: Cambridge University Press.

Bromwich, D. & G. Kateb (eds) 2003. *On Liberty: John Stuart Mill*. New Haven, CT: Yale University Press.

Capaldi, N. 2004. *John Stuart Mill: A Biography*. Cambridge: Cambridge University Press.

Gray, J. 1996. *Mill on Liberty: A Defence*, 2nd edn. London: Routledge.

Grote, G. 2000. *A History of Greece* [1846–56]. Bristol: Thoemmes. [Reprint of the 4th edn (1872) in 10 vols.]

Hamburger, J. 1999. *John Stuart Mill on Liberty and Control*. Princeton, NJ: Princeton University Press.

Hare, R. M. 1981. *Moral Thinking: Its Method, Levels and Point*. Oxford: Clarendon Press.

Harsanyi, J. M. 1992. "Game and Decision Theoretic Models in Ethics". In *Handbook of Game Theory*, vol. 1, R. J. Aumann & S. Hart (eds), 669–707. Amsterdam: North-Holland.

Mill, J. S. 1965 [1848; 7th edn 1871]. *Principles of Political Economy*. See Robson (1963–91), vols II & III.

Mill, J. S. 1969 [1861]. *Utilitarianism*. See Robson (1963–91), vol. X, 203–59.

Mill, J. S. 1977 [1859]. *On Liberty*. See Robson (1963–91), vol. XVII, 213–310.

Mill, J. S. 1981 [1873]. *Autobiography*. See Robson (1963–91), vol. I, 1–290.

Mill, J. S. 1984 [1869]. *The Subjection of Women*. See Robson (1963–91), vol. XXI, 259–340.

Posner, R. A. 2003. "*On Liberty*: A Revaluation". See Bromwich & Kateb (2003), 197–207.

Rawls, J. 1993. *Political Liberalism*. New York: Columbia University Press.

Riley, J. 1988. *Liberal Utilitarianism*. Cambridge: Cambridge University Press.

Riley, J. 1998. *Mill on Liberty*. London: Routledge.

Riley, J. 2000. "Defending Rule Utilitarianism". In *Morality, Rules and Consequences*, B. Hooker, E. Mason & D. Miller (eds), 40–70. Edinburgh: Edinburgh University Press.

Riley, J. 2005a. "Mill's Doctrine of Freedom of Expression". *Utilitas* **17**(2), 1–33.

Riley, J. 2005b forthcoming. *Mill's Radical Liberalism*. London: Routledge.

Riley, J. 2005c forthcoming. *Maximizing Security: A Liberal Utilitarian Theory of Justice and Rights*. Oxford: Oxford University Press.

Robson, J. M. (ed.) 1963–91. *The Collected Works of John Stuart Mill*, 33 vols. Toronto: University of Toronto Press.

Skorupski, J. (ed.) 1998. *The Cambridge Companion to John Stuart Mill*. Cambridge: Cambridge University Press.

Ten, C. L. 1980. *Mill on Liberty*. Oxford: Clarendon Press.

Further reading

The standard edition of the text is *On Liberty* (1977) in J. M. Robson (ed.), *The Collected Works of John Stuart Mill*, 33 vols (Toronto: University of Toronto Press, 1963–91), vol. XVII, 213–310. Among the many other editions currently in print, D. Bromwich & G. Kateb (eds), *On Liberty: John Stuart Mill* (New Haven, CT: Yale University Press, 2003) includes a balanced introduction to Mill's life and work by Bromwich, a stimulating reading of the text by Kateb, who downplays Mill's utilitarianism, and four highly uneven critical assessments of Mill's liberal doctrine by, respectively, Jean Bethke Elshtain, Owen Fiss, Richard A. Posner and Jeremy Waldron.

6

Søren Kierkegaard
Philosophical Fragments

C. Stephen Evans

Søren Kierkegaard lived a short but intense life from a literary point of view. Born in 1813, he died in 1855 in the midst of a controversial attack on the state church of Denmark. In his forty-two years of life, his published writings fill 25 volumes in the latest English translation, not including his voluminous *Journals and Papers*. Many of the published works were attributed by Kierkegaard to pseudonyms. This was not an attempt to hide his authorship; in many cases he put his name on the title page as "editor" and it was well known in Copenhagen that he was the author of the works. Rather, the pseudonyms are like fictional characters that Kierkegaard created, whose views and lifestyle may be quite different from Kierkegaard's own.

Kierkegaard was far from an academic philosopher, and in many ways not primarily a philosopher at all. He liked to think of himself as a kind of missionary, who had been assigned the task of "reintroducing Christianity into Christendom". The idea of "Christendom", according to Kierkegaard, involved a confusing illusion. People born into a Christian country come to believe that they are Christians regardless of whether or not they have any Christian convictions that shape their lives. Kierkegaard thus saw his task as one of helping people who are already "Christians of a sort" to become Christians in truth.

This missionary task, however, required philosophical work. Kierkegaard thought that his contemporaries had "forgotten what it means to exist" as an individual human being, and since Christianity is primarily a way of existence

159

it follows that his contemporaries also failed to understand Christianity, even if they were baptized members of a Christian church. Kierkegaard thus sets himself the task of reflecting on and describing the nature of human existence, so that the Christian message can be heard again. This brings him into direct conflict with the great German philosopher Hegel, and his Danish followers. Kierkegaard sees Hegel as the quintessential philosopher of Christendom, since Hegel had given a speculative interpretation of history that sees the Christian culture of Europe as the culmination of the coming of the kingdom of God on earth. The Hegelians, while claiming to have given a justification of Christianity, have actually betrayed it by confusing Christian existence with the cultural achievements of Europe. Hegel, according to Kierkegaard, misunderstands Christianity by considering it to be a kind of intellectual doctrine that can be better articulated through philosophy. Hegel, and other progenitors of liberal Protestantism such as Kant, had generally sought to develop a foundation for Christian belief in human reason. On this view it is not necessary to see Christianity as a religion founded on a special revelation from God; the truths of Christianity can be recognized without any appeal to such an authority.

Kierkegaard's book *Philosophical Fragments or a Fragment of Philosophy*, published in 1844, is a subtle polemic against this sort of liberal Protestantism. However, before looking at the content of the book, some attention must be given to its literary form. Although both the first draft and a final draft had Kierkegaard's own name affixed as author, at the last minute Kierkegaard decided to attribute the book to a pseudonym, Johannes Climacus, about whom I shall say more later. Kierkegaard put his own name on the book as "editor", and a few changes were made to the text that appear to reflect the decision to make the book pseudonymous. Thus, as with many of Kierkegaard's works, an interpretive problem is posed right at the outset: whose "voice" is heard in the book? Does *Philosophical Fragments* reflect Kierkegaard's own views or rather those of the enigmatic Johannes Climacus?

Kierkegaard attached a "First and Last Declaration" under his own name to *Concluding Unscientific Postscript to Philosophical Fragments* (also attributed to Johannes Climacus). In this "Declaration" he acknowledges he is the creator of his pseudonymous authors but claims that the views they embody are not necessarily his own, and thus asks the reader to separate him from the pseudonyms: "Therefore, if it should occur to anyone to want to quote a particular passage from the books, it is my wish, my prayer, that he will do me the kindness of citing the respective pseudonymous author's name, not mine".[1] Given this request, it seems hazardous simply to take *Philosophical Fragments* as giving us Kierkegaard's own thoughts.

Nevertheless, many commentators have done just that. Niels Thulstrup, for example, takes *Fragments* as giving us a definitive understanding of how Kierkegaard understood the central elements of Christian dogmatics, especially the doctrine of the atonement.[2] *Fragments* is seen as a book in which "Kierkegaard raises philosophical and Christian problems one after the other and gives his solutions, which open one's eyes to ever-widening perspectives".[3]

Recently more literary-minded scholars have protested against this kind of "blunt reading", claiming that attention must be paid to the literary form of Kierkegaard's authorship, particularly to the prevalence of irony in the works. Roger Poole, for example, protests against the attempt to see Kierkegaard against the background of orthodox Christian thought. As Poole sees things, Kierkegaard has no doctrines to propound or defend, but wants to provoke the reader to think things through for herself: "Kierkegaard's text does not offer itself to be the object of the question, 'What does it mean?' It offers itself as the proponent of the question 'What do you think?'"[4]

Philosopher James Conant, while taking an approach very different from that of Poole, also sees the "Johannes Climacus" literature as fundamentally ironical, interpreting the "Revocation" Climacus appends to the end of *Postscript* as similar to the conclusion of Wittgenstein's *Tractatus Logico-Philosophicus*. In the *Tractatus* Wittgenstein explains that the person who really understands his book will understand the book's statements to be nonsense.[5] Conant takes the Climacus literature to be another attempt to say what cannot be said but only shown, and thus any interpreter who summarizes the book's message inevitably gets it wrong. Interpretations such as those of Poole and Conant force us in thinking about *Philosophical Fragments* to confront the literary structure of the book along with the problem of pseudonymity that structure poses.

The ironical character of *Philosophical Fragments*

It seems to me to be beyond doubt that *Fragments* is a genuinely pseudonymous work. After all, Kierkegaard did make the decision to affix the pseudonym, and he did revise the book after making that decision. Even if the number of revisions is relatively small, the final product reflects Kierkegaard's judgement as to what the character he invented and named "Johannes Climacus" would say. Even if Kierkegaard had made no revisions to the work at all after changing the authorship to the pseudonym, the decision for the pseudonym would be decisive. It is not at all unusual for an author to recognize the true import of a work while the work is in process, and the fact that Kierkegaard decided only late in the game, so to speak, that *Fragments* should not be attributed to himself, does not mean that Kierkegaard's intentions can be ignored. For better or worse, the book that was published was one that Kierkegaard did not wish to be regarded as written by himself. The literary-minded scholars are surely right to insist that we take the pseudonym seriously.

Furthermore, I think that it is highly likely that the decision to opt for the pseudonym is related to the fundamentally ironical character of the book. Both Climacus, in *Postscript*, and Kierkegaard himself, in his *Journals and Papers*, comment on a review of *Fragments* by a German theologian. Both agree that although the theologian accurately summarized the contents of the book, he nevertheless fundamentally misunderstood it by missing the irony that pervades the work.[6]

However, although the book is certainly pseudonymous and fundamentally ironical in character, this does not mean that it contains no serious philosophical content. Kierkegaard himself, in his doctoral dissertation on *The Concept of Irony*, distinguishes two different forms of irony: "The most common form of irony is to say something earnestly that is not meant in earnest. The second form of irony, to say in a jest, jestingly, something that is meant in earnest is more rare."[7] I will try to show that the irony that pervades *Philosophical Fragments* is this second, rarer form of irony. The irony does not fundamentally lie in *what* is said in the book but rather in *how* what is said is said. The book makes serious claims that Kierkegaard himself would surely regard as correct, but it makes those claims in the form of an extended jest.

The problem of faith and history

Probably the clearest clue to the overall character of *Philosophical Fragments* is found in the questions posed on the title page: "Can a historical point of departure be given for an eternal consciousness; how can such a point of departure be of more than historical interest; can an eternal happiness be built upon historical knowledge?" By "eternal consciousness" Climacus clearly has something like immortality or the Christian concept of "eternal life" in mind. It is a commonplace that Christianity, in contrast to most other religions such as Hinduism and Buddhism, connects the acquisition of eternal life to particular historical beliefs. It is through believing in Jesus of Nazareth, and trusting in his atoning death and resurrection, that the Christian achieves eternal life, both as a present possession and as a future hope in the form of the promise of the resurrection of the body. If we had any doubt that Climacus means to discuss the problems posed by this Christian attempt to link historical faith with eternal life, he makes the point emphatically clear near the end of *Fragments*:

> As is well known, Christianity is the only historical phenomenon that despite the historical – indeed, precisely by means of the historical – has wanted to be the single individual's point of departure for his eternal consciousness, has wanted to interest him otherwise than merely historically, has wanted to base his happiness on his relation to something historical. (*PF*: 109)[8]

Why should these questions seem pressing in Kierkegaard's day? To some degree the basic problem is one that would occur in any time and place. Does it really make sense to think that a human being's eternal destiny might hinge on whether certain historical beliefs were true? However, the questions were especially pressing in the early part of the nineteenth century in Europe, since the advent of historical Biblical criticism had undermined the confidence of many in the historical accuracy of the Biblical narratives about the life of Jesus and other events. Kierkegaard was well aware of these developments in Biblical scholarship. His response, however, is not to engage in an apologetic strategy by marshalling historical evidence, but rather to raise philosophical questions about the roles played by history and historical evidence in the development of Christian faith. His creation Johannes Climacus does this by the development of a "hypothesis" that may be viewed as an extended thought experiment about the importance history may have for an individual's eternal destiny.

The "Socratic" view of "the Truth" and the "B-hypothesis"

The basic plan behind *Philosophical Fragments* is to compare and contrast two alternative accounts of how "the Truth" can be learned by human beings.[9] The baseline, so to speak, is provided by exploring what Climacus calls the "Socratic" view of the Truth. In most of Kierkegaard's works, Socrates is admired and extolled as providing a kind of "inwardness" that is an analogue to the inwardness of Christian faith. *Fragments* is somewhat different. Although Socrates is still presented as a great and exemplary figure, the emphasis in the book is on the differences between Socratic and Christian views, rather than the similarities. The figure of Socrates presented is a very Platonic one; Climacus attributes to Socrates the Platonic doctrine of recollection along with a belief in the immortality of the soul.[10]

What kind of truth is Climacus discussing? It is not just any old truth that Climacus has in mind. It becomes clear in the course of the book that the possession of the Truth is equivalent to the religious concept of salvation. The person who has the Truth is the person who is fully human, who is all that a human being should be, and who understands what human life is all about. Climacus goes so far as to say that a person who acquires the Truth undergoes an essential transformation and becomes a new creature (*PF*: 19). If I have the Truth I have achieved my destiny, and for Climacus this destiny includes an eternal happiness.

The discussion of the Socratic view of the Truth begins in Chapter 1 with the quandary Plato discusses in the *Meno*. It appears that the truth cannot be learned, because to learn the truth one must be ignorant of it. However, the person who is ignorant of the truth would not be able to recognize it even if the truth were found. Climacus says that the Socratic solution to this difficulty is found in the doctrine of recollection, in which no person is truly ignorant of the Truth and "learning" turns out to be recollecting (*PF*: 9).

Socrates is credited with a profound and consistent expression of this perspective on the Truth. Since every human being already possesses the Truth, Socrates viewed himself as a midwife whose task was to help others bring out the Truth they already possessed. Thus the best disciple of Socrates, the one who has learned the most from him, is the student who realizes that essentially he owes nothing to Socrates. Furthermore, and most crucially, the "moment" in which the learner is helped by Socrates to see that the Truth is already possessed has no essential importance. For in the same moment that the learners recognize that they have the Truth, they also realize that they have always possessed this Truth, that the Truth is an eternal possession. The significance of such a moment of discovery is thus said to be "vanishing".

Climacus clearly sees this "Socratic" view of truth not simply as an invention of Plato. Rather, in some way, this Platonic/Socratic view is seen as the paradigm for any religion or philosophy that holds that human beings possess within themselves the capability of achieving salvation.

Having developed this Socratic position, Climacus abruptly switches tracks in the middle of Chapter 1, and begins in Section B to develop an alternative position. The motivation for doing this is not made clear; he simply begins with a hypothetical statement: "If the situation is to be different [from the Socratic one], then the moment in time must have such decisive significance that for no moment will I be able to forget it ..." (*PF*: 13). The project simply seems to be to invent an account of the Truth and how it is learned that will be genuinely *different* from the Socratic account. Thus, employing simple logic, if the Socratic account says "*p*", then the alternative must say "not-*p*".

The Socratic view holds that the particular moment in time in which the Truth is acquired has no essential importance. Thus, in developing his alternative, which I will call the "B-hypothesis", the moment must be regarded as having crucial importance. On the Socratic view the disciple really owes the teacher nothing; thus the B-hypothesis posits that the learner owes everything to the teacher. On the Socratic view the teacher is only a midwife who does not give the disciple anything the disciple did not already possess. On the B-hypothesis the teacher gives the learner "the Condition" for understanding the Truth. Since this Condition is what makes it possible for the learner to be what he or she truly is, the giving of such a Condition is like giving new life. The teacher then is someone who recreates the disciple, gives birth to a new creature, and Climacus says that such a teacher must be seen as "the God", using the definite article to mimic the way Plato refers to the deity.

When logically developed, this B-hypothesis differs from the Socratic view at many points. On the Socratic view the state of the learner preceding the encounter with the teacher is essentially the same as after the encounter. However, on the B-hypothesis the learner's preceding state must be one of lacking the truth, of being in error, a state that Climacus decides to call "sin", because he argues that this state of untruth must be traced to the learner's own free will (*PF*: 14–15). Such a learner will indeed owe the teacher everything, and the transition the learner undergoes is aptly described as a conversion resulting in a new birth (*PF*: 18–19). The teacher who gives the condition is described not as a midwife, but as a saviour, a deliverer and a judge, for we are surely responsible and accountable to someone who has given us new life in this way (*PF*: 17–18).

A simple analogy from the realm of vision may help clarify the distinction between the two views. According to the B-hypothesis a human being is like a person who is blind, and the teacher is similar to the person who heals by giving the blind person the power to see. On the Socratic view, however, a person who does not see is like a person whose eyes happen to be closed. The person essentially already has the power to see, and only needs to be shown how to use that power.[11]

Having developed the logical outline of the B-hypothesis in Chapter 1, Climacus goes on in Chapter 2 to develop the project still further, employing his imagination as well as his intellect in a "poetical venture". Here he asks why God would become our teacher, and answers that the only conceivable motive would be self-giving love. Since God needs nothing from us, his love, unlike the loves we human beings are familiar with, is in no way self-interested. God desires only our good.

However, Climacus claims that any love affair between God and sinful human beings is fraught with difficulty. A love affair between unequals is always problematic, but the difference between rich and poor human beings, or educated and uneducated human beings, pales by comparison with the difference between God and sinful human beings. How can the inequality be overcome and the love-relation consummated?

In a powerful and imaginative analogy, Climacus tells the story of the powerful king who fell in love with a simple maiden. Although he insists that no human analogy really is adequate to describe the divine–human relationship, still he tells a story "in order to awaken the mind to an understanding of the divine" (*PF*: 26). A king who fell in love with a peasant might worry about whether the woman can really love him. He cannot simply order her to love him; genuine love cannot be coerced. And if he simply brings the woman to the palace and dazzles her with his riches and power, he may rightly worry if it is truly himself that the woman loves. In the fairy tale, the king of course solves the problem by donning a disguise and wooing the woman in the guise of a simple peasant. In so doing he risks rejection, but it is the only way he can engender love that is truly love, a love that will be a free response on the part of the woman.

In a similar way, Climacus suggests that if God wishes to become our teacher he would descend to our human level and woo us as a human being. The difference, and it is an important one, is that the God, being omnipotent, does not merely take on a human disguise but actually has the power to become fully human.[12] A God who took such action would, like the king, risk rejection. The learner may misunderstand and even be offended. Only in this way, however, Climacus suggests, could the God communicate to the sinful learner God's own nature as pure love and make possible a genuine response.

In the remainder of the book Climacus explores the nature of the B-hypothesis and how on this view the learner could acquire the Truth. Chapter 3 looks at human attempts to gain knowledge of God, either through "proofs" of God's existence or through a "negative theology" that tries to define God as that which is beyond human reason. Climacus tries to show that from the point of view of the B-hypothesis such attempts are doomed to failure. We can only come to know God if God appears in history as a human teacher, although this event must appear to human reason as a "paradox". (I shall say more about this later.) If human reason insists on its own autonomy and self-sufficiency it will react negatively to this paradox (offence), but it is possible, when the passion of faith is present, for human reason and the paradox to be united in a friendly relationship.

The last two chapters ask what role historical evidence might play in coming to know the God who is assumed to have appeared in history. The answer is essentially the same, both for the disciple at firsthand, who lives at the time of the God's appearance in history (Chapter 4), and for the later disciple who must rely on an historical report (Chapter 5). The historical evidence, whether consisting of direct, firsthand observation or testimony that has been handed down, provides the occasion for faith. However, no amount of historical evidence is sufficient by itself to produce faith, nor can one say that any particular amount of historical evidence is necessary for faith. Rather, faith is a gift from God, something that God creates in the disciple when the disciple encounters God in human form.

What is the point of this extended comparison between the Socratic view and the B-hypothesis? At least on the surface, the comparison is not drawn in order to argue the superiority of one over the other. The book concludes with a "Moral", in which Climacus affirms that he has certainly shown that his alternative hypothesis contains new developments in comparison with the Socratic view, but hastens to add that this does not mean it is truer:

> This project indisputably goes beyond the Socratic, as is apparent at every point. Whether it is therefore more true than the Socratic is an altogether different question, one that cannot be decided in the same breath, inasmuch as a new organ has been assumed here: faith; and a new presupposition: the consciousness of sin; and a new decision: the moment; and a new teacher: the god in time.   (*PF*: 111)

If Climacus does not argue that his invention is truer than the Socratic view, what is the point? The real target is not Plato or Socrates, but contemporary thinkers such as the Danish followers of Hegel and perhaps other progenitors of liberal Protestant Christianity such as Kant. Such views undermine the importance of an authoritative divine revelation by claiming that the truths of religion can be grounded in reason. Thus humans do have the Truth "within" them. These thinkers describe their view as Christianity while putting forward views that are indistinguishable from those of Socrates.

If we make the plausible assumption that the B-hypothesis is intended as an analogue to Christianity, Climacus's target is clear: "But to go beyond Socrates when one nevertheless says essentially the same as he, only not nearly so well – that at least is not Socratic" (*PF*: 111). The position held by followers of Hegel and other liberal Protestants might be correct; human beings may have within them, at least as a community, the capacity for the divine. However, it cannot be correct to describe such a "Socratic" view as Christianity, at least if Climacus is correct in showing that his B-hypothesis (Christianity in a jesting disguise) is logically incompatible with the Socratic view.

The role of the interlocutor: seeing the irony

The reader will have already recognized the suspicious resemblance between the B-hypothesis and Christianity that I just called attention to. Climacus has not exactly been coy about what he is up to, mixing the philosophical language of Plato with obvious Christian terms such as "saviour". In case, however, anyone is too dim to recognize that his "invention" is really not an invention at all, in each chapter we hear from a critical interlocutor, who interrupts Climacus to object to the proceedings. Thus, at the end of Chapter 1, Climacus introduces an objection like this:

> But perhaps someone will say, "This is the most ludicrous of all projects, or, rather, you are the most ludicrous of all project-cranks, for even if someone comes up with a foolish scheme, there is always at least the truth that he is the one who came up with the scheme. But you, on the other hand, are behaving like a vagabond who charges a fee for showing an area that everyone can see. You are like the man who in the afternoon exhibited for a fee a ram that in the morning anyone could see free of charge".
>
> (PF: 21, translation modified)

The interlocutor has in effect charged Climacus with plagiarism for introducing as his own invention the Christianity that everyone in Denmark can recognize.

Climacus' response can only be described as mock penitence: "Maybe so. I hide my face in shame". He is unruffled by the accusation of plagiarism, preferring instead to question the interlocutor about who the real author of the story is. Climacus suggests that the real reason for the interlocutor's annoyance is that Climacus has passed off as his own work something that no human being has authored or could author (*PF*: 21–2).

Essentially the same conversation occurs at the end of Chapter 2, where Climacus imagines "someone" claiming that his composition is "the shabbiest plagiarism ever to appear, since it is nothing more or less than what any child knows" (*PF*: 35). In response Climacus says that his plagiarism is perhaps not so bad, since it is so easily discovered, and he extends the suggestion he had made in Chapter 1 that his "poem" is not a human invention by explicitly proposing that the story comes from "the God". Similar conversations occur at other key points in the book.

The ironical form of the book is now completely evident. Any child in Denmark who had been catechized would know that Christianity is a religion grounded in a special revelation from God, a revelation that occurred decisively in the person of Jesus of Nazareth, understood as God incarnate. Christianity posits that human beings are sinful, incapable of saving themselves through any philosophical insights or self-help programmes. The Christian message is one that comes from God and it is one that human beings neither authored nor could have authored; it is a message about God's plan to do for human beings what human beings cannot do for themselves. The thought experiment of Climacus is indeed an extended jest in that it involves an attempt to invent a view whose content is supposed to be something that no human being could invent.

The irony that pervades the book is thus evident. However, the irony is indeed the "rarer" kind of irony in which something serious is said in the form of a jest, rather than the "common" kind in which something that is apparently serious is really only a jest. To Climacus, and doubtless to Kierkegaard, the "editor" of the volume, it is obvious that a religion such as Christianity is logically distinct from a system of thought that posits that human beings do have the capacity through unaided reason to understand themselves. That Christianity is not just Platonism in somewhat different language is a logical platitude that Kierkegaard could not have intended ironically to undermine. What is ironical is that the intellectual confusion in modern European theology and philosophy has made it necessary to make such a basic logical point in the form of an ironical jest. Through Climacus, Kierkegaard can thus remind his readers of what they already know, by communicating in the form of a jest that a religion that stands or falls on the basis of a claim to revelation cannot be identified with a humanly invented philosophical system.

Seeing the ironical point of *Philosophical Fragments* by no means exhausts the richness of the book's philosophical content, however. In the remainder of this essay, I shall discuss in more detail two of the more philosophically interesting sections of the book. The first issue concerns the nature of the incarnation understood as a paradox and its relation to reason. The second issue deals with the question of whether religious beliefs with historical content must be based on historical evidence.

The absolute paradox and its relation to reason

What does Climacus mean when he says that the appearance of the God in human form would be "the absolute paradox"? The claim that a particular human being is God is paradoxical, he says, because God must be conceived as something absolutely different from a human being. Thus, the idea of an incarnation involves the idea of something absolutely different from a human being becoming a human being. However, this explanation does not help very much; we need to know more about the nature of the difference.

It is tempting to interpret Climacus as thinking of the "absolute difference" between God and human beings as a metaphysical difference, and many commentators have assumed this is the case. On this reading, God is omnipotent, eternal, omniscient, omnipresent and so on, while human beings have the complement of all these properties. The claim that God has become a human being would then be a logical contradiction. To say that God became a human being is like saying that a circle has become a square, and the tension between faith in the incarnation and reason would be clear and stark.

It is true that Climacus says that the paradox involves a "contradiction" (*PF*: 88). However, Climacus frequently uses the term "contradiction" to refer to what we would term an "incongruity" rather than a logical contradiction. For example, he says in *Postscript* that human existence itself includes a contradiction, because of the incongruity between our ideals and our actual achievements, and also that all humour revolves around a "contradiction", for example the contradiction between the upward gaze of a comedian doing a pratfall and his simultaneous downward descent.[13] Hence the use of the term "contradiction" is not here decisive.

Actually, there are very good reasons to doubt that Climacus thinks that an incarnation involves a logical contradiction. For one thing, in order to clearly see that the idea of an incarnation involves a logical contradiction one must have a relatively clear grasp both of what it means to be God and what it means to be a human being. Climacus, however, is sceptical about our understanding of both. He says that even Socrates, "that simple wise man of old", did not really understand human nature (*PF*: 37). And Climacus denies that we have any speculative, philosophical knowledge of God and God's nature. When he says that God is "the Unknown", he means it, and he argues that human attempts to grasp God, whether positive or negative, amount to the production of idols (*PF*: 45). We are too ignorant of both God and human beings to *know* that the idea of the incarnation is logically incoherent.

Of course, our ignorance implies that we also do not know that an incarnation is logically possible. And this ignorance is quite consistent with the view that an incarnation might *seem* or *appear* to be impossible, or at least that it will appear to us to be highly unlikely or improbable. Climacus himself says an incarnation would have just this character; he describes it as "the strangest thing of all" and "the most improbable" thing (*PF*: 52, 101). These descriptions do not imply that the incarnation is logically impossible, but simply that it is the kind of thing that we shall find difficult or impossible to believe.

At one point Climacus actually distinguishes the two different senses in which he uses the term "contradiction" and makes it clear that he is not thinking of the logical sense when he describes the paradox as a contradiction. He says that if a disciple of the God receives "the Condition" of faith from the God, while a later disciple receives it from that first disciple, this would involve a contradiction that would result in "meaninglessness" (*PF*: 101). The reason this is so is that the person who gives a human being the Condition is the God, and the above scenario would imply that the same individual is both God and not-God, since he both receives the Condition from the God and gives the Condition to another. This kind of logical contradiction must be distinguished from the case of the paradox:

> That meaninglessness, however, is unthinkable in a sense different from our stating that that fact and the single individual's relation to the god are unthinkable. Our hypothetical assumption of that fact and the single individual's relation to the god contains no self-contradiction, and thus thought can become preoccupied with it as the strangest thing of all. (*PF*: 101)

Climacus actually makes it perfectly clear that the "absolute difference" between God and human beings that makes the incarnation paradoxical to us is not a metaphysical difference. Of course there are metaphysical differences between God and human beings, at least on the traditional view that God is our creator and we are his creatures. However, Climacus says that those differences would not be the basis of an absolute difference, since if God is our creator then there would be some similarity between God and human beings:

> But if the god is to be absolutely different from a human being, this can have its basis not in that which man owes to the god (for to that extent they are akin) but in that which he owes to himself or in that which he himself has committed. What, then, is the difference? Indeed, what else but sin, since the difference, the absolute difference, must have been caused by the individual himself. (*PF*: 47)

Climacus seems to hold the view, then, that we cannot know that an incarnation is possible or impossible, but such a thing does seem highly unlikely or improbable to us because our sinfulness does not allow us to understand God or God's ways. An incarnation motivated by pure self-giving love is an event that we have no other experience of, and if Hume is right in thinking that we estimate probability at least partly on the basis of the frequency with which events of a certain type occur, then we can understand why we might think the probability of such an event is small indeed.[14]

What, then, is the relation between reason and faith in the paradox, according to Climacus? The traditional options are that faith should either be conceived as something that is in accord with or grounded in reason, something that is above reason, or something that is against reason. On my reading, Climacus certainly does not hold the first view. The paradoxicalness of the incarnation rules out basing faith on reason. The second view seems closer to the mark. The incarnation is something that is to reason incomprehensible, something beyond the limits of reason that reason is not competent to evaluate.

However, although the incarnation is not a logical contradiction and thus is not fundamentally against reason, there is a tension between reason and faith that Climacus wants to emphasize and not downplay. We must be careful here. The tension is not a necessary one, but it is nevertheless prevalent and real. The tension arises from what we might term the imperialistic character of human reason: its natural reluctance to acknowledge that it is subject to limits or that there are realities it cannot understand. Climacus says that when reason encounters the paradox: "The understanding certainly cannot think it, cannot hit upon it on its own, and when it is proclaimed the understanding cannot understand it and merely detects that it will likely be its downfall. Insofar, the understanding has much to object to …"(PF: 47).[15]

However, Climacus immediately goes on to assert that this negative reaction on the part of reason is not the only possible one. There is an ambivalence in reason in that the limit that it fears and resists is also what it is seeking: "in its paradoxical passion the understanding does indeed will its own downfall" (PF: 47). If reason insists that it has no limits and refuses to recognize anything it cannot understand, then it will be offended by the paradox. However, offence is not the only possible reaction. The alternative to the passion of offence is the passion of faith, a condition in which "the understanding and the paradox happily encounter each other in the moment, when the understanding steps aside and the paradox gives itself" (PF: 59).

Climacus tries to illustrate faith and offence as the two possible ways reason may react to the paradox by using an analogy drawn from the realm of romantic love, even though he acknowledges that this provides an "imperfect metaphor" (PF: 48): "Self-love lies at the basis of love, but at its peak its paradoxical passion wills its own downfall. Erotic love also wills this, and therefore these two forces are in mutual understanding in the moment of passion, and this passion is precisely erotic love" (PF: 48). Climacus then draws the analogy: "So also with the paradox's relation to the understanding, except that this passion has another name, or, rather, we must simply try to find a name for it" (PF: 48).

What light does this shed on the relation between faith and human reason? We must first seek to understand what is being said about love. I think Climacus means to say that the original ground of romantic love for another is self-love. When people fall in love they are initially seeking their own happiness; when I begin to fall in love I find joy and pleasure in the company of this other enchanting person. However, when a person begins to love another person deeply, there is a transformation. As I begin to care about the one I love I begin to weigh her happiness more highly than my own. Or, to put it more paradoxically, to be happy I become willing to sacrifice my own happiness, because this is what love demands. In some way this passion of love is supposed to be similar to the happy passion that allows reason and the paradox to be on good terms, the passion Climacus names "faith" in the next chapter.

Of course, not every person is able to fall in love. Climacus describes a selfish person who "in self-love shrinks from erotic love". Such a person can neither understand nor commit to genuine love (*PF*: 48). This kind of selfish self-love is supposed to illuminate the unhappy reaction of reason to the paradox that Climacus calls "offence".

One important point that Climacus is making is that both faith and offence are indeed passions. Human reason is not a neutral judge in this matter, and when reason accuses the paradoxical revelation of being "absurd" it is not, as it would like to appear to be, simply rendering a dispassionate verdict that is grounded in objective evidence.

This is not surprising, since this revelational paradox must itself be seen as a kind of accusation against human reason, and a person who is not willing to acknowledge the truth of the accusation will naturally resent the charge. We must remember that it is sin that is supposed to make it impossible for human beings to understand God's true nature. It is certainly possible that there are limits to human reason; in fact, that there are some limits is virtually indisputable. The question concerns the nature of those limits and the ability of human reason to recognize them. Climacus spins a story in which human reason is limited by its sinfulness, and he claims that a reason that is willing to acknowledge those limits can be on good terms with God's revelation. A reason that stubbornly insists that it has no limits and that what it cannot understand must be nonsense will naturally be offended.

But must not reason have some ability in order to recognize its own limits? The answer to this is clearly yes. If the passion of faith is one in which reason and the paradox are on good terms, then it must be possible for reason to recognize its damaged character and respond positively to God's offer of healing, and this implies that reason, although damaged, is not completely destroyed. But that is precisely the view Climacus offers. The definition he gives of faith is that faith is a condition in which reason "yields itself" or "surrenders itself". It is reason that does the surrendering. Even though reason could not discover its limits apart from God's revelation, it still has a choice as to whether to recognize those limits once they have been revealed.

It is this fact that allows Climacus to hold that human beings still have some responsibility in the matter; he does not see faith simply as a condition that God creates in an individual without the individual's consent, as might be the case for some form of extreme Calvinism. Rather, he insists that the "act of consciousness" in which a person discovers his own untruth is one to which "the Socratic principle applies: the teacher is only an occasion, whoever he may be, even if he is a god, because I can discover my own untruth only by myself" (*PF*: 14). This, he says, is "the one and only analogy" between the B-hypothesis and the Socratic view of the Truth (*PF*: 14).

Climacus thus attempts to turn the critical attacks on the rationality of the incarnation back on the attacker. When reason accuses the paradox of being absurd, the proper response of faith is to view these attacks as providing "an indirect testing of the correctness of the paradox" (*PF*: 51). The attacks of reason are actually an echo, an "acoustic illusion", in which the self-understanding of revelation is repeated by reason as if it were an objection. To this the paradox replies, "It is just as you say, and the amazing thing is that you think it is an objection, but the truth in the mouth of a hypocrite is dearer to me than to hear it from an angel and an apostle" (*PF*: 52).

The content of the B-hypothesis, understood as a pretended "invention" that embodies the heart of the Christian revelation, is supposed to be something that human reason cannot understand. What reason could have hit upon on its own would not need to be revealed by a divine teacher. Thus, the fact that the content of the Christian revelation turns out to be something human reason cannot fully grasp is not an objection, but precisely what one would expect to be the case if that revelation is a genuine one.

One would hardly expect that this argument would convince a critic of the Christian revelation that the revelation is genuine. How can the issue be decided? Perhaps there is no neutral body of evidence that can be appealed to. However, that is at least one of the points Climacus wishes to make. Faith and offence are both possibilities when reason confronts this paradoxical revelation. Which response is chosen, on his view, will be shaped by such factors as a person's willingness honestly to recognize his or her own selfish character that blocks a person from understanding God's self-giving love. Neither response is determined by rational evidence.

Faith and historical evidence

The claim of Climacus that rational evidence does not and should not determine the response of a person to the claim that God has become incarnate goes against a widely held assumption. We normally think that beliefs with historical content must be based on historical evidence. There is strong historical evidence that George Washington was the first president of the United States, so that is a reasonable historical belief. However, there is little evidence for the famous story that George Washington chopped down a cherry tree as a boy and then confessed to his father, and so historians consider the story a non-historical myth. One would naturally think, then, that to believe that Jesus of Nazareth was God incarnate one would have to have historical evidence for this claim.

Nevertheless, in "inventing" his B-hypothesis, Johannes Climacus rejects the idea that belief in the God's appearance can or should be determined by evidence or by the lack of evidence. However surprising this view may be, Climacus does present arguments on its behalf, and I shall show that his view is quite similar to those of some other contemporary philosophers of religion who defend what has come to be called "Reformed epistemology".

The primary arguments Climacus gives are found in the "Interlude" between Chapters 4 and 5. He begins with an analysis of historical beliefs in general. To use Humean language, Climacus says that historical beliefs are a species of "matters of fact" and matters of fact can never be logically demonstrated.[16] The events themselves are only contingently true, since they have undergone the change of "coming into existence". What is contingently true cannot be understood as necessary, but this is what a logical demonstration requires (*PF*: 72–8).

Historical knowledge in the proper sense (as opposed to what we might call "natural history") is contingent in a double sense. Such events, because they involve free human decisions, include a "coming into existence [human action] within a coming into existence [nature]" (*PF*: 76). We have not only the uncertainty included in any matter of fact but a new level of uncertainty that corresponds to the contingency of free human behaviour. The apprehension of history then requires the negation of this uncertainty, and Climacus says that this is what faith or belief (the Danish word for both is *tro*) amounts to (*PF*: 81). The ancient sceptics are cited to show that beliefs of this sort are not determined simply by evidence (*PF*: 82–5). Fundamentally, the sceptic willed to be a sceptic, but the logical gap between our evidence and our beliefs is what allowed the sceptic to be a sceptic. It follows that those of us who are not sceptics have the beliefs we do because we do not want to be sceptics. We want to have beliefs. The human will thus plays a key role in faith or belief, not in the sense that we can simply manufacture beliefs at will but in the sense that what we wind up believing is fundamentally shaped by our deepest desires. The idea is not that we can perform a mental act and thereby turn beliefs on and off, but rather something close to Hume's claim that reason is the "slave of the passions". For Kierkegaard to will something is simply to have a fully formed desire, a desire that will lead to results.

All of this is true for what Climacus calls "ordinary" belief, beliefs about ordinary historical events. Even in ordinary cases, evidence alone does not produce belief. If we want to be sceptics that option is open to us, although such scepticism may not be easy because life has a way of eliciting belief from us. However, the idea of God becoming a human being creates special difficulties. Here we have the uncertainty that is present in all historical beliefs combined with the special uncertainty that the historical event in question is a paradox, something reason cannot understand. Climacus calls this faith or belief "in the eminent sense". When dealing with faith in the eminent sense, there is no way to establish the probability of the event by looking at the historical evidence. Perhaps in ordinary cases, evidence can at least make an event probable. However, in this case we have no way of estimating the probability of the event: no way of determining how likely it is that God would become a human being.

Suppose that I observed an ordinary-looking human being who claimed to be God. Even if this person appeared to perform stupendous miracles, and seemed to be perfectly morally good, it is hard to see how these historical facts could warrant the claim that the individual was divine. Or so Climacus claims, since he says one would always have the counter-evidence that the individual appears to be an ordinary human being, and all our experience suggests that such creatures are not gods. Human reason cannot understand how the creator of the universe could come to be a part of that universe, and, if human beings are sinful, perhaps we human beings cannot even recognize the character of the divine love such an incarnation would manifest.

One might think that if historical evidence is not sufficient to warrant belief then one must opt for unbelief, and that faith would then be irrational. However, Climacus does not see things this way. Since the content of the revelation, if true, is something that human reason would not expect to understand and acquire evidence for, our failure to find historical evidence that directly leads to belief is not decisive.

How, then, does faith arise if it not based on evidence? According to Climacus it is a gift, something produced in the individual by "the God" when the individual encounters God. For those who lived at the time of the God's historical appearance, this encounter might be mediated by actually seeing or hearing the God. For later generations, the encounter would be mediated by historical reports. In both cases, Climacus says that such historical evidence would be the "occasion" for faith, but that faith is actually something that God himself creates within the individual (*PF*: 69–70, 100). As we saw above, this does not imply that the individual has no choice in the matter, since the individual may refuse to recognize the sinfulness that necessitates the creation of the faith that makes the person a new creature. Faith for Climacus is "the condition" that allows the individual to apprehend the Truth, and each individual, whether a temporal contemporary, or later follower, must receive the condition personally from the God (*PF*: 103).

We can now understand why the acquisition of faith is not dependent on historical evidence. Even the greatest possible amount of historical evidence would not by itself be sufficient to lead to the kind of personal transformation that is equivalent to the acquisition of faith. Neither can one specify any particular amount of evidence as necessary for such a transformation, for it is conceivable that God could use a mere scrap of paper with a few scant words of testimony as the occasion for such a transformation (*PF*: 104).

Climacus's claim that historical evidence is neither sufficient nor necessary for faith does not imply that such evidence is entirely irrelevant to or without value for faith, although it is not clear that Climacus himself recognizes this. Although God could develop faith without evidence, it is also possible that evidence is one of the normal means God employs to create faith in an individual. In so far as a person is committed to some historical belief "*p*" it is hard to see how one could be indifferent to evidence that bears on the truth of "*p*". For example, a Christian would hardly be indifferent if some historian claimed to have overwhelming evidence that the story of Jesus was concocted in the eighth century. After all, a belief that is not based on evidence could still be defeated or overturned on the basis of evidence. However, it is difficult in practice to imagine any historical discoveries that would make it impossible to hold to historical Christian beliefs.

Kierkegaard and Reformed epistemology

Contemporary philosophy of religion has seen the development of a debate between evidentialists and non-evidentialists with respect to essential religious beliefs. Evidentialists, including defenders of religious belief such as Richard Swinburne as well as critics of belief, hold that a justified belief must be based on evidence. Non-evidentialists, notably Reformed epistemologists such as

Alvin Plantinga, reject this view along with its underlying epistemology. Most evidentialists have been epistemological internalists, holding that whether a belief is justified or even amounts to knowledge depends partly on its being based on reasons to which we have internal, conscious access. Reformed epistemologists reject this view in favour of epistemological externalism, which holds that a belief may be "warranted" (to use Plantinga's terminology) even if it is not based on any evidence to which we have access. My beliefs that there is an external world in front of me and that the people around me have conscious minds similar to my own are warranted even if I cannot give any good philosophical arguments for them. The beliefs are warranted because, to paraphrase Plantinga, they are the product of "faculties designed to reach truth that are working properly in the kind of environment in which they were designed to function."[17]

Externalists in general seem to be attracted by an intuition that knowledge requires us to be in the right relation with external reality, a relation that allows our beliefs to "track" with reality. However, we may not always be able to tell, just by accessing our consciousness, that we are in such a relation. We may not be able to prove that we are not being deceived by a Cartesian evil demon or that we are not brains in vats. If such conditions hold, then too bad for us. If they do not, then perhaps knowledge is possible.

Plantinga has now applied this kind of epistemology to the question of whether Christian beliefs are warranted. Plantinga had argued in earlier work that belief in God could be "properly basic", grounded in experiences that God has designed to evoke faith in himself, but without those experiences functioning as providing propositional evidence for God's existence.[18] In *Warranted Christian Belief*, Plantinga develops what he calls the "Extended Aquinas–Calvin Model" in which full-blooded Christian beliefs, including those with historical content, are viewed as beliefs that are not based on evidence. Rather, these beliefs are the product of faith, something God creates in the person when that person encounters God's revelation.[19] Plantinga argues that if Christianity is true then this is a plausible account of how Christian truths could be known, and he argues that there are no cogent objections to this model that do not presuppose the falsity of Christianity. From the point of view of Plantinga's externalist epistemology, in which a true belief gets converted to knowledge if it is produced by a process that is designed to attain truth and is working reliably in the right circumstances, Christian beliefs can be viewed as knowledge, at least by anyone who does not claim to know that Christianity is false.

There are certainly differences between Plantinga and the views Kierkegaard has Climacus develop in *Philosophical Fragments*. Some of these differences are real and some are merely apparent.[20] However, for both thinkers the historical beliefs that are part of Christian faith are fundamentally the work of God and not directly based on evidence. The plausibility of such an account is linked to the externalist epistemology that accompanies it. From the perspective of the kind of classical foundationalism characteristic of Enlightenment epistemologies, such views appear wrong-headed, for knowledge requires that our beliefs be based on certain evidence. If, however, we give up the view that human beings are godlike knowers capable of refuting scepticism, in favour of the view that whether we can know and what we can know depend on how we happen to be related to the reality we are trying to know, then the views of Kierkegaard and Plantinga make sense. Neither has provided, or even attempted, a neutral defence of Christian beliefs. Instead, they have raised the question as to whether such beliefs can truly be considered at all from a neutral perspective.

Notes

1. Søren Kierkegaard, *Concluding Unscientific Postscript*, H. V. Hong & E. H. Hong (eds and trans.) (Princeton, NJ: Princeton University Press, 1992), 627.
2. Niels Thulstrup, "Commentator's Introduction", in *Philosophical Fragments*, D. Swenson (trans.), H. V. Hong (rev. trans. and commentary) (Princeton, NJ: Princeton University Press, 1962), xlv.
3. *Ibid.*, lxxxv.
4. Roger Poole, "The Unknown Kierkegaard: Twentieth-Century Receptions", in *The Cambridge Companion to Kierkegaard*, A. Hannay & G. D. Marino (eds), 48–75 (Cambridge: Cambridge University Press, 1998), 62.
5. See James Conant, "Kierkegaard, Wittgenstein, and Nonsense", in *Pursuits of Reason*, T. Cohen, P. Guyer & H. Putnam (eds), 195–224 (Lubbock, TX: Texas Tech University Press, 1993).
6. For the response of Climacus to the review, see Kierkegaard, *Concluding Unscientific Postscript*, 274–7n. For Kierkegaard's comments see *Søren Kierkegaard's Journals and Papers*, vol. V, H. V. Hong & E. H. Hong (eds and trans.) (Bloomington, IN: Indiana University Press, 1978), 284, entry #5827.
7. Søren Kierkegaard, *The Concept of Irony*, H. V. Hong & E. H. Hong (eds and trans.) (Princeton, NJ: Princeton University Press, 1989), 248.
8. All parenthetical page references are from Søren Kierkegaard, *Philosophical Fragments*, H. V. Hong & E. H. Hong (eds and trans.) (Princeton, NJ: Princeton University Press, 1985).
9. Nineteenth-century Danish capitalized all nouns. Thus, a translator must make a decision as to whether a noun is being used as a proper noun or a common noun. For reasons that will become clear below I think that the term *Sandheden* should be translated as "the Truth" to indicate that it is a particular truth is the object of the discussion.
10. By "the doctrine of recollection", Climacus means to refer to the Platonic view that human beings have an innate knowledge of "the Forms": universal concepts understood as eternal realities, which were known prior to birth but have been "forgotten",

obscured and covered over. Learning is thus a recalling of these truths that were known when the soul existed apart from the body. Plato himself sees this innate knowledge as evidence that the human soul itself has an eternal character, and Climacus follows Plato in linking the two ideas.

11. My thanks to the editor for suggesting this analogy.

12. For a fuller discussion of this "kenotic Christology" see my "The Self-Emptying of Love: Some Thoughts on Kenotic Christology", in *The Incarnation*, S. T. Davis, D. Kendall, SJ, & G. O'Collins, SJ(eds), 246–72 (Oxford: Oxford University Press, 2002).

13. See Kierkegaard, *Concluding Unscientific Postscript*, 516n, where there is a discussion of the "contradiction" between an upward gaze and a downward ascent.

14. I don't mean to suggest here that Climacus (or Kierkegaard) has been directly influenced by Hume, although there may well be some indirect influence from Hume through Hamann, a German thinker much influenced by Hume. Kierkegaard read Hamann carefully and cites him in *Philosophical Fragments*.

15. By "reason" I have in mind our human capacity to draw and justify conclusions on the basis of argument and evidence. Kierkegaard actually uses the Danish term "*Forstanden*", translated properly as "understanding". Of course Hegel and other philosophers of the period make a distinction between "understanding" (*Verstehen*) and reason (*Vernunft*). However, I think it is clear that this distinction has no importance for Kierkegaard, since he does not, like Hegel, think that human beings have a "higher capacity" of reason that allows them to know the Infinite, but rather wants to argue that our human intellectual capacities are strongly limited. Hence I have used "reason" and "understanding" interchangeably in discussing Kierkegaard's view.

16. To repeat a point made earlier, although Kierkegaard apparently did not read Hume, and there may be no direct allusion to Hume here, it is likely that Hume's philosophy had some influence on Kierkegaard via Hamann.

17. See Alvin Plantinga, *Warrant and Proper Function* (Oxford: Oxford University Press, 1993), for a fuller account of warrant that takes account of several technical points here ignored.

18. See Alvin Plantinga, "Reason and Belief in God", in *Faith and Rationality*, A. Plantinga & N. Wolterstorff (eds) (Notre Dame, IN: University of Notre Dame Press, 1983).

19. See Alvin Plantinga, *Warranted Christian Belief* (Oxford: Oxford University Press, 2000), 241–89.

20. See my "Externalist Epistemology, Subjectivity, and Christian Knowledge: Plantinga and Kierkegaard" in *Vernünftig*, R. Berndt (ed.), 13–40 (Würzberg: Echter Verlag, 2003).

References

Conant, J. 1993. "Kierkegaard, Wittgenstein, and Nonsense". In *Pursuits of Reason*, T. Cohen, P. Guyer & H. Putnam (eds), 195–224. Lubbock, TX: Texas Tech University Press.

Evans, C. S. 2002. "The Self-Emptying of Love: Some Thoughts on Kenotic Christology". In *The Incarnation*, S. T. Davis, D. Kendall, SJ, & G. O'Collins, SJ(eds), 246–72. Oxford: Oxford University Press.

Evans, C. S. 2003. "Externalist Epistemology, Subjectivity, and Christian Knowledge: Plantinga and Kierkegaard". In *Vernünftig*, R. Berndt (ed.), 13–40. Würzberg: Echter Verlag.

Kierkegaard, S. 1978. *Søren Kierkegaard's Journals and Papers*, vol. V, H. V. Hong & E. H. Hong (eds and trans.) (Bloomington, IN: Indiana University Press, 1978).

Kierkegaard, S. 1985. *Philosophical Fragments*, H. V. Hong & E. H. Hong (eds and trans.) . Princeton, NJ: Princeton University Press.

Kierkegaard, S. 1989. *The Concept of Irony*, H. V. Hong & E. H. Hong (eds and trans.). Princeton, NJ: Princeton University Press.

Kierkegaard, S. 1992. *Concluding Unscientific Postscript*, H. V. Hong & E. H. Hong (eds and trans.). Princeton, NJ: Princeton University Press.

Plantinga, A. 1983. "Reason and Belief in God". In *Faith and Rationality*, A. Plantinga & N. Wolterstorff (eds), 16–91. Notre Dame, IN: University of Notre Dame Press.

Plantinga, A. 1993. *Warrant and Proper Function*. Oxford: Oxford University Press.

Plantinga, A. 2000. *Warranted Christian Belief*. Oxford: Oxford University Press.

Poole, R. 1998. "The Unknown Kierkegaard: Twentieth-Century Receptions". In *The Cambridge Companion to Kierkegaard*, A. Hannay & G. D. Marino (eds), 48–75. Cambridge: Cambridge University Press.

Thulstrup, N. 1962. "Commentator's Introduction". In *Philosophical Fragments*, D. Swenson (trans.), H. V. Hong (rev. trans. and commentary). Princeton, NJ: Princeton University Press.

Further reading

There are two English translations of *Philosophical Fragments*. The most recent is in the *Kierkegaard's Writings* series: Søren Kierkegaard, *Philosophical Fragments*, H. V. Hong & E. H. Hong (eds and trans.) (Princeton, NJ: Princeton University Press, 1985). The older translation is *Philosophical Fragments*, D. Swenson (trans.), H. V. Hong (rev. trans. and commentary)(Princeton, NJ: Princeton University Press, 1962). Kierkegaard himself attributes one other of his pseudonymous books to "Johannes Climacus": *Concluding Unscientific Postscript*, H. V. Hong & E. H. Hong (eds and trans.) (Princeton, NJ: Princeton University Press, 1992). All of Kierkegaard's published works are available in *Kierkegaard's Writings*, 26 vols, H. V. Hong & E. H. Hong (eds) (Princeton, NJ: Princeton University Press, 1978–2002).

The following books about *Philosophical Fragments* are highly recommended: C. S. Evans, *Kierkegaard's Fragments and Postscript: The Religious Philosophy of Johannes Climacus* (Atlanta Highlands, NJ: Humanities Press, 1983) (reprinted in 1999 by Humanity Books, an imprint of Prometheus Books) and *Passionate Reason: Making Sense of Kierkegaard's Philosophical Fragments* (Bloomington, IN: Indiana University Press, 1992); H. A. Nielsen, *Where the Passion Is: A Reading of Kierkegaard's Philosophical Fragments* (Tallahassee, FL: Florida State University Press, 1983); and R. C. Roberts, *Faith, Reason, and History: Rethinking Kierkegaard's Philosophical Fragments* (Macon, GA: Mercer University Press, 1986). A fine collection of articles about *Philosophical Fragments* can be found in R. Perkins (ed.), *International Kierkegaard Commentary: vol. VII, Philosophical Fragments and Johannes Climacus* (Macon, GA: Mercer University Press, 1994).

The following books about Kierkegaard are also recommended, although they do not necessarily focus specifically on *Philosophical Fragments*: J. Collins, *The Mind of Kierkegaard*, 2nd edn (Princeton, NJ: Princeton University Press, 1983); P. Gardiner, *Kierkegaard* (Oxford: Oxford University Press, 1988). J. D. Mullen, *Self-Deception and Cowardice in the Present Age* (Lanham, MD: University Press of America, 1995); and M. Westphal, *Kierkegaard's Critique of Reason and Society* (University Park, PA: The Pennsylvania State University Press, 1991).

7

Karl Marx
Capital

Tom Rockmore

This chapter will discuss Marx's conception of political economy as illustrated in *Capital*. Marx's conception of political economy is based on his philosophical views. I see no way to separate them. This chapter will discuss some of the differences between Marxian and "orthodox" political economy, then take *Capital* as the illustration of the Marxian approach, and end with some further remarks about Marx's conception of political economy. In discussing *Capital*, emphasis will be placed on a simple presentation of Marx's main points. I shall cite a large number of passages from the book in order to help the reader to perceive the flavour of Marx's writing and to understand Marx in Marx's own words.

In order to be clear about Marxian political economy, it will be necessary to free it from Marxism. Marxism insists on the discontinuity between Marx and Hegel, Marxian political economy and philosophy. I shall be insisting, on the contrary, on the continuity between Marx and Hegel, and Marxian political economy and philosophy. Similarly, orthodox, or mainstream, economics insists on the difference in kind between economics and politics, whereas Marx underlines their continuity and, as a direct consequence, calls attention to the intrinsically political character of economics. The main point I shall be making is that Marxian political economy and mainstream economy are not directly comparable, but different, and that at a time when Marxism seems to have declined in a way that cannot be recovered, the Marxian approach to political economy has never been more relevant.

On understanding Marx

Marxism is the series of doctrines mainly due to Engels, the first Marxist, and adopted on political grounds by a series of writers who claim to speak in Marx's name. Marxism generally sees Marx as breaking with Hegel and with philosophy in general. Since Marx's position is not independent of, but rather dependent on, his view of philosophy, we need to see Marx as criticizing Hegel (and hence any kind of philosophy), but as remaining within Hegel's overall position and, more generally, within philosophy.

To the best of my knowledge, no important Marxist denies the supposed continuity between Marxism and Marx. Marxists generally present Marxism as the further development of Marx's views. Marxism generally includes claims that Marx is not a philosopher, or that he began in philosophy, but later left it behind. He is most often described as a political economist, and Engels is often described, as he described himself, as the philosopher of Marxism. Marxism, hence Marx's position as well, is routinely held to reject what Marxists call bourgeois philosophy, and hence not only to criticize, but to reject, Hegel.

The Marxist descriptions of Marx and Marxism typically stress discontinuity between Marx and the philosophical tradition. This discontinuity was called into question through the tardy publication of such early Marxian writings as the *Paris Manuscripts* (1964b) and the *Grundrisse* (1970b). These texts focused attention on continuity between Marx and philosophy, or between the later Marxian emphasis on political economy and the early Marxian emphasis on philosophy. The emphasis on continuity between the early Marx and the late Marx in turn suggests a discontinuity between Marx and Marxism, and between Marx and the Marxist view of Marx. It also called attention to the importance of his early studies in philosophy, which had until then appeared irrelevant, for the formulation of his position.

The Marxist reading of Marx, which was initially formulated by Engels (Engels 1941 [1888]) and which has been routinely accepted by Marxists, non-Marxists and anti-Marxists alike, has been a main and continuing obstacle over many years to understanding Marx. The relation of Marx to Hegel is mentioned by almost everyone who writes on Marx, but it is rarely studied in detail. The Marxist reading of this relation is mainly based on a single passage in *Capital*, where Marx obscurely indicates that his own position is the inversion of Hegel's. In this context he makes the famous remark about dialectic, which is frequently cited: "With him it [i.e. dialectic] is standing on its head. It must be turned right side up again, if you would discover the rational kernel within the mystical shell" (Marx 1975: 19).

Marx is here using an inversion metaphor, which occurs frequently in his writings. This metaphor was popularized slightly earlier in Feuerbach's studies of religion (Feuerbach 1957). Yet whatever Marx means by this metaphor, there is no way to show that his own position is the "inversion" of Hegel's. And there is also no way to show that as a result of the supposed inversion he either breaks with Hegel or, more radically, leaves philosophy behind.

Marxism typically asserts that Marx is a political economist, and that in that role he simply rejects Hegel, or Hegelian idealism. The idea that, in coming to grips with Hegel, Marx left philosophy reflects the young Hegelian view, famously stated by the great German Romantic poet Heinrich Heine, Hegel's former student and a friend of Marx, that philosophy comes to a peak and to an end in Hegel (Heine 1986). Yet the suggestion that any criticism of a philosophical position could result in an extra-philosophical position is false in general and as concerns Marx.

Marx took his PhD in philosophy at a time when the debate was still dominated by Hegel. Every philosopher identifies and criticizes the supposed deficiencies of others in the course of formulating another position intended to correct them. In criticizing Kant, Hegel no more leaves philosophy behind than, in criticizing Hegel, Marx leaves philosophy behind. Marx's relation to Hegel is similar to Hegel's relation to Kant.

Marx is the thinker in the immediate post-Hegelian debate who remains closest to Hegel. It is incorrect to think that Marx can somehow be reduced to Hegel, or that in reacting to Hegel Marx somehow breaks out of philosophy. It is rather correct to understand Marx's position as arising through his effort to criticize, continue and complete Hegel's position through further work within the connected domains of philosophy and political economy.

Marxian philosophy

There is much confusion in the literature about the relation of Marx to philosophy, hence about the basic outlines of his philosophical position. Since Hegel was the dominant philosopher in Germany when Marx was a student, it is hardly surprising that Marx's philosophical views develop in the first place through a critique of Hegel's. The confusion is partly due to two exaggerated claims. One is the belief that Marx's position differs not only in degree but also in kind from Hegel's. The other is the conviction, widespread after Hegel, that in Hegel philosophy reaches its peak and its end. Taken together, these two claims yield the inference that Marx's position differs from philosophy itself. If this were correct, then Marx simply could not be a philosopher in any relevant sense. In fact, philosophy does not come to an end but continues after Hegel, and Marx develops a philosophical position that criticizes as well as develops key insights found in German idealism, within which Hegel's position belongs.

Marx is a philosopher of modern industrial society whose approach applies certain philosophical insights developed in German idealism with respect to the problem of knowledge in working out a theory of the modern social context. In simplest terms, Marx's theory of modern industrial society is based on a revised view of the German idealist approach to knowledge through the idea that we know only what we construct. In German philosophy, this insight originates in Kant's critical philosophy. Kant is an epistemologist who proposes a theory of knowledge based on a so-called Copernican revolution in philosophy, or the enigmatic claim, which we cannot discuss here, that in the final analysis we know only what we "construct". The post-Kantian German idealist tradition develops this insight beyond Kant. What for Kant is an abstract theory of the conditions of the possibility of knowledge whatsoever, or in the most general sense, becomes in such post-Kantians as Fichte, Schelling and Hegel a theory of knowledge rooted in and inseparable from the social context.

The key change is a shift towards philosophical anthropology. As a result, Kant's abstract theory of the philosophical subject gives way to finite human beings. Kant's austere epistemological construction of the cognitive object is replaced by the social construction of human society through historical time. Hegel, to whom Marx reacts, proposes a theory of knowledge, or cognition, as a phenomenology of conscious experience, and a theory of society as the historical result of the human efforts at self-realization in the nation-state that is the modern form of the ancient Greek city-state.

Marx continues the post-Kantian move towards philosophical anthropology in transforming and building on its specifically Hegelian form. A simple way to describe Marx's philosophical position is to say that he further transforms the Kantian insight that we know what we in some sense construct by proposing, on the basis of a theory of human beings as active, a theory of human society, human being and human knowledge.

Marx's philosophical position centres on a conception of the subject. According to Marx, a person is basically active. Our activity, which takes two basic forms, is directed toward two ends: work, or labour, in which we produce products in order to meet our reproductive needs, such as food, clothing and shelter, without which we would cease to exist; and what one can call free human activity with the aim of developing one's capacities, hence oneself as an individual. In a society based on private property, people become workers in the course of meeting their reproductive needs. In and through their work, they produce products, and a series of social relations governing the status of workers and owners, and in the process themselves as workers. Work serves to meet reproductive needs but, in reducing the human individual to the economic role of meeting one's immediate reproductive needs, is unrelated to developing one's specific human capacities. The latter is possible only outside the economic process, which, Marx believes, must eventually be brought under control in order to create free time in which one can develop one's own talents in ways that may have nothing at all to do with economics, but everything to do with realizing oneself as a fully individualized human being.

It is obvious, if we are to create the real possibility of development of everyone, that we need to increase economic development to a point at which human beings can be at least partly freed from the daily round. By the same token, Marx sees the transition from capitalism to communism as loosening the hold of mere economic gain on the great mass of people. The overall interest in human self-development in modern industrial society impels Marx to construct a theory of the modern world based finally on a theory of finite human being, or a philosophical anthropology, which requires a detailed analysis of the economic component of the modern world, in short an analysis of modern industrial society, which reaches its highest point in *Capital*.

Marx, Hegel and political economy

How does this relate to political economy? Like Hegel, when Marx turns to political economy he is not opposing economics to philosophy. Marxism emphasizes a supposed discontinuity between Marx and Hegel. On the contrary, the continuity between these two thinkers is startling and instructive. Both are concerned with the realization of human freedom in the modern social context. Hegel, who studied political economy as it existed in his own times, was well aware that meaningful freedom depends on economic conditions. Hegel's interest in political economy is an important aspect of his overall position. Like Hegel and, more recently, the Indian economist and Nobel laureate Amartya Sen (Sen 1999), Marx also thinks that economic development is a necessary prerequisite to meaningful freedom.

Private property is central to the modern state and, on some analyses, also central to the realization of human freedom. A useful way to grasp Marx's understanding of political economy, including its relation to philosophy, is his reaction to Hegel's views of property.

Like Marx, Hegel studies modern industrial society, or capitalism, through the lens of private property. The crucial difference between their respective views of modern industrial society, hence the crucial difference between their respective positions, can be expressed through different conceptions of property. A simple way to put the point is to say that Hegel takes a legal approach to property, which Marx transforms into an economic approach.

In the *Philosophy of Right* Hegel treats property as a legal right acknowledged by law, valid in civil society, and protected by contract (Hegel 1967: §§208, 217, 218.) He is sensitive to the failure of modern liberal economy to solve the persistent problem of poverty (*ibid.*: §203), and worried about its possibly destabilizing consequences. According to Hegel, in the modern state, the abstract principle of freedom is actualized in the protection of property through what he calls the administration of justice (*ibid.*: §§ 209–29).

In "Contribution to the Critique of Hegel's Philosophy of Right", Marx complains that civil society, as distinguished from the state within which it is a subset, is in fact very different from and more important than Hegel's grasp of it. According to Marx, capitalism produces conflicts between individuals within civil society that the state cannot resolve since it largely functions to protect the interests in private property that generate the conflicts. Hegel postulates an identity of interest between individuals and the state. Yet Marx insists that the single most important factor is the role of private property in civil society. It is, then, not the state that determines civil society, but rather civil society and, prior to it, the institution of private property that determine the state.

From a Marxian perspective, Hegel provides a phenomenological (or kinematic description) of modern society centred on a legal view of property. Yet he does not analyse the central economic motor of capitalism, since he treats property in a juridical, and not an economic, sense. Marx, who grasps the economic function of property as the central element in modern industrial society, substitutes a dynamic analysis for Hegel's descriptive analysis of the modern world. For Marx, capitalism is based on the private ownership of the means of production, or private property. He thinks of the origin, functioning of and possible alternative to modern capitalism in the wake of the Industrial Revolution in terms of the central institution of private property.

The publication history of *Capital*

Capital is both the name of a book and a reference to a specific concept in a conceptual framework intended to understand modern liberal market-driven economy, or capitalism.

The publication history of *Capital* is a good example of Marx's chronic inability to bring his work to completion. This enormous study has come down to us as three fat volumes plus the additional three huge tomes intended to make up the fourth volume, and finally published as *Theories of Surplus Value*. The first volume of *Capital* is the only one actually published by Marx himself. The second and third volumes were largely ready in manuscript during the 1860s. Marx did not die until 1883, some sixteen years after the appearance of the first one in 1867. But he was in poor health most of the time and he was unable to finish the rest of the work.

The publication history of *Capital* reflects a series of changes introduced into Marx's original publication by his own and other hands, as Engels edited and directed the translation into English. It is an open question as to how closely Engels's textual emendations correspond to Marx's own intentions. Changes concern even the number of chapters. Anyone who has ever looked at the German original knows it is divided into 25 chapters that, in English translation, have swollen to 33 chapters.[1]

Capital has long been widely acknowledged as Marx's masterpiece, and in any case his principal economic work. Marx spent forty years working on *Capital*, beginning with his first systematic studies of political economy in Paris in 1843.[2] This suggests that his writings are contributions to the realization of a single project that, after many twists and turns, finally culminates in *Capital*. Certainly, numerous ideas that appear in fragmentary or undeveloped form in earlier writings here receive detailed, or more detailed, treatment. Yet this huge work, which is already enormous by normal standards, is no more than a small unfinished fragment of the much larger project Marx set for himself in the *Grundrisse*, in which the discussion of capital was intended to make up no more than the first of six books.

Marx's style here is clear, certainly clearer than the vast majority of his other texts. The pedagogical value is high, perhaps higher than in any of his other writings. In composing this book, he obviously made great efforts to be understood and to present his arguments in the simplest possible way. Continuing a practice that goes back to his earliest texts, Marx here cites abundantly from a wide variety of literature, often in the original language. As before, his great erudition, which by now has become simply enormous, shows itself in numerous references in different languages that enlighten but do not obstruct the reading. Marx's attention is once again focused on England, the most important country in the world market, where capitalism is most developed. The pages of the work are literally replete with concrete references, revealing detailed knowledge, about virtually any imaginable aspect of English political economy.

After his failure to embark on an academic career, Marx rejected ordinary standards as merely symptomatic of a socially distorted form of society. But in *Capital* he produced a model study and critique of political economy, which fully exhibits all the normal criteria of an academic work on the highest level. An unusual feature that appears now is his frequent reference to, and quotation from, his previous writings. It is as if he already knew, when he published this volume, that its successors were unlikely to appear and he desired to "locate" it with respect to his already enormous corpus of writings.

Prefatory materials to *Capital*

Marx begins the Preface to the first German edition by justifying his concentration on English political economy since England provides the classic example – although he claims his theories apply to Germany as well – of the "development of social antagonisms that result from natural laws of capitalist production" (Marx 1975: 9). Since the Industrial Revolution began in England, capitalism is naturally more advanced there as well. Marx now describes his aim as "to lay bare the economic law of motion of modern society" (*ibid.*: 10). Since the economic base is prior to everything else, and since modern society emerged from the Industrial Revolution, Marx's intention is to provide a general theory of modern industrial society in economic terms.

He now describes the situation of English capitalism as manifesting "tendencies working with iron necessity toward inevitable results" (*ibid.*: 9). This suggests, perhaps unwisely in view of the continued success of modern liberal economy since that time, that the evolution of capitalism must necessarily follow a single prescribed path including its rise and then unavoidable fall. It is more realistic to say that due to changes since Marx's time, such as the ability of governments to affect the economy in such ways as unemployment insurance, pensions and so on, these tendencies are best understood as probable consequences.

In prior writings, Marx has consistently based his theories on the Hegelian idea that human beings meet what can be called their reproductive needs through various kinds of productive activity within civil society. He now indicates that his interest does not lie in individuals as such, but rather only as they embody the different interests of modern industrial society. He is not concerned with a particular "capitalist" or "landlord", since "individuals are dealt with only in so far as they are the personifications of economic categories, embodiments of particular class-relations and class-interests" (*ibid.*: 10). As if to underline this important point, Marx later repeats it in similar language in the chapter on exchange, where he notes that "the characters who appear on the economic stage are but the personifications of the economic relations that exist between them" (*ibid.*: 95).

According to Marx, the science of political economy presupposes for its existence a stable form of society, that is, a society without fundamental social changes, one in which the basic concepts and laws of political economy will continue to hold, rather than a transitory historical phase. Political economy is the theory of modern industrial society, or capitalism, which excludes basic social change. On the contrary, Marx's view of the development of social antagonisms, or contradictions, within capitalism is based on the supposition that the emerging class struggle is transforming society. Ricardo, a near contemporary English economist, was naive in thinking that the various antagonisms of modern industrial society (e.g. wages and profits, profits and rent, and so on) constitute a so-called law of nature. Why? Because his ahistorical viewpoint fails to note that society changes, often in basic ways. In this context, Marx makes the following general comment about political economy:

> In so far as Political Economy remains within that horizon, in so far, i.e., as the capitalist régime is looked upon as the absolutely final form of social production, instead of as a passing historical phase of its evolution, Political Economy can remain a science only so long as the class-struggle is latent or manifests itself only in isolated and spo-radic phenomena. (Marx 1975: 14)

In other words, in this passage Marx is pointing to the historical limit of political economy conceived as a science of a stable social context. For if in practice the social context turns out to be unstable, then political economy in this precise sense no longer applies.

The first chapter of *Capital*

The main text of volume one of *Capital* is divided into eight parts. The first part is divided into three chapters, which respectively concern commodities, exchange and money, or the circulation of commodities. Marx begins *Capital* with a detailed discussion of commodities.

The account of commodities repairs a lacuna in Marx's writings while continuing a shift in emphasis. The term "commodity", which has occurred much earlier in Marx's writings, occurs rarely until the *Grundrisse*, where it occurs frequently. Marx now literally constructs his theory upon the concept of the commodity, which, for this reason, becomes the central concept, the conceptual basis, of his view of modern industrial society.

In recentring his account of political economy on the commodity, Marx completes a shift in emphasis in his writings. In the *Philosophy of Right*, Hegel stresses the impact of modern liberal economy everywhere in society, for instance concerning the family through remarks on family capital (Hegel 1967: §§170–72) and the division created by civil society between the individual and his family (*ibid.*: §238). Marx's early texts on Hegel criticize him for neglecting the human dimension that is central to Marx's account of philosophy and economics in the *Paris Manuscripts*. In later texts Marx increasingly emphasizes that modern economics forms a system that can be studied as a science. In *A Contribution to the Critique of Political Economy*, Marx refocuses his discussion from the individual to the commodity as the central element of a society based on private property. It is only in *Capital* that, through detailed studies of the effect of capitalism on individuals, the former theme returns with a vengeance.

The reason for beginning with an analysis of commodities is clear: Marx is interested in neither a modern industrial society as such, nor a static, self-preserving, homeostatic system, but rather in the way modern industrial society functions and evolves with respect to the realization of human goals for human beings. Capitalism is defined by the institution of private ownership of the means of production, or private property. But the condition for capitalism to function is the exchange process based on the exchange of commodities.

Marx begins his exposition of commodities and money in noting that social wealth takes the form of "an immense accumulation of commodities" (Marx 1975: 45). What is a commodity [*die Ware*]? Basically, it is a tangible external object that satisfies a human need of whatever kind, that is exchanged, and that has an exchange value. Now everything useful, that is useful to satisfy a need, can be regarded from the different perspectives of quality or quantity. On this basis, Marx now reintroduces a distinction between use value and exchange value, which was already known to Aristotle.[3] A thing is useful because it has a use value, or serves a purpose. "The utility of a thing makes it a use value" (*ibid.*: 46). Use value is intrinsic to the commodity. Exchange value, on the contrary, which is extrinsic to a thing, is a relative, or variable, value that can be had for a thing, be it another thing or money. Since use value, which is qualitative, cannot be expressed in quantitative terms, "exchange value is the only form in which the value of commodities can manifest itself or be expressed" (*ibid.*: 48).

In order to understand the value of commodities, Marx turns to work, or labour. His central insight, which is anticipated by Locke, Hegel and others, is that labour confers value on products. Since labour, which produces use value, depends on pre-existing materials that themselves have value, it is not the only source of value.

Modern science arose when, through certain simplifying assumptions, a way was found to apply mathematics to nature. Marx similarly simplifies the calculation of the exchange value in suggesting that in all cases it can be represented as a multiple of average labour-power. "The labour … that forms the substance of value, is homogeneous human labour, expenditure of one uniform labour-power". In other words, the value of an object is "the amount of labour socially necessary, or the labour-time socially necessary for its production" (*ibid.*: 49). Things that take the same time to produce should have the same exchange value.

The view that value is calculated in terms of labour is stated earlier in different ways by other writers. As formulated by Marx, it is an application of the Hegelian view, mentioned above, that in the process of production the work of individuals is "crystallized" or "objectified". The objectification of the work of different individuals in products is the same in all commodities. In the *Grundrisse*, Marx drew a distinction between labour and labour capacity. In developing this distinction, he pointed out that labour is measured by labour time. More or less labour time is required to produce different commodities, such as sewing machines or cars. Yet in all cases exchange value is a function of labour time.

Different types of use value are the result of different types of labour. Productive activity creates use value. Marx, who acknowledges that human productive activity can take many forms, both qualitatively and quantitatively, considers it in the first place as human labour in general.

In order to understand the form of exchange value, Marx relates it to money. He distinguishes between the relative value of the materials that go into making a thing, and the thing, which has a value calculable in what he calls equivalent form, or monetary units. Value is created by the congealed, or concretized, form of human labour power, which does not itself have any value, but acquires it in taking the form of an object. "Human labour-power in motion, or human labour, creates value, but is not itself value. It becomes value only in its congealed state, when embodied in the form of some object" (Marx 1975: 61) In a word, labour power is accumulated, or stored up in, or again given concrete form as the product.

Since one commodity can be exchanged for another, commodities have equivalent form. The underlying idea, that is, that particularity is lost in the way that the value of one commodity is calculated on the basis of another, depends on a concept of value. In a pertinent remark on Aristotle, Marx notes that for historical reasons the Greek philosopher was prevented from arriving at a concept of value. He was aware of the value of commodities. Yet since he lived in a society founded on slavery, he could not grasp "[t]he secret of the expression of value, namely, that all kinds of labour are equal and equivalent" (*ibid.*: 70).

Marx points out that all products have use value, although it is only at a certain stage in social evolution that "a product becomes a commodity" (*ibid.*: 72). The social character of human labour can, however, be represented in abstract, average form.

> The general value-form, which represents all products of labour as mere "congelations" of undifferentiated human labour, shows by its very structure that it is the social résumé of the world of commodities. That form consequently makes it indisputably evident that that in the world of commodities the character possessed by all labour of being *human* labour constitutes its specific social character.
>
> (*Ibid.*: 78)

Marx innovates in describing what he calls the fetishism of commodities. A commodity is mysterious since the relation between producers takes the form of a relation between products (*ibid.*: 82). In other words, the central relation is not that between individual human beings, but rather that between objects that are assumed to have an intrinsic value, in independence of people, through ignorance about the social process through which value is constituted. Producers do not come into contact before the exchange of commodities. It follows that the social character of the labour that goes into production is manifest only in exchange. More precisely, it is directly manifest through the products exchanged and indirectly through their producers. As he points out, there is absolutely no connection between the value of commodities as products of labour and their physical attributes. What is mysterious is, as he writes in a famous passage, "a definite social relation between men, that assumes, in their eyes, the fantastic form of a relation between things" (*ibid.*: 83).

Marx's claim can be understood if we recall that, in exchange, we presuppose homogeneous human labour (*ibid.*: 84). This labour converts each and every product into "a social hieroglyphic" (*ibid.*: 85), while at the same time the monetary form of the world of commodities conceals instead of disclosing the social character of private labour and the relations between producers. Marx has in mind the fact that in a society dominated by the productive process, which we do not control but which rather controls us, its real nature is concealed. Now this is not the case in, say, feudal society, where there is barter or payment in kind, since there is no commodity exchange. And it will not be the case in a society of free individuals, where the social relations of the individual producers and their relations to their work and their products will supposedly be straightforward.

Marx's point is that our ability to think correctly about the economic process depends on being able to distance ourselves from its influence over us. For the process of production only loses its mystical aspect when we emerge from the economic yoke to work according to our own plan. Marx illustrates his claim by referring to the classical school of political economy, which reaches its high point in David Ricardo. According to Marx, the classical school has so far sought but failed to understand the concept of value, since it has never grasped the relation between labour as use value and labour as exchange value. This remark reaffirms Marx's conviction that a proper understanding of the difference between use value and exchange value is key to understanding modern industrial society.

Further remarks on *Capital*

Since there is no space here to describe *Capital* in any detail, it will be sufficient to make some rapid descriptive remarks. Chapter 2, which is very short, discusses "Exchange" by proceeding from the object, or commodity, to its owner. Marx has earlier considered the labour that creates use values in simplified fashion as homogeneous labour-power. He now extends the same courtesy to those implicated in the economic process, all of whom are fictiously considered as a function of their respective roles. Marx is not denying that, say, Henry Ford played a specific role in the creation of the assembly line. Yet what a particular individual does in a particular situation is irrelevant to the fact that that person functions in the general economic framework. The reason is rather that "the characters who appear on the economic stage are but the personifications of the economic relations that exist between them" (Marx 1975: 95). In other words, rather than consider particular persons as such, Marx considers particular persons as illustrations of general roles in modern industrial society.

The longer third chapter studies "Money, or the Circulation of Commodities" in some detail. In three sections, Marx distinguishes between the measure of value, the medium of circulation and money. Marx, who assumes that gold is the so-called money-commodity, or again the universal measure of value, immediately observes that it only functions in this way because the value of commodities is commensurable, or expressible as a function of what he calls realized human labour in so many units of precious metal, which expresses the quantity of human labour necessary to produce the thing.

The first transformation of the commodity into money brings about the second transformation of money into a commodity, as Marx points out. Since for every purchase there is a sale, the money that results from it becomes available for a further purchase. The so-called "metamorphosis of a commodity", that is, a sale followed by a purchase, make up "a circular movement, a circuit" (*ibid.*: 121). This circuit is merely one among many which, taken together, compose *"the circulation of commodities"* (*ibid.*: 122, original emphasis). The difference between barter and the circulation of commodities lies in the fact that no seller is obliged to become a buyer. In a word, unlike direct barter, in the case of circulation a direct identity does not obtain.

In Chapter 4, Marx begins to consider the accumulation of capital, a topic that has been in abeyance, lurking on the horizon as it were, ever since the important discussion of surplus value in the *Grundrisse*. There he developed the idea of surplus value as unpaid labour. Here he draws the consequence of that idea in showing that the fact that commodity exchange produces surplus value automatically leads to the accumulation of capital, which he regards as the inherent aim of capitalism.

Marx begins by pointing out that capital takes the form of money, as opposed to property in the form, say, of land. There is a distinction in kind between mere money and money that is capital. Since money constantly begets more money, capital is self-expanding, constantly adding to its value through the generation of surplus value, which increases the original value. In short, value begets value, since in and through the circulation of capital as money, the generation of surplus value in the form of an increase in money leads to the accumulation of capital.

In itself, this idea is very old, as Marx shows in a lengthy footnote to Aristotle, who more than two thousand years earlier distinguished between oeconomic, roughly the art of making a living, and chremastic, or engaging in trade with the idea of absolute wealth. In Marx's account, Aristotle was already aware that the circulation of money through commodity exchange leads on to riches (Marx 1975: 163n.).

Although surplus value originates in circulation, this does not explain *why* it originates. The solution to this puzzle will require lengthy discussion throughout most of the rest of Volume 1. Marx makes a start in the next chapter in his analysis of labour power. His suggestion is that surplus value is the result of the difference between the sum paid for labour power, which creates use value in producing a commodity, and its exchange value. Labour power is by definition what is exercised to produce use value. Individuals are forced to sell their labour power for the simple reason that, in order to live, much less to live well, they require a means of subsistence, hence must meet such basic needs as food, clothing and shelter.

The accumulation of capital depends on the production of surplus value, whose real presupposition is the existence of commodities. Surplus value is not produced in a barter economy, in which products are directly exchanged for other products or services but not for money. It is produced only in an economy in which use value and exchange value are separated, thereby transforming products into commodities to be exchanged for money. What the worker has to offer, his only commodity, is his labour power, whose price is fixed by what he needs to continue to subsist. The wages the capitalist pays for labour power are fixed before production. The value of the commodity, or product to be exchanged, is a function of the use value produced. The worker and capitalist come together out of their own interests. The worker sells his labour power in order to meet his subsistence needs and the capitalist buys the same labour power, which is for sale, for which he pays wages or a salary, with the idea of selling the commodity for more than his costs in virtue of the surplus value.

In Chapters 5–9, Marx discusses types of surplus value, beginning, in Part III, with "[t]he production of absolute surplus value". Marx begins by pointing out that the capitalist buys labour power in order to produce use value in the form of a commodity. The product of the production process, or use value, goes to the capitalist. Examination of labour in so far as it creates value concerns mere quantity unrelated to quality. For purposes of calculating the amount of value, it is necessary to reduce skilled labour to so-called average social labour.

It is obvious that an increase in labour increases total value in preserving the original value, say, of the factory including its machines. Value lies in the objects, and the means of production, such as machines, do not contribute to use value more than they lose in being operated. In the process, the use value of the machines is consumed, or used up, by the worker who adds value to the product. On this basis, Marx claims that value is not used up or reproduced, since "[i]t is rather preserved" (Marx 1975: 217). It follows that "surplus value" is (measured by) "the difference between the value of the product and the value of the elements consumed in the formation of that product, in other words of the means of production and the labour power" (*ibid.*: 219).

During what Marx calls surplus labour time, the worker creates surplus value for the capitalist which, "for the capitalist", as Marx sarcastically writes, "has all the charms of a creation out of nothing" (*ibid.*: 226). It follows that the rate of creation of surplus value is represented by the ratio between surplus labour and necessary labour. Obviously, the owner of the means of production has every interest in prolonging the working day in order to maximize profit. Marx illustrates this point through a reference to a contemporary Oxford economics professor, Nassau W. Senior, who in 1837 argued that at the time, when a mill worker could not be obliged to work more than 12 hours per day during the week and 9 hours on Saturdays, "the whole net profit is derived from the last hour".[4]

With this example as a lead-in, Marx next turns to an account of "The Working Day" in Chapter 10. This long discussion (some 70 pages) rehearses the rather dreadful conditions of labour, particularly child labour, which prevailed during the period. In *The Wealth of Nations*, Adam Smith notes that poverty is very unfavourable to bringing up children.[5] Marx goes a great deal further. In a striking passage, he writes that "Capital is dead labour, that, vampire-like, only lives by sucking living labour, and lives the more, the more labour it sucks" (Marx 1975: 241). There is no natural limit to the working day. As the capitalist profits by its extension, and as the worker only represents a source of labour time, the capitalist has every interest in extending the working day.

The long discussion of absolute surplus value in Part III is followed by an even longer discussion of the "Production of Relative Surplus Value" in Part IV. Marx distinguishes between absolute surplus value, which is produced by lengthening the working day, and relative surplus value, which is due to reducing necessary labour time. At stake is the possibility for the owner of the means of production to increase profits while shortening the time during which the worker must be paid. The idea is either to reduce wages or to increase efficiency. The result of technological innovation is to increase the productivity of labour, hence to increase surplus value. The solution to the question lies not in shortening the working day, but in shortening the working time. This has the double effect of making commodities cheaper and increasing their surplus value.

Marx touches rapidly on the division of labour in manufacture and on the social division of labour. Division of labour, which arises naturally and spontaneously, for instance in the family, is enormously developed through the separation between town and country – a point already made in *The German Ideology* (Marx & Engels 1973) in the development of commodity exchange. "The foundation of every division of labour that is well developed, and brought about by the exchange of commodities, is the separation between town and country" (Marx 1975: 357). Large-scale manufacture typical of modern industrial society requires the prior development of division of labour. He ends this chapter in noting that the simple restriction of a worker to repetitive movements converts him into a mere beast.

In the very long Chapter 15, "Machinery and Modern Industry", Marx hammers away at the point that the progress of modern industrial society is dearly paid for in the sacrifice exacted of the workers, who literally give up everything that characterizes the good life and even life itself for others in pursuit of capital. The result of the introduction of machines is that instead of using tools the worker is transformed into a mere appendage of the machine, which in effect takes his place. A machine, in displacing human beings, only increases the amount of work that can be accomplished, and hence the value that can be created.

It is clear that the introduction of machinery is often harmful to the individual worker. Turning now to the factory, Marx observes that the introduction of machinery tends to replace skilled workers by unskilled ones, who, unable to perform skilled labour, merely tend the machines through repetitive motions.

Some economists argue that the introduction of machinery frees up capital to employ workers elsewhere. But Marx contends that displaced workers only find new work through the investment of new capital. Marx further notes that the factory system allows overproduction, which in turn produces pressure to diminish wages in order to sell commodities more cheaply, for instance in the cotton industry.

As Marx repeatedly stresses, capitalism is centred not on the production of commodities, but rather on the production of surplus value. The relation of the owner of the means of production to the worker is to a person whose labour power creates surplus value. He ends with a splendid passage, which summarizes the difference between political economy and his basic insight that modern industrial society centres on the control of unpaid labour:

> Capital, therefore, is not only, as Adam Smith says, the command over labour. It is essentially the command over unpaid labour. All surplus labour, whatever particular form (profit, interest, or rent) it may subsequently crystallize into, is in substance the materialization of unpaid labour. The secret of the self-expansion of capital resolves itself into having the disposal of a definite quantity of other people's unpaid labour.   (Marx 1975: 534)

In considering "The transformation of the value (and respectively the price) of labour power into wages" (*ibid.*: ch. 19), Marx states his controversial version of the labour theory of value as a function of the work required to produce a given commodity: "But what is the value of a commodity? The objective form of the social labour expended in its production" (*ibid.*: 535). Labour, which is the source of value, has no value in itself. Its price is determined by the law of supply and demand. But the expression "price of labour" should be taken as "the price of labour power", which is calculated in the form of wages. In Marx's opinion, the fact that the value of labour is always less than the value it produces is concealed in the concept of wages in which the unpaid labour is hidden.

The accumulation of capital is central to capitalism. Marx addresses accumulation in two phases: Part VII, "The Accumulation of Capital", studies how this occurs in modern industrial society in some detail. The discussion of simple reproduction is based on the insight that production is in fact a process of reproduction. In the process of producing new products in order to supply wages to the worker and profit to the owner of the means of production, production ultimately reproduces itself.

Capital is composed of variable capital and constant capital, which is invested in buildings, machinery and so on. Since the latter is consumed in the process of production, all capital eventually becomes accumulated capital, or the accumulation of surplus value. It follows that the starting point of capitalist production, which lies in the separation between labour and its product, or labour power from its objective conditions, is constantly reproduced through simple reproduction within the process of production. More precisely, the result of the normal functioning of the productive process is to increase capital for the capitalist. Yet the worker, who creates that wealth, but sells his labour power to do so, has no means of acquiring it. Now accumulation of capital not only needs capitalists to supply the objective conditions of production; it also requires workers to produce commodities. A further result is that the process in effect produces the worker as a worker. The more general point is that in its normal functioning capitalist production reproduces the separation between labour-power and the means of labour, between what the worker provides and what the owner of the means of production provides, between the subjective and the objective conditions of production. Hence not in abnormal but rather in normal times it produces and reproduces the conditions for exploiting the worker. It follows that the process of production produces commodities, profit, and reproduces the structure of capitalism itself.

In the account of simple reproduction, Marx argues that in the course of production capital is turned into accumulated capital. He studies this theme in more detail in Chapter 24, under the heading "The Conversion of Surplus-Value into Capital". Surplus value, which is contained in the product, becomes capital when it is transformed into money. Now only what belongs to the process of production can be converted into capital. Surplus value can be converted into capital because it furnishes the conditions for continuing the process of production in the form of new capital. In this way, capital constantly creates new capital.

Chapter 25, on the general law of capitalist accumulation, which closes this part, is both longer – about a hundred pages – and more detailed than the preceding chapters. Marx is here concerned with two themes discussed as early as the *Paris Manuscripts*: the way in which capitalism literally produces its own supply of workers, and the effect of the accumulation of capital on individual workers. In order for capital to grow, that part invested in variable capital, or labour power, must increase. It follows, as classical economy already knew, that increase in profit depends on an increase in workers.

The accumulation of capital is due to various factors, such as the increase in the number of workers, or increased productivity. Naturally, the accumulation of capital brought about by workers impacts on the working population. An increase in productivity, for instance, turns workers into surplus workers, who soon join the ranks of the unemployed. Conversely, if there were not enough workers, wages and salaries would rise, hence undercutting the development of capital. At all times, there must be enough workers, including a certain number of workers unemployed or partially employed, to maximize the expansion of capital.

In general the more capital increases the more workers make up the industrial reserve army waiting to find jobs. Marx argues that the various mechanisms that increase productivity tend to dehumanize workers. The wider point, which has been made many times before, is that workers impoverish themselves as a direct result of bringing about an increase in wealth.

The eighth and last part of the book treats "The So-called Primitive Accumulation" in a series of eight very short chapters, together taking up some sixty pages. Primitive accumulation precedes and makes possible capital accumulation. Money and commodities, which are distinct from capital, can only become capital on the double condition that the owner of the means of production is willing to employ workers, and workers are willing to sell their labour-power. A worker who possesses his own means of production, for instance a self-employed farmer, is only willing to work for someone else if he loses these means, in this case the farm.

Marx, who notes that this process is different in different lands, studies it in England where it assumed a classic form. The disappearance of serfdom by the end of the fourteenth century led to a situation in which a majority of the population consisted of free peasant proprietors. This situation was altered in the late-fifteenth and early-sixteenth centuries as the peasants were driven from the land. The wholesale usurpation of the common lands was the direct result of the rise of Flemish wool manufacturers, in turn leading to the transformation of farmland into pasture, which was then enclosed starting in the late-fifteenth century. The dispossession of the peasants, which was later continued in different ways, such as the spoliation of Church property at the time of the Reformation, transformed them over time into a proletarian workforce later able to supply labour as industry developed in urban areas. This series of expropriations of the peasants "conquered the field for capitalist agriculture, made the soil part and parcel of capital, and created for the town industries the necessary supply of a 'free' and outlawed proletariat" (Marx 1975: 723).

Marx provides detailed accounts of the atrocious living conditions of this "free" proletariat. In 1530, during the time of Henry VIII, those who refused to work were whipped on the first offence, mutilated on the second and executed on the third as enemies of the state. Primitive accumulation, the same process that dispossessed the English peasants, created the capitalist farmer, the home market for industrial capital, and finally the industrial capitalist. Expropriation of the peasants created the great landed proprietor, whose capital increased in value as the prices of agricultural produce (e.g. corn, wool, meat) rose. By the same token, the destruction of rural domestic industry created a market for industrial products that were bought by peasants who, through expropriation, were transformed into workers.

The final two chapters, Chapter 33, "The Modern Theory of Colonisation", and Chapter 32, "Historical Tendency of Capitalist Accumulation", appear to be out of their natural order in respect to the argument in the book. The former treats colonization, a theme that belongs to the different forms of primitive accumulation, whereas the latter brings the discussion of Part VIII and of the volume to a close in a brief comment on the prospects of modern industrial society.

In Chapter 32, conceptually the final piece of the argument, Marx ends his great book with a rapid remark, taking up a theme already discussed in earlier writings, such as the *Paris Manuscripts*, on the weak long-term prospects for modern industrial society in virtue of the tendency of capital to accumulate. Since his earliest writings, he has consistently presupposed a distinction between private property, or private ownership of the means of production, and social or collective property, which belongs not to individual capitalists, but to everyone. Historically, the process of development passes from the stage in which individuals exploit their private property to a further stage in which capitalists exploit the work of others. In the normal course of events, small capital is transformed into bigger and bigger capital through a process of centralization in which "One capitalist always kills many" (Marx 1975: 750). Marx contends that in following its own tendency to increase, capital multiplies but, when the conditions for maintaining private property become sufficiently difficult, it finally destroys private property and capitalism itself. "Centralization of the means of production and socialization of labour at last reach a point where they become incompatible with their capitalist integument. Thus integument is burst asunder. The knell of capitalist private property sounds. The expropriators are expropriated" (*ibid.*: 750).

Marx's political economy and contemporary economics

After this rapid account of some main themes of the first volume of *Capital*, I turn even more rapidly to some remarks on the relation between Marxian and contemporary forms of political economy. According to Marx, individuals, who are active in producing commodities in order to meet their subsistence needs, are unable, within the framework of modern capitalism, to meet their human needs, or needs to develop as individual human beings in ways related to their individual capacities. Such human needs can be met, if at all, only outside the framework of modern capitalism and, according to Marx, after the transformation of capitalism into communism.

Marx's model of political economy offers moral criticism in terms of a possible alternative. For instance, in a discussion of the rate of surplus value, Marx draws attention to the distinction between necessary labour time, or the time a person must work to meet subsistence needs, and surplus labour time. The alternative is a form of society in which the individual is not dependent on an autonomous economy, whose innate goal is to maximize profit by exploiting human beings. In such a society, the individual, who still needs to meet subsistence needs, is however, free, beyond this point, to do as one wishes.

Marx's view of political economy has long been criticized from the perspective of orthodox economics. For the most part these criticisms miss the mark since they fail to enter into the spirit of his position. In part, the difference concerns the difference between political economy and economics. As already noted, for Marx, but not for orthodox economics, economics is intrinsically political. Mainstream economists acknowledge a link between economics and the social context in a way that suppresses the political dimension of economics. Two examples from recent non-Marxist economics in English will suffice to make this point. According to Lionel Robbins, "Economics is the science which studies human behavior as a relationship between ends and scarce means that have alternative uses".[6] More recently, Allan Drazen has argued that political economy begins with the observation that actual policies differ from optimal policies.[7]

Orthodox economics, in studying aspects of the economy, such as labour, trade and so on, is concerned to enable different sectors of the economy to function optimally in purely economic terms, without respect to the effect of the so-called optimal function of capitalism on human beings. The silent assumption is that rigorous discussion of liberal capitalism with a view to perfecting it is in the interests of all concerned, and that such a commitment is not a political choice. The question of whether economics exists to serve human political interests, whether it should be judged by its contribution, say, to the realization of human freedom, is not a question mainstream economists are now debating. To put the point bluntly: from the perspective of human wellbeing, orthodox economy, to the extent that it considers human beings at all, is committed to some version of Adam Smith's famous invisible hand theory, which resurfaced in the US some years ago as so-called supply side economics.

Marx, who takes the economy as a whole, is less interested in the maximal functioning of liberal capitalism than in its short- and long-term prospects, and in the real possibility of an acceptable alternative economic model. In a nutshell, Marx's aim is human wellbeing, which he believes is better served not by making liberal capitalism work, and work better, or even work well, but by replacing it. This leads to clearly different analyses of economic situations. Whereas orthodox economics might be interested in opening new markets to increase gross national product, hence per capita earnings, in the long run Marx is not interested in growing the economy as an end in itself as much as in restricting its influence over individuals.

Some (orthodox) objections to Marxian political economy

Mainstream, or orthodox, economics and Marxian economics are working with irreducibly different, incompatible models. Criticisms that apply to one model often do not apply to the other. Mainstream economics aims at rigorous knowledge of what is the case. More precisely, it is directed towards a rigorous grasp of so-called economic reality, a grasp that is often expressed through sophisticated mathematical models, in which problems, such as inflation, are solved (or resolved) by manipulating interest rates and so on. Marxian political economy is less interested in how to deal with inflation than in its likely effect on individual wellbeing and, for that reason, on the viability of various forms of liberal capitalism.

Different views of economics obviously lead to different views of what should be done in particular situations, and even to different views of the outstanding problems. In pointing to differences between Marxian and mainstream economics it is not my intention to claim that the former is beyond reproach. There are many difficulties in Marxian political economy, such as the so-called labour theory of value. I am not suggesting that the theory is acceptable or that it is beyond criticism. I am rather examining the conditions under which it can reasonably be criticized.

All criticisms are obviously not equal. Marx, who knew the political economy of his day in detail, formulated an alternative to it. Standard objections to Marxian political economy are often formulated from a mainstream perspective incompatible with it. Often those who criticize Marx simply do not know enough about his theories to formulate pertinent criticisms of them. They are more concerned to defend approaches to which they are committed by formulating criticisms on that basis than to take the considerable trouble to enter deeply in Marx's rival theories. Such criticisms are external and, for that reason, less pertinent\e, and also less telling than criticisms that are formulated from within Marx's theories.

Three examples will suffice to illustrate this general point. The standpoint of orthodox economics is often internalized uncritically by economists and non-economists alike as a basis of criticism. According to Jürgen Habermas, the German social theorist, Marx's theory of economic crisis is inadequate.[8] Such crises are due not to intrinsic contradictions in modern industrial capitalism, but rather to difficulties in the steering mechanism in modern society. A different objection, based on a preference for an economic system based on demand, is advanced by János Kornai, an economist who judges Marxian economics through the distinction between so-called resource-constrained and demand-constrained systems.[9] A third objection directed to Marx's conception of value was famously formulated by Eugen Böhm-Bawerk, the Austrian economist, at the end of the nineteenth century. According to Böhm-Bawerk, Marx's theory is built on an overly selective, hence defective, theory of value. For Böhm-Bawerk, Marx simply omits, say, psychological factors, as well as comparative rarity, from the theory.[10]

All three objections miss the mark. Habermas's objection is based on a change in capitalism as a result of which it allegedly overcomes its so-called "crisis ridden form of economic growth.[11] That is doubtful since even now it is arguable that capitalism is in crisis. The terrorist attack on the World Trade Center on 11 September 2001, and the subsequent wars in Afghanistan and in Iraq can hardly be understood without taking a long series of economic factors into consideration. The fact that the industrialized world is so rich and becoming richer while a series of Muslim countries have largely stagnant economies, all of which can now be seen on television, is an obviously destabilizing factor. Kornai's objection follows his commitment to the allegedly weaker economic functioning of demand-constrained systems. Although historically political Marxism led in that direction, and although there are still corners of the world that function, or at least try to function, according to this model, that is not anything Marx either recommends or explicitly discusses.

Kornai's objection is based on practical experience of communism in Hungary, but little or no knowledge of Marx's writings. Böhm-Bawerk's objection, on the contrary, follows from detailed study of the third volume of *Capital*, whose argument conflicts with his own theories of capital and interest, including his earlier critique of the first volume of *Capital*. On the basis of his adherence to the so-called subjective theory of value, which he favours, Böhm-Bawerk objects to Marx's allegiance to the labour theory of value.

Böhm-Bawerk's classic criticism was answered by the Marxist economist Rudolf Hilferding.[12] Did he understand Marx's theory of value, as Hilferding denied? Is it licit to assume as correct a different theory as the basis of criticism? According to Leszek Kolakowski, the Polish philosopher, who adopts the positivistic pose that Marx's law of value cannot be verified or refuted, Hilferding does not answer Böhm-Bawerk so his refutation is inconclusive.[13] Yet even if Marx's theory of value turned out not to be scientific in the positivistic sense currently favoured by mainstream economics, that only counts as a criticism if Marxian political economy ought to have respected the scientific standards utilized in orthodox economy. But to judge Marx by standards he rejects is to miss the point.

Conclusion: Marx and contemporary economics

In the final analysis, Marx, who rejects mainstream economics, and mainstream economists are concerned with different themes. Yet it would be hasty and incorrect to infer that Marxian political economy is therefore false or at best simply irrelevant. On the contrary, it has never been more relevant. For much of the twentieth century, political systems with opposing worldviews were engaged in a dangerous competition that finally ended with the sudden disappearance of institutionalized Marxism in Europe and much of the world. At the beginning of the new century, we live at a time when globalization is an all but accomplished fact, when any real alternative to capitalism has disappeared from the horizon, when we have entered upon a wager forced upon us by prevailing circumstances about the future of the world whose outcome is still unknown, and when institutionalized Marxism has largely disappeared. Yet Marx's insistence that economics is not an end in itself, but must be judged in terms of the success or failure in realizing human beings as individuals, has never been more relevant.

Notes

1. There are only seven parts in the German original. Part VIII in the translation, which has been quarried without comment from part VII in the original first volume, contains a long Chapter 24 with seven subsections, which, in translation, each become separate chapters alongside the original Chapter 25. Is it unclear how to justify this change in Marx's text and none is given.
2. See *Marx-Engels Collected Writings*, vol. 23, 843n.1.

3. See Aristotle, *Politics*, I, 9, 1257a.
4. Nassau W. Senior, *Letters on the Factory Act*, as it affects the cotton manufacture, cited in Marx, *Capital: A Critical Analysis of Capitalist Production*, F. Engels (ed.), S. Moore & E. Aveling (trans.), in *Marx-Engels Collected Writings*, vol. 35 (New York: International Publishers, 1975), 233. Marx was so impressed by this idea that he repeats it again later in the volume. See *ibid*.: 592.
5. See A. Smith, *An Inquiry into the Nature and Causes of the Wealth of Nations*, E. Cannan (ed.), intro. by M. Lerner (New York: Random House, 1937), 79.
6. L. Robbins, *An Essay on the Nature and Significance of Economic Science* (London: Macmillan, 1932), 16.
7. See A. Drazen, *Political Economy in Macroeconomics* (Princeton, NJ: Princeton University Press, 2000), 5.
8. See J. Habermas, *Legitimation Crisis*, T. McCarthy (trans.) (Boston, MA: Beacon Press, 1975), 24–31, 50–61.
9. See J. Kornai, "Resource-Constrained versus Demand-Constrained Systems", *Econometrica* 47(4) (July 1979), 801–20.
10. See P. M. Sweezy (ed.), *Karl Marx and the Close of His System by Eugen Böhm-Bawerk & Böhm-Bawerk's Criticism of Marx by Rudolf Hilferding* (New York: Augustus M. Kelley, 1949), 3–118.
11. See Habermas, *Legitimation Crisis*, especially Pt. II: "Crisis Tendencies in Advanced Capitalism".
12. See *ibid*.: 121–96.
13. See L. Kolakowski, *Main Currents of Marxism*, 3 vols, P. S. Falla (trans.) (Oxford: Clarendon Press, 1978), vol. 2, 296–7.

Bibliography

Aristotle 1984. *Politics*, B. Jowett (trans.). In *The Complete Works of Aristotle*, 2 vols, J. Barnes (ed.), vol. II, 1986–2129. Princeton, NJ: Princeton University Press.

Drazen, A. 2000. *Political Economy in Macroeconomics*. Princeton, NJ: Princeton University Press.

Engels, F. 1941. *Ludwig Feuerbach and the Outcome of Classical German Philosophy*, C. P. Dutt (ed.). New York: International Publishers.

Feuerbach, L. 1957. *The Essence of Christianity*, G. Eliot (trans.). New York: Harper & Row.

Habermas, J. 1975. *Legitimation Crisis*, T. McCarthy (trans.). Boston, MA: Beacon Press.

Hegel, G. W. F. 1967. *The Philosophy of Right*, T. M. Knox (trans.). Oxford: Oxford University Press.

Heine, H. 1986. *Religion and Philosophy in Germany*, J. Snodgrass (trans.). Albany, NY: SUNY Press.

Kolakowski, L. 1978. *Main Currents of Marxism*, 3 vols, P. S. Falla (trans.). Oxford: Clarendon Press.

Kornai, J. 1979. "Resource-Constrained versus Demand-Constrained Systems". *Econometrica* 47(4) (July), 801–20.

Lukács, G. 1971. *History and Class Consciousness*, R. Livingstone (trans.). Cambridge, MA: MIT Press.

Marx, K. 1964. "Contribution to the Critique of Hegel's Philosophy of Right: Introduction". In *Early Writings*, T. B. Bottmore (ed. and trans.), 41–60. New York: McGraw-Hill.

Marx, K. 1964. *Paris Manuscripts*. In *Early Writings*, T. B. Bottmore (ed. and trans.), 61–220.
New York: McGraw-Hill.

Marx, K. 1970. *A Contribution to the Critique of Political Economy*, S. W. Ryazanskaya
(trans.), M. Dobb (ed.). New York: International Publishers.

Marx, K. 1970. *Grundrisse: Foundations of the Critique of Political Economy*, M. Nicolaus
(trans.). Harmondsworth: Penguin, in association with *New Left Review*.

Marx, K. 1975. *Capital: A Critical Analysis of Capitalist Production*, F. Engels (ed.), S. Moore
& E. Aveling (trans.). In *Marx-Engels Collected Writings*, vol. 35. New York: International
Publishers.

Marx, K. & F. Engels 1973. *The German Ideology*, part 1, C. J. Arthur (trans.). New York:
International Publishers.

Robbins, L. 1932. *An Essay on the Nature and Significance of Economic Science*. London:
Macmillan.

Sen, A. S. 1999. *Development as Freedom*. New York: Knopf.

Smith, A. 1937. *An Inquiry into the Nature and Causes of the Wealth of Nations*, E. Cannan
(ed.), intro. by M. Lerner. New York: Random House.

Sweezy, P. M. (ed.) 1949. *Karl Marx and the Close of His System by Eugen Böhm-Bawerk &
Böhm-Bawerk's Criticism of Marx by Rudolf Hilferding*. New York: Augustus M. Kelley.

Further reading

The literature on Marx is vast. Here are a few suggestions. P. Anderson, *Considerations on Western Marxism* (London: New Left Books, 1976) gives a good account of main forms of Western Marxism. S. Avineri, *The Social and Political Thought of Karl Marx* (Cambridge: Cambridge University Press, 1970) provides a careful, unbiased study of Marx's social and political thought. I. Berlin's biography, *Karl Marx: His Life and Environment* (Oxford: Oxford University Press, 1978), is interesting and well written, but hostile. G. A. Cohen, *Karl Marx's Theory of History: A Defense* (Princeton, NJ: Princeton University Press., 2000) provides the initial analytic philosophical study of Marx. M. Henry, a leading French phenomenologist, treats Marx as a philosopher of human reality in *Marx: A Philosophy of Human Reality*, K. McLaughlin (trans.) (Bloomington, IN: Indiana University Press, 1983). L. Kolakowski, earlier a leading Marxist thinker, offers a detailed but often idiosyncratic history of Marxism in *Main Currents of Marxism*, 3 vols, P. S. Falla (trans.) (Oxford: Clarendon Press, 1978). G. Lukács, *History and Class Consciousness*, R. Livingstone (trans.) (Cambridge, MA: MIT Press, 1971) is the single most important Marxist contribution to philosophy. T. Rockmore, *Marx After Marxism* (Oxford: Blackwell, 2002) provides an accessible, non-Marxist introduction to Marx's main philosophical writings. R. P. Wolf, *Understanding Marx: A Reconstruction and Critique of Capital* (Princeton, NJ: Princeton University Press, 1984) gives a careful philosophical account of *Capital*.

8

Friedrich Nietzsche
The Genealogy of Morals

Rex Welshon

Although no single book presents all of Nietzsche's thinking on any of the many topics in which he takes an interest, *The Genealogy of Morals* comes as close as any to capturing the general aim of his mature work. It is sober, detailed, philosophically and psychologically astute, historically challenging, scholarly and a joy to read. Composed in 1887 and intended as a sequel to *Beyond Good and Evil (BGE)*, *The Genealogy of Morals (GM)* is an extended argument in defence of a clear thesis. That thesis is that an analysis of moral values will reveal that their value lies almost exclusively in the social support they provide for the herd or slave elements of a society and not, as is claimed on their behalf, the ethical guidance they provide for all of us. According to Nietzsche, moral values are, again contrary to what is typically claimed on their behalf, self-interested and, since self-interested, not binding on everyone. At best, they are binding only on those for whom they promise to provide some relief from the suffering of life. The premises behind these surprising judgements are often controversial and go to some of our most deeply held assumptions about ourselves and our moral values. As we shall see, Nietzsche goes so far as to deny that we are all alike in a morally relevant way. He thinks that what we can say about human nature discloses morally relevant differences across humans that are substantive, deep and ineliminable. We are so different from one another that there cannot be a universally binding evaluative framework.

The body of *The Genealogy of Morals* is divided into three essays, each with its own topic. In the first essay Nietzsche investigates the history of herd moral values by contrasting the distinction between good and bad, on the one hand, and good and evil, on the other. In the second essay he analyses the emergence of the psychological capacity for guilt and bad conscience, a cornerstone for the development of modern moral values. And in the third essay he investigates the implications of the ascetic moral values of chastity, humility and poverty.

Essay I

The question of Essay I is this: how did herd morality became the dominant form of evaluation, so dominant that we do not even recognize that it is a perspective taken by a particular class of people on evaluation and not something universal in scope? Genealogy is designed to answer this question. Genealogy is a uniquely Nietzschean enterprise, a peculiar kind of history, but at its simplest a familiar form of reasoning. With certain contemporary phenomena as its objects of explanation, genealogy devises hypotheses about the antecedents of those phenomena and then tries to confirm the hypotheses by investigating evidence in their support. In this, Nietzschean genealogy is not markedly different from other kinds of history. What makes it peculiar is four-fold. First, genealogy denies that contemporary practices can always or even usually be read back into the distant past and found at the origin of those practices. Secondly, genealogy denies that the origin of evaluation has much in common with its contemporary descendants. Thirdly, genealogy denies that contemporary practices always represent an improvement over that which caused them. Fourthly, genealogy is unabashedly perspectival in a way that typical histories pretend not to be. Nietzsche is quite happy to allow that his is not an objective history of moral values; after all, he does not think there can be such a thing.

The first and second aspects of genealogy just noted are particularly interesting divergences from typical histories, so let us focus on them in greater detail. Nietzsche first claims that from the contemporary value of some social practice or some psychological characteristic we cannot infer that that practice or characteristic had that value when it first developed. Hence, the contemporary value of some practice or characteristic cannot explain its initial emergence and cannot be assumed to explain its subsequent development. One direct implication of this genealogical point is that the modern assumption that herd morality is valuable and that herd values are, and have always been, valuable for everyone, may be rejected. Far from being universal, herd values are, he thinks, valuable only for some. Far from being immutable, herd values are an historical product, contingent creations of particular groups of people, designed to serve their interests. Far from being intrinsically valuable, herd values are, where they are valuable at all, valuable instrumentally. Genealogy also shows that the emergence of herd values is explained not, as moral defenders would have it, as our recognition of some universally held and trans-historical "moral sense" whose dimensions and structure are delineated by herd moral concepts, but as the result of a struggle between the herd and the nobility, a struggle that the herd has won.

So, in the initial section of Essay I, Nietzsche has a good laugh at the expense of British moral historians who, convinced of the truth of utilitarianism and social Darwinism, read them back into history and place them at the embryonic stages of moral development. Utilitarianism was the dominant form of moral theory in the nineteenth century and, in its contemporary guise as decision theory, it remains the moral theory most frequently discussed by philosophers. According to utilitarianism, the moral *good* is maximal net happiness. Maximal net happiness is what we should aim at when we make moral decisions and that which serves as the criterion of goodness of our actions. Given two actions A and B, the one with the maximal net happiness – say A – is the better of the two; so, since, in this context, A is the *best* thing to do, it is the morally *right* thing to do, and since it is the right thing to do, A is what we *ought* to do. Social Darwinism is the claim that evolutionary development guarantees both that only those individuals who are best adapted to their social environment will live long enough to pass on their genes and that, as a result, those gene lineages that have survived the longest and are most widely distributed are the best adapted.

The moral historians alluded to in the first essay are accused of thinking that we moderns are the cream of the evolutionary crop and that since maximal net happiness is what the utilitarian's moral theory claims is morally good, it must be that when moral values first developed they did so as the result of a similar line of reflection. Nietzsche finds both claims preposterous. There is, he thinks, no reason to think that the modern European is the best that evolution can muster. On the contrary, he thinks that the modern European is mediocre and vicious. And, being a well-trained classical philologist, he is in a peculiarly well-qualified position to counter the utilitarian potted history of morality. He thinks that, at the beginnings of evaluation, there was nothing like nineteenth-century utilitarian considerations in the reflections that resulted in the creation of moral values. His explanation of the origin of moral values is quite different: there are, he claims, two senses of "good", to each of which there is an opposing term. In the first sense of "good", call it "noble good", the opposing term is "bad". In the second sense of "good", call it "moral good", the opposing term is "evil".

Nietzsche thinks that the evaluative distinction between noble good and bad originated entirely within the noble classes of a society. Those who were blessed by birth or by attainment to be members of the highest castes of society, those with the greatest privileges and the noblest spirits, called themselves good and those lower in social rank bad (*GM* I 2). Nietzsche offers etymological evidence for this hypothesis: "*schlecht*", the German word for "bad", is related to "*shlicht*", the German word for "plain" (*GM* I 4). We might trace a similar history with the English words "bad" and "base". Nietzsche hypothesizes that the nobility, who in earliest days were identical with those whom he calls the masters, first designated themselves as good and the rest as bad. The masters are truthful among themselves (*GM* I 5), spontaneous, open and trusting, unable to take injuries seriously, self-controlled (*GM* I 10), delicate, loyal, prideful and friendly (*GM* I 11). But when they are not among themselves they are little better than animals:

> There they savor a freedom from all social constraints, they compensate themselves in the wilderness for the tension engendered by protracted confinement and enclosure within the peace of society, they go *back* to the innocent conscience of the beast of prey, as triumphant monsters who perhaps emerge from a disgusting procession of murder, arson, rape, and torture, exhilarated and undisturbed of soul, as if it were no more than a students' prank, convinced they have provided the poets with a lot more material for song and praise. One cannot fail to see at the bottom of all these noble races the beast of prey, the splendid *blond beast* prowling about avidly in search of spoil and victory; this hidden core needs to erupt from time to time, the animal has to get out again and go back to the wilderness: the Roman, Arabian, Germanic, Japanese nobility, the Homeric heroes, the Scandinavian Vikings – they all shared this need.   (*GM* I 11)

This is a particularly notorious passage, for the reference to the blond beasts was used by the German Nazis to justify their eugenic project of creating a master race of Aryans. They should have read Nietzsche more closely: the blond beast of prey does not refer to Germans or blond Europeans at all but to the lion and the lion in noble human beings. It is glaringly obvious that he does not mean to be identifying the blond beast of prey with the blond Germans; after all, he includes Arabs and Japanese among the blonds.

The contrary value of the noble sense of good is bad. Bad consists in the denial of noble values and bad people are those who exemplify such ignoble values. The ignoble slaves are dishonest, strategic, distrustful, resentful, uncontrolled, crude, disloyal, humble and unfriendly. They are common, base and weak, sycophantic and greasy people.

It is a great temptation to read Essay I as valorizing the masters as ideals for all historical epochs and for all cultures. *This is a mistake*. Even if the masters of *The Genealogy of Morals* are the best *their* ancient society has to offer, it does not follow that they exemplify the best *any* society has to offer, and, in particular, it does not follow that they exemplify the best *our* society has to offer. Those who make this mistake fail to heed the second unique aspect of Nietzschean genealogy, that from the archaic value of some social practice or psychological characteristic we cannot infer that that practice or characteristic has that value now. The anachronistic apologists who endorse noble savage models of human flourishing as a viable model of contemporary human flourishing ignore this aspect of genealogy. For Nietzsche, the masters are one, extremely crude, example of a kind of human being that justifies humanity, but they are irredeemably limited by their intellectual dullness, their inability to see beyond their own self-glorification, and their lack of psychological depth (*GM* I 6). To think that the masters of Essay I provide a contemporary ideal is to ignore the psychological depth and character that two thousand years of Christianity has bred in us. Indeed, any contemporary attempt to "rediscover" the blond beast within us is doomed to fail because our image of what that life could be were we only a master is hopelessly distorted by selectivity, biased representation and a longing to escape contemporary life. We might find *something* by roaming wild places, looking for blood and honour, tanning deer hides to make our own clothes, drinking bad wine, banging drums, dancing and attacking people. However, the conditions that made the masters exemplars of their time – poorly developed technology, an ineffective economic system, primitive psychology – make the attempt to revert now to their example little more than a wrongheaded relic. It is also likely to get us arrested, which just makes the point: *we* are no longer who *they* were.

In addition to the distinction between noble good and bad, a distinction that is the result of noble evaluation, there is another distinction, that between moral good and evil. This distinction is the exclusive product of the herd, the slave elements of society. The herd species of goodness emerges when those who are bad according to the noble valuation – the base and common – view themselves as good and the denial of their characteristics as evil. The herd evaluation presents a fairly straightforward reversal of noble valuations. Noble valuations are autonomous and made independently of any comparison with the common, the base; herd valuations, on the other hand, are the product of individuals who are self-reflective and whose thoughts about themselves are mediated by their knowledge that they are weak (*GM* I 10). Their actions are fundamentally *reactions* and their values are fundamentally *reactive* values, reactions against the perceived threat posed by the powerful to their survival (*GM* I 13). The slaves are passionless, pale and meek; they denigrate their bodies, express pity, practice charity, believe in other worlds where their fortunes are reversed and hope that they can achieve that world. And evil for them is that which they fear, namely power.

The agents of the slave revolt in moral evaluation are, of course, the weak and the ignoble. But Nietzsche makes it clear in Essay I that the slave revolt would never have been successful were it not for organized religion's recruitment of the slave's cause. Christianity in particular provides the slaves with a worldview wholly consonant with their hopes to find a reason for their suffering and to undermine the powerful. Christianity supplies the argumentative ammunition the slaves take into battle against the powerful, an arsenal of metaphysical claims, psychological explanations, promises, threats, social institutions and justifications for their aggressive reactions against the powerful, whom they loathe.

The slave revolt in morality is successful because Christianity more than any other social institution has enlisted the herd's decadence and resentment against the powerful. Both "decadence" and "resentment" are technical terms in Nietzsche's work. "Decadence" refers to psychological dispositions and character traits that are contrary to a healthy life and the social and cultural institutions that buttress and support those dispositions and traits. When Nietzsche identifies someone as a decadent, he refers not, as we might, to a libertine or a wastrel, but to someone who either chooses, or is so constituted as to be unable to avoid choosing, activities, behaviour and conduct that are unhealthy and contrary to human flourishing. These activities and behaviour can be physical behaviours or social actions, cognitive activity, such as particular beliefs or patterns of them, or affective behaviour, such as particular emotions or attitudes or patterns of them. Any such activity or behaviour qualifies as decadent when it either directly expresses or helps cultivate a state of being contrary to human flourishing.

A small digression to unpack some of these dense claims will help avoid misunderstanding. Nietzsche insists repeatedly that thwarting human flourishing is contrary to life itself. What can that mean? Nietzsche takes life to be the criterion of all evaluation. By this he means, among other things, that all evaluation is undertaken in the service of furthering and enhancing life. A person is decadent in the deepest Nietzschean sense of the term because he presumes to affirm that life is not worth living. Nietzsche thinks that this is absurd: it is, he believes, impossible to coherently assert that life is not worth living. For since the decadent must be alive to assert that life is worthless, his continued existence exhibits his ongoing belief to the contrary. Therefore, as Nietzsche notes, the decadent who asserts that life is not worth living cannot but be a liar. Not surprisingly, despite inveighing against willing, the decadent continues to will, even if what is willed is, in the end, contrary to what makes life itself possible. We shall return to this issue.

Decadence is thus contrary to human flourishing because it is contrary to life itself. It would be most helpful, then, were Nietzsche to specify that in which he takes human flourishing and life to consist. Unfortunately, he does not do so here, and nor, to be perfectly honest, are there extended discussions of human flourishing or of life in any of his published books (although *Beyond Good and Evil* has more to say about these matters than any other particular book). Instead, we have to piece together his views from a variety of different sources. We can say this much. A life is healthy when it allows us to flourish; we flourish when we exercise and augment our power; and we exercise and augment our power when we cultivate and deploy those psychological traits that permit us to impose structure and form on ourselves, thereby helping us overcome ourselves and then become who we are. Among the traits that, when cultivated to the point where they become the causes of our decisions and actions, constitute flourishing are separation and love of solitude, spiritual independence, discipline, disdain for equality of human beings, love of enemies, pride and courage. These are Nietzsche's core virtues.

It is obvious that human life, especially the life that we have inherited over the last few millennia, is more tortured, self-referential and self-aware than other kinds of lives. Thanks to our evolution from brutes to decadents (the description of which is the subject of *The Genealogy*), our kind of life is much more complex than the masters of Essay I. No better description of the promise our kind of life holds out for us is to be found than this one, from *Beyond Good and Evil*:

> That commanding something which the people call "the spirit" wants to be master in and around its own house and wants to feel that it is master; it has the will from multiplicity to simplicity, a will that ties up, tames, and is domineering and truly masterful. Its needs and capacities are so far the same as those which physiologists posit for everything that lives, grows, and multiplies. The spirit's power to appropriate the foreign stands revealed in its inclination to assimilate the new to the old, to simplify the manifold, and to overlook or repulse whatever is totally contradictory – just as it involuntarily emphasizes certain features and lines in what is foreign, in every piece of the "external world," retouching and falsifying the whole to

suit itself. Its intent in all this is to incorporate new "experiences," to file new things in old files – growth, in a word – or, more precisely, the *feeling* of growth, the feeling of increased power.

(*BGE* 230)

Since life is the criterion of value and since this description is of our kind of life, Nietzsche thinks it can serve as a criterion of value. Where life as described is enhanced, that is, where power is enhanced, we have flourishing and health, and where life as described is thwarted, that is, where power is thwarted, we have decadence and sickness. *The Anti-Christ* (*AC*) puts it into an infamous slogan: "What is good? All that heightens the feeling of power, the will to power, power itself in man. What is bad? Everything that is born of weakness" (*AC* 2).

Consider, then, a particular psychological state – pity – as an example of a decadent state. Pity is one of a number of types of concern for another's suffering, others being empathy, sympathy, compassion and mercy. What distinguishes pity from these others is that pity conserves suffering and multiplies it. Pity is occasioned by another's suffering but is conjoined with a disposition to keep that suffering alive and salient as a symptom of a claimed deep understanding of the despair that this earthly life engenders. That is the *conserving* part of pity. Secondly, when we pity another person's suffering we add our own suffering to that of others. That is the *multiplying* part of pity. Finally, pitying convinces us that such suffering is inevitable and that, as a result, it actually has moral value. Our suffering becomes a criterion of our faith and right thinking.

Nietzsche thinks this is madness. He does not deny that there is suffering; indeed, he believes that there is a lot of it, and he acknowledges that the worst thing about it is not its existence but its pointlessness. The point here is that pity provides those who have no other explanation of their suffering a wholly *fictitious* explanation of it. As any institutional representative of Christianity is happy to point out, we disobeyed God and were cast out of Eden in order to suffer. It is the *human lot* to suffer. Pity serves as a tactic for revealing the ubiquity and appropriateness of suffering and our culpability in it. Nietzsche puts it this way:

"I suffer: someone must be to blame for it" – thus thinks every sickly sheep. But his shepherd, the ascetic priest, tells him: "Quite so, my sheep! Someone must be to blame for it: but you yourself are this someone, you alone are to blame for it – *you alone are to blame for yourself!*"

(*GM* III 15)

Once we are convinced that pity is the suitable response to suffering, the game is up. Upon this epiphany, the Christian jumps in not only with an explanation of our suffering and our guilt, but a cure for it as well: believe in God, subject yourself to the church as His earthly representative and prepare yourself for heaven by doing what the church tells you to do. It is a wonderful package deal. The Christian makes us sick and then offers the potions that purport to cure the sickness. In short, Christianity *invents* most of the pain it pretends to cure, parades that invention around as if it were a *discovery* about the human condition, *prescribes* a cure for it and then *supplies* everything necessary to induce dependence. But since the sickness is fictional, the prescribed cure just gets us hooked on a regime of tranquilizers that makes us ever more diseased.

Consider resentment next. "Resentment" refers to a set of psychological dispositions and character traits. A psychological disposition or character trait is an instance of resentment when it is a state of anger or frustration whose cause is insult or injury to oneself or recognition of one's decadence and weakness. But that cannot be all there is to resentment, because there are lots of instances of anger and frustration caused by someone else hurting or insulting us that are not resentful. We must also add that a resentful state is such a state of anger or frustration coupled with the recognition that direct reprisal against the responsible agent is likely to lead to further injury or insult. It is, thus, only human beings who are properly capable of resentment because only human beings are conscious and sufficiently complex to recognize their own weakness and to plot and strategize as a response to that recognition. Some paradigm examples of resentful states are, of course, resentment, revenge, corrupt desires for insulting others, envy, self-pity and other-directed pity, and desires for retribution. Some examples of products of resentment are strategies to weaken the agents of insults and consolation strategies to make ourselves feel better.

It is hard to overemphasize the importance that resentment plays in Nietzsche's assessment of the herd's psychological profile. Nietzsche believes that contemporary Europe is dominated by resentful evaluative codes, even to the extent that those who should, by rights, be exempt from their reach feel themselves bound by them and even to the extent that those who fight against them tend only to add further twists to those codes without understanding that their reaction against those codes is actually determined by them. This is, after all, why the slave revolt in morality has been victorious. When even the most powerful are constrained by herd values in voicing their opposition to them, those herd values set the agenda. Those who oppose herd values now start their opposition so deeply influenced by those values that any reversion to the masters is anachronistic foolishness and any wilful assertion of independence from them empty rhetoric. For better or worse, those of us who want to oppose

Christian values have to start by admitting that we too uphold them and are thoroughly stained by them.

It is no surprise, then, that Nietzsche actually identifies *himself* with those for whom herd values are values (although his reasons for valuing them are different). In *Ecce Homo* (*EH*) he identifies himself with the decadent product of two thousand years of the slave revolt (*EH* "Why I am So Wise"). Why does he do this? The answer is that he recognizes that saying "no" to the slave revolt in morality, to resentment, to Christianity, is to say "no" to ourselves, and that is incompatible with loving our fate, a requirement for flourishing that Nietzsche makes repeatedly. While it is tempting to think that we can simply turn away entirely from our personal and cultural pasts through an act of free will and head off bravely in a new direction, such a negation is no more possible than the wilful reversion to the masters. Both are romantic delusions. Loving our fate (*amor fati*) – an ability Nietzsche came, late in his life, to think was necessary for a good life – requires that we become and overcome who we are. It is self-deception to think that we are nothing to begin with and can become whoever we want to be by an act of will.

Essay II

Essay II is a most surprising essay. After the first essay one might expect Nietzsche to advocate a wholesale repudiation of the herd. However, Nietzsche resists temptation and instead offers a genealogical account of the development of another pair of phenomena: guilt and responsibility. Why this turn? Nietzsche thinks these two capacities are essential for understanding ourselves as moderns and essential for understanding how we moderns might yet flourish in the bowels of herd morality. To overcome who we are and to express our power now we must first understand who we are. Essay I offered part of an answer; Essay II offers another part by tracing the development of our modern sense of guilt and responsibility. Nietzsche's thesis is that the prerequisites of guilt are also the prerequisites for the best and noblest things we can do with ourselves now. In short, realizing human excellence now entails the development of some of the very personality characteristics that herd morality has implanted in human beings.

The first pair of character traits are self-identity at a time (synchronic identity) and self-identity over time (diachronic identity). Both of these are necessary for a sense of responsibility for the actions we perform. After all, in order to be responsible for what we do now, we have to know that who we are now is the same as who we were ten minutes ago and who we will be in ten minutes' time. Responsibility is, in turn, necessary for bad conscience and guilt, which in turn are necessary for the highest forms of autonomy, self-creativity and nobility. So, without all of them – synchronic and diachronic identity, responsibility and bad conscience (guilt) – the highest forms of human excellence available to us now cannot obtain. What is needed, then, is a genealogy of responsibility and the bad conscience. Here, punishment is relevant, because it explains the initial appearance of responsibility.

Nietzsche's genealogy reveals that responsibility was developed through a mutilating, bloody and deadly regime of techniques that ingrained a sense of identity at and over time. The original purpose of punishment is unknown – perhaps the enjoyment of inflicting pain on others – but one initial consequence of punishment is that memory is ingrained in human beings. As Nietzsche notes, only that which is most painful will be burned into memory. Since memory entails continuity over time, that is, diachronic identity, it is to the mechanisms of memory inducement that Nietzsche calls attention, providing a list of mechanisms that, over the course of history, have been used for this purpose. The sadistic catalogue includes:

> stoning ... breaking on the wheel ... piercing with stakes, tearing apart or trampling by horses ("quartering"), boiling of the criminal in oil or wine ... the popular flaying alive ... cutting flesh from the chest, and also the practice of smearing the wrongdoer with honey and leaving him in the blazing sun for the flies.　　　*(GM* II 5)

That is *our* past, a past of using proportional pain to communicate to victims that they are now the same person as the person who earlier committed a transgression. So, even if we do not know what the original purpose of punishment was, we can, Nietzsche thinks, hazard that the first social consequence achieved by punishment was to instil, through inflicting proportional pain, a sense of diachronic identity and with that a sense of prudential responsibility. As he notes, the "actual *effect* of punishment must beyond question be sought above all in a heightening of prudence, in an extending of the memory, in a will henceforth to go to work more cautiously, ... in a kind of improvement in self-criticism" (*GM* II 15).

Once the appropriate sense of prudential responsibility was ingrained, punishment should have reached the end of its utility. Yet punishment did not evaporate just because its original consequence was realized. How do we explain the continuation of punishment? Nietzsche's answer is not kind. He thinks that the occurrence of punishment is always underdetermined by any single social function and that it continues after prudential responsibility is established because it is repeatedly endowed with new functions. For example, punishment makes not just the debtor but also the creditor more predictable and humane, and it prevents arbitrary rampaging by unpaid creditors. Woven through all of these various functions of punishment is the public display of punishment, the *festivity* of inflicting pain on others. One of the constants in European, indeed, most, societies is the spectacle of publicly imposing pain:

> To see others suffer does one good, to make others suffer even more: this is a hard saying but an ancient, mighty, human, all-too-human principle to which even the apes might subscribe; for it has been said that in devising bizarre cruelties they anticipate man and are, as it were, his "prelude." Without cruelty there is no festival: thus the longest and most ancient part of human history teaches – and in punishment there is so much that is *festive!* (*GM* II 6)

Such elements are present even today. Every time a convicted murderer is executed anywhere in the United States, hundreds of people gather at the prison walls to celebrate the death announcement. As painful as it may be to admit to ourselves, Nietzsche's fundamental point is thus borne out: whatever the humanitarian and political goals of punishment have been, may be now, or will be in the future, they have always co-existed and will probably continue to co-exist side by side with the spectacle of inflicting physical or psychological pain.

For all of our viciousness, Nietzsche is prepared to admit that over the past two thousand years the need for and the pleasure taken in spectacles of cruelty have moderated somewhat. For, as we become tamer – more predictable, less prone to outrageous rampages, refined, guilty, "spiritualized" – so too does the need for flaunting pain become less salient. Even if, for instance, hundreds gather outside the prisons where convicts are put to death, it is significant that these death celebrants must now wait *outside* the prison. Many nations have abandoned capital punishment altogether and most of those that still use it do not carry it out in public, preferring instead to sequester the condemned away from all but those deemed necessary to witness death.

This spiritualization of cruelty culminates for Nietzsche in eventually overcoming corporal punishment altogether, with mercy:

> It is not unthinkable that a society might attain such a *consciousness of power* that it could allow itself the noblest luxury possible to it – letting those who harm it go *unpunished*. "What are my parasites to

me?" it might say. "May they live and prosper: I am strong enough for that!"

The justice which began with, "Everything is dischargeable, everything must be discharged," ends by winking and letting those incapable of discharging their debt go free: it ends, as does every good thing on earth, by *overcoming itself*. This self-overcoming of justice: one knows the beautiful name it has given itself – *mercy*; it goes without saying that mercy remains the privilege of the most powerful man, or better, his – beyond the law.   (*GM* II 10)

Here, Nietzsche mentions power and the role that it plays in distinguishing the best elements of a society from its worst. Although the will to power is not discussed at length in the *Genealogy*, it is clearly presupposed in this and other passages.

There is a problem with Nietzsche's explanation of punishment. The kind of responsibility it instils is prudential, not moral. The debtor knows that his actions are his, and so knows that if he does not repay the debt, he is likely to forfeit – depending upon the size of the debt – some part(s) of his body, his spouse or his life. But moral responsibility and a sense of guilt are deeper than prudential responsibility, for they are internally imposed states of mind and not just prudent responses to external threats. So we need to add to the explanation of prudential responsibility some additional resource to explain moral responsibility and the bad conscience. Nietzsche thinks this additional resource is the "internalization of man" (*GM* II 16), the psychological revolution attending our gradual immersion into complex human societies, where outwardly directed drives are turned inwards.

When we become civilized we lose the primitive vent for our instincts in war and dancing and turn those instincts for mastery over others and things inwards on ourselves in cruelty to ourselves. While this internal laceration is, at least initially, sick and leads to self-mutilation, it is also the most important psychological change humanity has experienced, for it deepens our psychology and makes possible entirely new forms of self-overcoming hitherto unknown and impossible. The following description of this transition is justly famous:

The man who, from lack of external enemies and resistances and forcibly confined to the oppressive narrowness and punctiliousness of custom, impatiently lacerated, persecuted, gnawed at, assaulted, and maltreated himself; this animal that rubbed itself raw against the bars of its cage as one tried to "tame" it; this deprived creature, racked with homesickness for the wild, who had to turn himself into an adventure, a torture chamber, an uncertain and dangerous wilderness – this fool, this yearning and desperate prisoner became the inventor of the "bad conscience."

Let us add at once that, on the other hand, the existence on earth of an animal soul turned against itself, taking sides against itself, was something so new, profound, unheard of, enigmatic, contradictory, *and pregnant with a future* that the aspect of the earth was essentially altered. Indeed, divine spectators were needed to do justice to the spectacle that thus began and the end of which is not yet in sight – a spectacle too subtle, too marvelous, too paradoxical to be played senselessly unobserved on some ludicrous planet! From now on, man is *included* among the most unexpected and exciting lucky throws in the dice game of Heraclitus' "great child," be he called Zeus or change; he gives rise to an interest, a tension, a hope, almost a certainty, as if with him something were announcing and preparing itself, as if man were not a goal but only a way, an episode, a bridge, a great promise—   (*GM* II 16)

Among many other claims made here, the most relevant for our purposes is that Nietzsche causally links the emergence of the bad conscience with the internalization of what were once outwardly directed drives. This is a little mysterious. Why should internalizing cruelty lead to the emergence of the bad conscience, the sense of guilt?

Nietzsche has an answer to this question. He abstracts away from all of the observable acts of cruelty against others to a drive to impose form (*GM* II 17). The mark of crude power is, he thinks, not observable bits of behaviour such as impaling a deer, but the drive behind those bits of behaviour, the drive to command, to impose oneself on others. Nietzsche insists that this drive is an instance of the drive of giving form to the world. Once our outwardly directed drives are thwarted, as they are when we enter into structured social and political relationships, they take as their object not others but ourselves. The internalized drive to impose form then takes not others but the self as its raw material and demands that it be stamped with direction, with structure, with discipline and control. As Nietzsche puts it: "This *instinct for freedom* forcibly made latent – we have seen it already – this instinct for freedom pushed back and repressed, incarcerated within and finally able to discharge and vent itself only on itself: that, and that alone, is what the *bad conscience* is in its beginnings" (*GM* II 17). Note that he does not say that the instinct of freedom turned inwards is *all* that the bad conscience is. But it is the primordial drive from which variants of the bad conscience develop. There are, in principle, many interesting developments of this primordial form of the bad conscience. Nietzsche focuses on two. The first is what Nietzsche calls "active bad conscience" (*GM* II 18), which is, he thinks, the soil from which everything beautiful and worthwhile grows. We shall return to this matter again in our discussion of Essay III. But we must confront the other form of bad conscience, for it is this second form that has become through Christianity the most familiar form of guilt.

Nietzsche's explanation of the moral sense of guilt – the moral bad conscience – is that the debt primitive peoples feel to their ancestors for their very existence continuously grows as the power of the tribe itself increases until the most powerful tribes convert their ancestors into gods. Since gods are transcendent beings, the debt owed to these gods becomes increasingly difficult to repay. Finally, with the Christian God, which, as Nietzsche notes, is the "maximum god attained so far" (*GM* II 20), the sense of debt becomes maximal, that is, unpayable in principle, and religious guilt is formulated. Religious guilt is the logical and psychological precursor to moral guilt. Moral guilt precipitates out of religious guilt the phenomenon of inflicting pain upon ourselves and the belief that we have fallen so far away from God that our debt to him for our existence is "irredeemable" (*GM* II 21). We cannot redeem the debt because our sin in the face of God is original, final and infinite. This will to find ourselves guilty "to a degree that can never be atoned for" (*GM* II 22) is moral guilt. Given his view of the matter, Nietzsche's despairing conclusion to the essay seems the only possible one: "Oh this insane and pathetic beast – man! What ideas he has, what unnaturalness, what paroxysms of nonsense, what *bestiality of thought* as soon as he is prevented just a little from being a *beast in deed!*" (*GM* II 22).

Essay III

Essay III is the most complex of the three essays composing *The Genealogy of Morals*, in part because it addresses so many issues, in part because it addresses what looks like a paradox. That paradox flows from the topic of the essay, the attraction of what Nietzsche calls "ascetic" values. These ascetic values – poverty, chastity and humility – form the core of the herd outlook resulting from the slave revolt in morality. They are typically used by the slave elements of society as a kind of anaesthetic against suffering, but, amazingly, they can also be used by others, such as philosophers, artists and other exemplars of human flourishing, for the noblest and most far-reaching experiments with life. The paradox that flows from the investigation is, then, this: how can self-abnegation be an expression of *power* both for the worst exemplars of humanity and for some of its best? Another way of putting the point is this: it looks like ascetic ideals are both systematically against life and yet necessary for some of the highest forms of life. We can even put the paradox as the conclusion of a simple argument: herd morality professes to lead us to a good life; but morality is decadent, so, as we have seen above, against life; yet herd morality's decadence must be a product of life; therefore herd morality is both against life and a product of life. That conclusion certainly looks like a self-contradiction. Nietzsche's response is that the paradox is only apparent.

Let us set the scene for Essay III by summarizing the results of the first two essays. According to Essay I, there has been a revolution in evaluation: the slave revolt. The result of the slave revolt is to invert noble forms of valuation. Herd evaluation makes the ideals of the slaves binding on all, the best and worst alike. Why then did the masters of Essay I succumb to the slaves' evaluation? Part of the answer comes in Essay II. The slave revolt in morality accompanies the development of the bad conscience, which, in turn, is a result of our immersion into social life. With an alternative system of evaluation and the bad conscience both in place, the morality salesmen come on the scene to prop up the slaves by justifying their existence. The slaves and their apologists then start to eat away at the nobility's sense of self-worth, difference and distance, eroding the nobility's confidence that what applies to it applies only to it and that what applies to the masses does not apply to it. Slowly, over the centuries, the moralists spread their infection through the masses, giving them a reason to live, but eventually they poison the noble classes as well, contaminating them with guilt about their wellbeing.

For all of the historical detail of Essays I and II, neither essay completely answers some fundamental questions. First, Essay I does not answer the question, *why* was the slave revolt successful? Essay I *describes* what happened, but it does not *explain* why the nobles did not simply turn their backs on the herd. And, secondly, why, of all of the ways the bad conscience can be dealt with, does Christianity and its prescriptions for the alleviation of suffering come to dominate all others? Again, Essay II *describes* the development of diachronic identity, responsibility and guilt, which are necessary for morality, but it does not *explain* how morality, Christian herd morality in particular, capitalized on them to become the pre-eminent mode of evaluation. So it is up to Essay III to answer these questions.

The key concept for unpacking these explanations is that of ascetic ideals, the values of chastity, humility and poverty. According to Nietzsche, there are two ways these values can be used. The first way is to think of them as a means to an end; the second is to think of them as intrinsic values. Call the first use the "non-moral" use of ascetic ideals; call the second the "moral" use of ascetic ideals. The first eleven sections of Essay III describe various non-moral ways in which ascetic ideals are used by artists and philosophers. He discusses artists in the first six sections and philosophers in the next five. Consider the manner in which philosophers use ascetic ideals. The philosopher uses chastity, humility and poverty both as protection against the herd and as bridges to independence from contemporary culture. Nietzsche discusses the first point in sections 9 and 10 of Essay III, noting that since philosophers are critics of dominant values, adopting ascetic ideals outfits the philosopher with a mask behind which she may continue her frightening work. Ascetic ideals are also used by philosophers for some of their own purposes, as a kind of attitudinal ensemble adopted for engaging in their work:

> What, then, is the meaning of the ascetic ideal in the case of a philosopher? My answer is – you will have guessed it long ago: the philosopher sees in it an optimum condition for the highest and boldest spirituality and smiles – he does *not* deny "existence," he rather affirms *his* existence and *only* his existence, and this perhaps to the point at which he is not far from harbouring the impious wish *pereat mundus, fiat philosophia, fiat philosophus,* **fiam!** [Let the world perish, but let there be philosophy, let there be the philosopher, *me!*].
>
> (*GM* III 7)

Cultivation of chastity, humility and poverty engender the conditions in which the philosophical animal "achieves its maximal feeling of power" (*GM* III 7). Otherwise put, the ascetic ideals are a means to augment their will to power. Since what is true of philosophers is true of other "great, fruitful, inventive spirits" (*GM* III 8), many truly great individuals have licence to practise them as well for, by their cultivation, discipline and self-overcoming are also cultivated. Philosophers see the ascetic ideals as means of expressing their own power and of becoming and overcoming who they are. Of course, they do not thereby condemn those who deny the value of ascetic ideals, for they recognize that their life is but one of a number of distinct kinds of flourishing life.

Moral asceticism is a different story. Moral ascetics make a blanket judgement against all of life. That is one of the things that set moral ascetics off from philosophers, who restrict use of the ascetic ideals to their own lives:

> The ascetic treats life as a wrong road on which one must finally walk back to the point where it begins, or as a mistake that is put right by deeds – that we *ought* to put right: for he *demands* that one go along

225

with him; where he can he compels acceptance of *his* evaluation of existence. (*GM* III 11)

So, unlike philosophers, who use ascetic ideals as instrumental values to enhance their peculiar kind of life as a means to the end of philosophical insight, moral ascetics affirm ascetic ideals as an intrinsic end, as the highest goal of *every* life. Moral ascetics reject life and compel others to agree with their disgust. Nietzsche makes the point evocatively by imagining another species investigating us from afar:

> Read from a distant star, the majuscule script of our earthly existence would perhaps lead to the conclusion that the earth was the distinctively *ascetic planet*, a nook of disgruntled, arrogant, and offensive creatures filled with a profound disgust at themselves, at the earth, at all life, who inflict as much pain on themselves as they possibly can out of pleasure of inflicting pain – which is probably their only pleasure. (*GM* III 11)

All those who seriously believe that ascetic ideals have any but limited instrumental use are included in this description and that, Nietzsche thinks, is everyone who thinks that herd values are universally binding. For herd values are nothing more than the popularized expression of ascetic ideals.

This sorry state of affairs is the end product of the slave revolt in morality. The ascetic, disgusted with life and resentful of those who are not, parades his self-loathing ideals around and insists that they apply to everyone and in particular to those who think other than he does. Those who are otherwise healthy succumb to this presentation because they share with the ascetic a sense of responsibility and guilt, the cognitive nodes to which the ascetic ideals attach like leeches. Once attached, those ideals suck the life-enhancing drives out of their host, leaving even the healthiest and most interesting desiccated shells of their former selves.

We now face the paradox fully. The ascetic's ideals drain all of the life-enhancing drives out of a life and yet he offers those ideals as a way to enhance all kinds of life. The only resolution to the paradox is to admit that the kind of life actually enhanced by ascetic ideals must already be so debased that only denying the conditions that make life possible in general make this particular kind of life endurable. It is only a sick, decadent and declining life, a life shot through with self-loathing, that could find the prospect of denying drives and affects a *tonic*, and as a possible prescription for health. Nietzsche puts the matter as follows:

Where does one not encounter that veiled glance which burdens one with a profound sadness, that inward-turned glance of the born failure which betrays how such a man speaks to himself – that glance which is a sigh! "If only I were someone else," sighs this glance: "but there is no hope of that. I am who I am: how could I ever get free of myself? And yet – I *am sick of myself!*"

It is on such soil, on swampy ground, that every weed, every poisonous plant grows, always so small, so hidden, so false, so saccharine. Here the worms of vengefulness and rancour swarm; here the air stinks of secrets and concealment; here the web of the most malicious of all conspiracies is being spun constantly – the conspiracy of the suffering against the well-constituted and victorious, here the aspect of the victorious is *hated* ... What do they really want? At least to *represent* justice, love, wisdom, superiority – that is the ambition of the "lowest," the sick. And how skillful such an ambition makes them! Admire above all the forger's skill with which the stamp of virtue, even the ring, the golden-sounding ring of virtue, is here counterfeited. They monopolize virtue, these weak, hopelessly sick people, there is no doubt of it: "we alone are the good and just," they say, "we alone are *hominess bonae voluntatis* (men of good will)". (*GM* III 14)

The psychology outlined here is at the core of Nietzsche's thinking about morality. All of us seek to be powerful individuals – strong, intelligent, goal-directed, creative, disciplined, rich in contradictions – but only a few ever achieve it, for it is difficult and causes a considerable amount of suffering. The rest of us are failures, know it, and are miserable as a result. We hate ourselves for our weakness, uselessness and redundancy, and we hate those who are demonstrably better. So we latch on to any evaluation scheme on which we, *qua* failures, are exemplars, especially if that also means laying low the powerful.

Christianity enlists this resentment by offering an explanation of our suffering, an explanation of its causes and a cure. According to Christianity and herd morality, the source of suffering is not our self-hatred, unrealized dreams and envy of the powerful, but our desiring power in the first place. Christianity's recommended cure for the suffering sometimes caused by our drives and passions is to extirpate the drives and passions altogether. Power itself and the desire for it are for the Christian the great sins. We who desire power are sinners and are therefore responsible for our own suffering (*GM* III 15). Christianity offers the ascetic values as a strategy to deaden the suffering caused by unrealizable desires for power. This is a classic consolation strategy:

extirpate passion and drive and the desires that follow from them and suffering will cease. Succeeding at this game is of course decadent, but the genius of Christianity and herd morality is that they offer evaluative systems that permit life's failures to succeed at *something*, even if what they succeed at is confounding the conditions of a healthy life. Life's failures become themselves by undoing the very conditions that make their life possible.

Thus is the paradox dissolved. The ascetic ideals are contrary to most *healthy* lives but consolations to *sick* and *unhealthy* lives. So, although they are, at best, instrumentally useful to some kinds of mental health, ascetic ideals are in the diseased necessary to avoid a nihilistic collapse. How then can Nietzsche criticize the moral ascetic? In the end, what Nietzsche objects to is the ascetic's universalization to everyone of what applies only to them. Herd morality inverts the natural order of values and thereby provide a reason for life's failures to feel good about themselves, but accomplishing that reversal requires disguising for ever its own perspectivity. Christianity and herd morality lie about their own perspectivity, deny altogether that they serve the interests only of a group. They pretend to be something that they are not and pretend not to be something that they are.

Nietzsche adds an extended discussion of science toward the end of Essay III, whose relevance becomes clear only when we realize that he is warning against an all too familiar temptation that emerges once religion loses its status as the ground of objective moral evaluation. Most people think that science can and will liberate us from and be an alternative to religion and morality. The great hope of the Enlightenment has always been to replace the superstition and myth of folk religion with the clarity and reason of scientific method and scientific truth. We see the consequences of this hope every day, in creationism/evolution debates, abortion debates, debates about insanity and mental illness, arguments about prayer in school and many others. These debates are inevitable given the assumption that the objective truths of science oppose myth and faith and given the expectation that the empirical findings of science will replace the metaphysical stories told be religion.

Nietzsche rejects such optimism in science. He is willing to allow that science can be deployed against Christianity and the absurdities of extra-sensory worlds, altruism and higher beings, but science itself is a secularized expression of exactly what it criticizes, asceticism stripped of metaphysical excess. As such, science is, Nietzsche thinks, the *best* ally moral asceticism can have. For both still rely on truth:

> This pair, science and the ascetic ideal, both rest on the same foundation – I have already indicated it: on the same overestimation of

truth (more exactly: on the same belief that truth is inestimable and cannot be criticized). Therefore they are *necessarily* allies, so that if they are to be fought they can only be fought and called in question together. (*GM* III 25)

Science, every bit as much as religion, *depends* upon the assumption that there is an objective world beyond all interpretation (even if it is no longer a heavenly realm) that licenses absolute truths that are equally binding on everyone. Likewise, science counsels abstraction from one's own life in order to view the world objectively, an intellectually twisted expression of the moral ascetic's adherence to chastity. Moreover, we have scientific labourers who practise humility before the truth and who, by suppressing their desires in order to devote their lives to their research, their labs and their books, practise poverty as well. Thus the practice of science is practical asceticism.

Nietzsche goes further than simply assimilating science to asceticism. He understands that science and asceticism are both attempts to stave off nihilism but are, for all that, nihilistic to the core. For, as he speculates:

> Man, the bravest of animals and the one most accustomed to suffer-
> ing, does *not* repudiate suffering as such; he *desires* it, he even seeks
> it out, provided he is shown a *meaning* for it, a *purpose* of suffering.
> The meaninglessness of suffering, *not* suffering itself, was the curse
> that lay over mankind so far – *and the ascetic ideal offered man mean-*
> *ing!* It was the only meaning offered so far; any meaning is better
> than none at all … In it, suffering was *interpreted*; the tremendous
> void seemed to have been filled; the door was closed to any kind of
> suicidal nihilism. (*GM* III 28)

Nihilism here refers to the collapse of all values and the despair that results from such a collapse. Nietzsche is explicit in his judgement about the role that ascetic ideals can play in salvaging otherwise unsalvageable lives. By making the nihilistic ascetic values binding on all, pointless suffering of the masses is replaced with suffering for a reason, namely, our infinite guilt. So the ascetic's suffering on behalf of his nihilistic ideals saves him from the nihilism of mean-ingless suffering.

For all of his suspicion that science is practically ascetic and nihilistic, Nietzsche is careful not to draw overly dismissive conclusions about science. He also suggests elsewhere, in *The Gay Science* and *The Anti-Christ* for instance, that there are many epistemological perspectives to adopt when gain-ing knowledge and that science is preferable to most others. How, then, can he both criticize science and praise it? One answer is that Nietzsche's assessment of science can be seen to be an instance of his general attitude about most things, namely, that we are well advised to refrain from dogmatic over-assertion on behalf of our beliefs. That attitude is, of course, a direct implication of Nietzsche's epistemological perspectivism. Nietzsche's perspectivism is a complex set of claims, and there is not sufficient space here to do all of them justice. However, one famous component of the view is that our knowledge varies as a function of the number of perspectives that can come into play:

> But precisely because we seek knowledge, let us not be ungrateful to such resolute reversals of accustomed perspectives and valuations … to *want* to see differently, is no small discipline and preparation of the intellect for its future "objectivity" – the latter understood not as "contemplation without interest" (which is a nonsensical absurdity), but as the ability *to control* one's pro and con and to dispose of them, so that one knows how to employ a *variety* of perspectives and affective interpretations in the service of knowledge …. There is *only* a perspective seeing, *only* a perspective "knowing"; and the *more* affects we allow to speak about one thing, the *more* eyes, different eyes, we can use to observe one thing, the more complete will our "concept" of this thing, our "objectivity," be.   (*GM* III 12)

For instance, if simple perceptual beliefs have a number of relevant perspectives for determining their justification, more complex beliefs will no doubt have many more perspectives that are relevant for determining whether we are justified in believing them. Of course, Nietzsche is not advocating that our justification for a belief consists simply in adding up a bunch of available perspectives and announcing that we have considered fifteen contexts in which the belief is true, *therefore* the belief is justified. For some perspectives are true but irrelevant, some relevant but false, and some relevant and uninteresting.

Nietzsche's epistemological perspectivism is a form of relativism, for it indexes truth and justification to perspectives, and that makes both truth and justification relative to those perspectives. However, Nietzsche's relativism is quite benign, for although truth is indexed to perspectives, he allows that there are statements and beliefs that are true not only in a particular perspective, but are true across perspectives, and this permits him to reject the conclusion that every truth is as true as the next. And even if his perspectivism about justification requires that it be indexed to a context or perspective, again he allows that there are cross-perspectival justification practices and that a measure of a belief's justification is that it can be submitted to cross-perspectival adjudication. So, again, Nietzsche may reject the conclusion that every reason for believing something is as good as the next.

Consider, then, a perspectivist account of science. That there can be a perspectivist science implies that there are features of science that Nietzsche admires. One such feature is the scientific method, which he regards as producing a much-desired mental rigour. A related positive feature is that adherence to the scientific method staves off superstition. This feature is cause for some of Nietzsche's greatest praise and it is the source of some of his greatest sorrow, for scientific method was in place in Greek and Roman culture and was then condemned by Christianity and lost during the Middle Ages. Finally, science does not commit a variety of common errors found in other perspectives. For example, since science needs only the apparent world as its domain of reference, it need not commit itself to the false division of the real *versus* the apparent world and, in its attention to natural phenomena, science can be non-moral. It is no wonder that herd moralists and religious types are compelled to attack science. Nietzsche makes the point in *The Anti-Christ* as follows: "it is all over with priests and gods if man becomes scientific! – *Moral*: science is the forbidden in itself – it alone is forbidden. Science is the *first* sin, the germ of all sins, *original* sin" (AC 48).

Still, for all of its virtues, the ongoing *practice* of science by scientists reveals their continued allegiance to the ascetic ideals and to the hope of yet discovering a body of objective truths that will warrant a universally accepted set of empirical findings and, perhaps, a universally binding set of moral evaluations. In this, scientists recapitulate the psychological dynamic of all decadents: rather than suffer meaninglessly, they will find some universal ideal in the service of which *their* suffering is meaningful. The search for objective scientific truth may in the end be as illusory as the search for God's truth, but so long as the illusion can be maintained, science entails and so justifies the ascetic sacrifices made in its name. Of course, the scientist's warrant against suffering lasts only so long as the scientist continues under the illusion that his ascetic regime is on a par with the moralist's ascetic regime and so is undone as easily as the moralist's. Then and only then – in the crucible of the debilitating nihilism that will follow – will the world be ready for Nietzsche's alternative hypothesis: will to power.

Conclusion

The Genealogy of Morals may seem unrelentingly negative and critical, especially of Christianity. Still, for all of his condemnation of Christianity and herd morality, we have to remember again that Nietzsche nowhere excludes himself from the criticism. He is relating his own history because he is discussing modern European history. Let us note, then, that in so far as Nietzsche allows that consciousness, guilt and a sense of responsibility are required for self-control and self-discipline, and in so far as ascetic ideals are still instrumentally viable, the debts we owe to herd thinking in general and Christianity in particular are enormous. It was, after all, in the herd – the weak, the decadent and the resentful – that such reflection and self-awareness first developed as a force for change. It was the herd that, in responding to the rapacious masters described in Essay I, turned their inevitably frustrated attempts to augment power against others inwards, thus claiming a direct victory over themselves and guaranteeing the indirect and eventual victory over the masters. They became those who had control of themselves and who overcame themselves in exhibitions of self-directed cruelty. And they also accomplished an indirect victory over the strong, but unreflective, masters. They burrowed into the mind of the master and have been watching it rot for a millennium.

No doubt the masters were a little mystified when the herd reacted against them by labelling them evil. After all, they were no more capable of being other than they were than a predator was. But the herd of slaves was different: their misery prompted them into brooding about things, reflecting on things and on themselves. They wanted explanations of their misery and solutions to it. In this process, they became interesting and devastatingly effective. Against the masters, the slaves were like insects, coming in droning swarms, infecting them with slave values and slave ways of thinking until the masters turned against themselves. After infection, the masters hobbled around in a stupor of domestication and civility, humbled not by any physical violence done against them, but by their own poisoned psyches.

A necessary condition for the slave revolt's success is that the masters had to be able to reflect on themselves. Otherwise, how would the self-doubt that the slaves contaminated them with ever find purchase? And that is the second crucial reversal introduced by the slave revolt and the second great debt we all owe to the herd. In the herd, conscious awareness and guilt first developed, and from them they spread into the masters. The development of consciousness and its attendant bad conscience fundamentally changed the human psyche and the future of humanity.

What had happened was nothing less than a Copernican revolution in psychology and morality. Copernicus reoriented astronomy, cosmology and theology by rejecting the view that the earth was the centre of the universe, replacing it with the heliocentric model with which we are all familiar. The slave revolt in morality was, if Nietzsche is right, of comparable significance. Where reflection had been a rare and sporadic episode quickly dismissed as a voice of gods, now it became an everyday occurrence. Where power in the masters had been exercised against the flesh of the weak and against enemies, power in the herd was internalized. Where the masters had once been the exemplification of a good life, they now became contemptible and barbaric relics of a bygone era. Where the slaves had once been the pawns of the masters, they now became the exemplars of a new regime of power, one focused inwards rather than outwards, a regime bent on power enhancement by self-improvement rather than by acts of violence against others. Refocusing our drive for power within our own bodies and psyches opened up worlds of refinement undreamt of by the one-dimensional masters, who were no more capable of becoming a Beethoven than a beet might be, no more capable of thinking about mathematics than a dog. And this Copernican revolution of our interior life was premised on the discovery and cultivation of reflective consciousness and guilt. It succeeded, of course, but, more importantly, it sowed the seeds for the extraordinary accomplishments of the past two thousand years and the even more astonishing future awaiting us if we could but liberate ourselves from our self-administered addiction to decadence and resentment.

Further reading

Collected works by Nietzsche in German

Colli, G. & M. Montinari (eds) 1975. *Werke: Kritische Gesamtausgabe Briefwechsel*, 24 vols in 4 parts. Berlin: Walter de Gruyter.
Colli, G. & M. Montinari (eds) 1988. *Sämtliche Werke: Kritische Studienausgabe in 15 Bänden*, Berlin: Walter de Gruyter.

The Genealogy *in English translation*

There is no reliable collection of Nietzsche's works in English currently available. Such a collection is under construction by Stanford University Press, under the general editorship of Ernst Behler. The following are the best English translations of *The Genealogy*:

1967. *On the Genealogy of Morals*, W. Kaufmann & R. J. Hollingdale (trans.). New York: Random House.
1994. *On the Genealogy of Morality*, C. Diethe (trans.). Cambridge: Cambridge University Press.
1996. *On the Genealogy of Morals*, D. Smith (trans.). Oxford: Oxford University Press.
1998. *On the Genealogy of Morality*, M. Clark & A. Swensen (trans.). Indianapolis, IN: Hackett.

Books about Nietzsche's views on morality and books on The Genealogy

Berkowitz, P. 1995. *Nietzsche: The Ethics of an Immoralist*. Cambridge, MA: Harvard University Press.

Clark, M. 1990. *Nietzsche on Truth and Philosophy*. Cambridge: Cambridge University Press.

Foucault, M. 1977. *Language, Counter-Memory, Practice: Selected Essays and Interviews by Michel Foucault*, D, F. Bouchard (ed.), D. F. Bouchard & S. Simon (trans.). Ithaca, NY: Cornell University Press.

Havas, R. 1995. *Nietzsche's* Genealogy: *Nihilism and the Will to Knowledge*. Ithaca, NY: Cornell University Press.

Hayman, R. 1980. *Nietzsche: A Critical Life*. Oxford: Oxford University Press.

Hunt, L. 1991. *Nietzsche and the Origin of Virtue*. New York: Routledge.

Kaufmann, W. 1974. *Nietzsche: Philosopher, Psychologist, Anti-Christ*, 4th edn. Princeton, NJ: Princeton University Press.

Leiter, B. 2002. *Nietzsche on Morality*. New York: Routledge.

Magnus, B. & K. Higgins (eds) 1996. *The Cambridge Companion to Nietzsche*. Cambridge: Cambridge University Press.

May, S. 1999. *Nietzsche's Ethics and His War on "Morality"*. Oxford: Oxford University Press.

Müller-Lauter, W. 1999. *Nietzsche: His Philosophy of Contradictions and the Contradictions of His Philosophy*, D. J. Parent (trans.). Urbana, IL: University of Illinois Press.

Nehamas, A. 1985. *Nietzsche: Life as Literature*. Cambridge, MA: Harvard University Press.

Richardson, J. 1996. *Nietzsche's System*. Oxford: Oxford University Press.

Richardson, J. & B. Leiter (eds) 2001. *Nietzsche*. Oxford: Oxford University Press.

Ridley, A. 1998. *Nietzsche's Conscience: Six Character Studies from the* Genealogy. Ithaca, NY: Cornell University Press.

Schacht, R. 1983. *Nietzsche*. New York: Routledge & Kegan Paul.

Schacht, R. (ed.) 1994. *Nietzsche, Genealogy, Morality*. Berkeley, CA: University of California Press.

Sedgwick, P. (ed.) 1995. *Nietzsche: A Critical Reader*. Oxford: Blackwell.

Sleinis, E. 1994. *Nietzsche's Revaluation of Values*. Urbana, IL: University of Illinois Press.

Solomon, R. (ed.) 1973. *Nietzsche: A Collection of Critical Essays*. New York: Anchor Books.

Staten, H. 1990. *Nietzsche's Voice*. Ithaca, NY: Cornell University Press.

Welshon, R. 2004. *The Philosophy of Nietzsche*. Chesham: Acumen.

Wilcox, J. 1974. *Truth and Value in Nietzsche: A Study of His Metaethics and Epistemology*. Ann Arbor, MI: University of Michigan Press.

Index